I, CAESAR

To Amanda

This book is published to accompany the television series entitled *I, Caesar* which
was first broadcast in 1997. The series was produced by
Seventh Art Productions for BBC Television and Arts & Entertainment Television Network
Written and produced by Phil Grabsky
Co-directed by Phil Grabsky and Peter Nicholson

Published by BBC Books,
an imprint of BBC Worldwide Publishing,
BBC Worldwide Limited, Woodlands,
80 Wood Lane, London W12 0TT

First published 1997
© Phil Grabsky 1997
The moral right of the author has been asserted

ISBN 0 563 38725 4

Design and map artwork by Design/Section, Frome
Graphic reconstructions by Liquid Television Graphics Ltd
© Seventh Art Productions/BBC/A & E
Picture research by Deirdre O'Day

Display copy set in Trajan, body copy set in Berkeley
Printed and bound in Great Britain by Butler & Tanner Ltd, Frome and London
Colour separations by Radstock Reproductions Ltd, Midsomer Norton
Jacket printed by Lawrence Allen Ltd, Weston-super-Mare

I, CAESAR

RULING THE ROMAN EMPIRE

PHIL GRABSKY

SPECIALIST RESEARCH
AND INTRODUCTION BY
DR PHILIP RANCE

BBC BOOKS

ACKNOWLEDGEMENTS

First and foremost, at a time when the increase in TV channels is paving the way for less choice in programming rather than more, I thank the BBC and A&E for continuing to finance productions such as these.

In particular I thank: Michael Attwell whose help and encouragement launched the whole adventure, Michael Jackson and Mark Thompson at the BBC and Michael Cascio and CarolAnne Dolan at A&E for their support, Steve Nam for his backing and, above all, Adam Kemp whose energy, time and insight have been fantastic.

At BBC Books, I thank: Doug Young and Charlotte Lochhead for their editorial skills, Deirdre O'Day for the picture reasearch and Kelly Davis for dotting the i's and crossing the t's.

At Seventh Art, on the production of the TV series, I thank: Fiona Kingsman, Lucy McLoughlin and Julia Wilkie – a better team of production staff I could not have wished for. Ali Ray and Sally Jenkinson for help and criticism, Mike Fox and Jonathan Partridge for their talented camerawork, their professionalism, inspiration and fun. Tony Miller for his help at the start of the project. Matthew Fox, Richard Hill and Dirk Nel for being superb camera assistants and great company. Mike Lax and Simon Farmer, expert sound recordists and as entertaining as ever. Alan MacKay and Phil Reynolds who understood the films I wanted to make and, through their editing brilliance, made them better. Mickey Portman for his perfect music. My parents and Anthony Haynes for reading the first draft and being honest. Dr Simon James and Chris Scarre for their input – and all the expert interviewees: Keith Hopkins, David Shotter, Andrew Wallace-Hadrill, Miriam Griffin, Peter Heather, Chris Kelly and Averil Cameron.

A final but special thanks goes to three people. First, to Philip Rance, researcher and 'oracle', forever calmly answering questions (no matter how often they had been asked before); secondly, to Peter Nicholson, his hard work and abilities have been invaluable; and lastly but above all, to Amanda Wilkie, the Head of Production and my partner at Seventh Art. Her input was the most important of all.

CONTENTS

FOREWORD
6

INTRODUCTION
**AN OVERVIEW OF
ROMAN HISTORY**
10

CHAPTER I
JULIUS CAESAR
18

CHAPTER II
AUGUSTUS
58

CHAPTER III
NERO
98

CHAPTER IV
HADRIAN
134

CHAPTER V
CONSTANTINE
172

CHAPTER VI
JUSTINIAN
208

**NOTES, BIBLIOGRAPHY
AND SOURCES**
248

INDEX
253

FOREWORD

As a television documentary-maker, I have been lucky enough to dip in and out of many cultures and societies. While making films throughout Europe, North Africa and the Middle East, I have repeatedly been struck by the appearance of Roman columns by the sides of motorways, headless statues in public parks and fragments of mosaic in the cellars of public buildings. From northern England to eastern Syria, from western Spain to southern Egypt – who could have ruled an empire that stretched so far? How on earth did they manage it?

Attempting to write a history of the Roman Empire is an enormous task. Two thousand years need to be considered – and then condensed into 60,000 words. There are many ways of approaching the subject but I decided to focus on six men, who all used the name Caesar – first as a family name and then as a symbol of imperial power and prestige. I feel these six reflect the history of Rome. Through accounts of their lives I hope to be able to illustrate the whole of what I believe to be the most significant empire in history.

On completing a series entitled *The Great Commanders* for Channel 4 in the UK and A & E in the USA, I began working with Dr Philip Rance in an attempt to break down the history of Rome into six manageable stages, each of which could be reflected by one man. To delineate the history in this way was, we realized, to walk on shifting sands but we felt it was important to mark out a course from start to finish in order to give some kind of structure, however imperfect, to both book and TV series.

The six stages we identified were 'the rise', 'the consolidation', 'life in Rome', 'life in the provinces', 'decline and transition' and 'fall and legacy'. Then the individuals were chosen to represent each stage. Julius Caesar, although born when the empire was well under way, represents the character of Rome's expansion. Augustus represents the consolidation and control of central power. Nero illustrates the effects of successful empire, the downside of a hereditary succession and the ability of Rome 'the empire' to run despite affairs in Rome 'the capital'. Hadrian represents the rising power and influence of the provinces. Constantine illustrates the reaction to the signs of decline. Justinian, 600 years after Julius Caesar, attempts to unify a divided and splintering empire but in effect marks the end of pan-Mediterranean unity and, in some ways, the end of the Roman Empire.

The individual stories are in themselves remarkable. The accomplishments seem incredible. For some Romans, life was nasty, brutish and short. For others, it was luxurious and stimulating.

And that, of course, is part of the appeal in studying Roman history. The parallels to our own lives are so striking that they are at times unnerving. All six of the lead players have their modern parallels: Julius Caesar the rebellious general, Augustus the public moralist with a family whose private sins he cannot control, Nero the spoilt teenager who becomes the most powerful man in the western world, Hadrian who keeps on the move to keep his position secure, Constantine who uses religion to try to unify his realm, and Justinian who retreats from view into the safety of his palace. All illustrate the truism that people don't change, only the date.

Producing the *I, Caesar* television series was a massive undertaking which involved 50,000 miles of travelling to 300 sites in over twenty countries. Few, if any, Romans would have been fortunate enough to travel so extensively. Each visit added colour to my understanding and served to illustrate how complex the histories are. There rage huge debates about many facets of Roman life and there are countless questions that remain to be answered. One of those questions is how relevant the emperor actually was to the majority of those who lived in the empire. Some say hardly at all – I disagree. Our day-to-day lives may seem unrelated to our monarch or president but that depends on their benevolence or otherwise. The man or woman who sits atop the pyramid of power can lead us to war (external or civil), famine or bankruptcy. Their potential to do good is often exceeded by their potential to do harm. Either way, we do not live in a vacuum. Likewise, the people of the Roman empire were affected, directly or indirectly, by their Caesars. Consequently, in order to understand the system, the history and the actions, I believe we must look to the Caesars first.

A sense of the glorious excitement of history – in particular Roman history – was partly stimulated in me by a classics teacher, Mr Grimsby, at school. How often our lives must be governed by the variable quality of those who educate us as children! Mr Grimsby's ability to breathe life into the lives of long-dead Romans fired in me an enthusiasm that has never waned. If I can pass on some of this wide-eyed wonder to those who read the words that follow, then I have, in part, succeeded.

BRITANNIA

GERMANIA

R. Rhine

GERMANIA
INFERIOR

BELGICA

● Trier

R. Danube

GERMANIA
SUPERIOR

RHAETIA

NORICUM

DACIA

LUGDUNENSIS

GALLIA

PANNONIA

MOESIA

AQUITANIA

Milan
●

Ravenna
●

ITALIA

NAISSUS ●

MACEDON

NARBONENSIS

CORSICA

● Rome

TARRACONENSIS

SARDINIA

HISPANIA

SICILIA

LUSITANIA

● Syracuse

BAETICA

Carthage
●

Mediterranean S

● Italica

NUMIDIA

MAURITANIA
CAESARIENSIS

AFRICA

MAURITANIA
TINGITANA

N

0   100   200   300 miles

0   200   400   600 km

The Roman emperor
Justinian's wars
ultimately failed to
recreate the lost
grandeur of the Roman
Empire, and arguably
weakened the eastern
provinces in the process.
His victories in the West
were transitory, and in
the East his successors
had to face the new
threat of Islamic
invasions. Never again
would Eastern and
Western Europe be
united. Justinian's
failure marked the end
of 'Rome' as a pan-
European reality. Yet,
as a political entity,
the Roman Empire
was to survive in the
East for many centuries,
until 1453 when
Constantinople fell to
the Ottoman Turks.

AN OVERVIEW OF ROMAN HISTORY

THE traditional foundation date of Rome is 753 BC. Sited on a group of hills beside the River Tiber in Latium, Rome's original growth was dependent on its control of the river crossing and of local salt deposits. Rome thus grew wealthy through the passage of trade between neighbouring peoples, notably the Etruscans to the north and the Greek colonies to the south. The culturally more advanced Etruscans played a dominant role in the development of early Rome. The Romans were originally ruled by kings, under whose leadership they achieved their first military successes against the neighbouring cities of Latium. According to tradition, the first of these kings was the city's founder, Romulus, but he and several of his successors are purely legendary. The last kings belonged to an unpopular Etruscan family. In 510 BC, members of the Roman aristocracy staged a revolution which overthrew the monarchy and established the Republic. The Republic was theoretically a partnership between the aristocracy, represented by the Senate, and the Roman People, gathered in various assemblies, in which the People held sovereign power. In reality it was a narrow oligarchy, dominated by a few powerful aristocratic families and clans. The aristocracy competed in open election for the offices of state, but power-sharing and brevity of political office aimed to prevent the dominance of any one man.

The course of Roman imperial expansion was slow and faltering, and beset with many reverses. By the middle of the third century BC, through a combination of sustained military effort and skilful diplomacy, Rome had come to dominate first her immediate neighbours and then the whole of Italy. This broader sphere of influence brought the Romans into collision with the North African city state of Carthage, whose extensive mercantile interests were threatened by Roman expansion. Rome's defeat of Carthage in the long and exhausting

Punic Wars (264–241 BC and 218–202 BC) left Roman domination of the western Mediterranean unopposed.

Thereafter the antiquated Hellenistic monarchies of the East rapidly crumbled in the face of Roman aggression. The wealth derived from conquest, and contact with the more advanced culture of Greece, transformed Roman society, and the resulting social and political tensions eventually led to the collapse of the Republic. By the end of the second century BC the aristocratic rivalries earlier fought out at city level were being played out on the wider stage of an empire. The old institutions of the city state were unsuited to running an empire, and Roman security increasingly required that greater political and military authority be placed in the hands of individuals. The last century of the Republic saw the state dominated by a series of politically ambitious generals, backed by what were effectively private armies. The last of these was Julius Caesar, whose conquest of Gaul had brought him immense prestige and wealth. Caesar's failure to accommodate the political aspirations of other aristocratic families, and the overtly monarchial character of his short-lived administration, ended in his assassination in 44 BC.

Caesar's assassination only led to renewed and brutal civil war, ultimately won by his nephew, and adopted heir, Octavian. Octavian, later renamed Augustus, was the first emperor and the architect of the imperial system. A statesman of consummate subtlety, over his forty-year rule (27 BC–AD 14) he steadily formulated a system of government which was essentially a monarchy, but one clothed in the trappings of a 'restored Republic'. With the deliberately vague title of *princeps* or 'first citizen', he avoided the mistakes of Julius Caesar, and took care to pay lip-service to Republican precedent. In reality, through his control of the legions, his immense wealth and his monopoly of patronage, Augustus ensured that his personal influence within the state was overwhelming. The pattern of Augustus's rule, the Principate, formed the basis of Roman political life for the next 200 years. This was a period of unprecedented internal peace, the *pax Romana*, during which the Empire flourished. The chief reason for Rome's success as an imperial power was the degree to which the conquered were offered a share in the society and politics of the conquerers. This period saw the gradual assimilation and Romanization of the provinces, with Graeco-Roman culture pervading every aspect of provincial life. Despite the persistence of local customs and languages, there was a fundamentally uniform culture from one end of the Empire to the other, based on a standard concept of 'civilization', underpinned by the widespread use of Latin and/or Greek.

The Romanization of the provinces, and the accompanying broadening of the political class, were reflected in the imperial succession. Augustus was succeeded by members of his own family, the Julio-Claudian dynasty, descendants of the ancient aristocracy of the Republic. The downfall of this dynasty with the death of Nero (AD 54–68) was followed by the Flavian Dynasty, Italian and bourgeois in origin, who in turn were succeeded by emperors from the provinces. Trajan (98–117), Hadrian (117–138), and Marcus Aurelius (161–180) were Spanish in origin; Antoninus Pius (138–161) was Gallic; the Severan Dynasty (193–235) North African and Syrian. The principal weakness of the Principate was that it lacked an effective mechanism for the succession, in part due to the very vagueness of the position of *princeps*. A constitutional fiction dictated that the *princeps* received his powers from the Senate, but real power had always rested on control of the legions, and in periods of political crisis it was the army that decided who would rule. At the end of a dynasty the succession was usually decided by bouts of civil war (as in 68–69 and 193–197), but these remained brief and were followed by the re-establishment of civilian rule on the model of the Augustan Principate. From the early third century, however, civilian government began to deteriorate as individual armies raised their candidates as emperor. There followed a prolonged period of civil war (235–284) in which emperors were raised and deposed in rapid succession. At the same time the Empire's frontiers were breached by new and more threatening enemies: the Goths in Europe, and the Sassanian Persians in the East. The combination of civil war and foreign invasion caused immense destruction and economic disruption in some parts of the Empire. One important consequence was to intensify the movement of political power away from the city of Rome and Italy to cities nearer the threatened frontiers, such as Milan, Trier and Antioch.

The situation was eventually restored in the later third century by a series of vigorous soldier emperors, but the strains of the third-century crisis fundamentally transformed the nature of imperial rule. Emperors were thereafter usually men of humble origins, who had risen through the ranks because of their military merit. The emperor, and his administration, assumed an overtly military character, in accordance with the backgrounds of the emperors and the increased strains on the Empire's security. These trends were to some extent formalized by Diocletian (284–305), who inaugurated a series of far-reaching reforms to the imperial system. He attempted to stabilize imperial security by increasing the size of the army and the bureaucracy, both of which demanded considerable increases in taxation. He also divided imperial rule between four individuals, a system known as the Tetrarchy. From their separate capitals each of the Tetrarchs was responsible for border defence and internal security. However, co-operation between these imperial colleagues proved illusory. Mutual suspicion between successive Tetrarchs led to renewed civil wars over twenty years, and ultimately saw the Empire fall to one man, Constantine (306–337).

Constantine had a profound impact on the course of imperial history. At first granting only religious toleration to the hitherto sporadically persecuted Christians, he later favoured this group as a source of strength to the Empire. The growth of Christianity was further boosted by Constantine's death-bed conversion, and thereafter state backing allowed this exclusive and intolerant religion to make considerable gains against traditional heterogeneous paganism. The transformation from a pagan to a Christian empire was not complete until the sixth century, but Roman emperors were hereafter effectively God's representatives on earth responsible for ensuring orthodoxy. Constantine was also responsible for the founding of Constantinople. A city of immense strategic importance, well placed to give easy access to both the European and the Asian provinces, the defensive nature of the site enabled it to survive for eleven centuries. Constantine did not originally intend it to be the new 'capital' of the Empire, as he still regarded Rome as the spiritual centre of the Empire, but his decision was a momentous one. For succeeding generations Constantinople was the 'New Rome' and grew to become the largest city in the Western world. The Roman Empire became increasingly orientated towards the East, and the centre of Roman civilization was no longer Rome and Italy, but Greek-speaking, Christian, eastward-looking Constantinople.

Despite Constantine's achievement, after his death the Roman Empire was rarely ruled by one man. Although there was still one Empire, its eastern and western halves were ruled by separate lines of emperors. Throughout the fifth century the two governments became increasingly hostile, and often failed to co-operate against renewed pressures from Germanic peoples and later the Huns. The eastern provinces, always wealthier, more populous and more urbanized than the West, were better able to cope with sporadic barbarian incursions. The West, however, facing more relentless and pervasive invasions and settlement by Germanic peoples, began to fragment politically. At the same time, its weak emperors, forced to employ barbarian mercenaries to secure their rule, became puppets in the hands of their generals. In 476 the line of Roman emperors that had lasted in Western Europe for five centuries came to an abrupt end with Romulus Augustulus, a powerless teenager, who was pushed aside by his own German general.

Although, for generations, historians have dated the fall of the Roman Empire in the West to 476, at the time this event was only significant because no new emperor was proclaimed in his place; few at the time would have seen this situation as permanent. While Germanic kingdoms were established upon the ruins of the western Empire, in the East the Roman Empire not only survived but flourished. At its heart lay Constantinople, an immense and wealthy city, a 'New Rome' rivalling the old in its splendour. Among the next generation of emperors was Justinian (527–565), whose reign saw the last attempt to reconquer the western provinces from their 'barbarian' rulers. Justinian was the last truly 'Roman' emperor, the last to view the Roman Empire as a pan-European entity. Initially undertaken to popularize his regime, Justinian's 'reconquest' made rapid and unexpected gains. His wars, however, ultimately failed to re-establish the political unity of the Mediterranean, and arguably exhausted the eastern provinces in the process. His successes in the West were transitory, and in the East his successors had to face the new threat of Islamic invasions. Never again would Eastern and Western Europe be reunited. Justinian's failure marked the end of 'Rome' as a pan-European reality. Yet, as a political entity, the Roman Empire, in the guise of the Byzantine Empire, was to survive in the East for many centuries, until 1453 when Constantinople fell to the Ottoman Turks.

> *Imperial Caesar, dead and turned to clay*
> *Might stop a hole to keep the wind away*
> *O, that that earth which kept the world in awe*
> *Should patch a wall t'expel the winter's flaw!*

> *William Shakespeare*, Hamlet, *Act V, Scene 1*

FORUM 1 – 85 BC

FORUM 6 – 300 AD

16

FORUM 2 – 49 BC

FORUM 3 – 46 BC

FORUM 4 – 14 AD

FORUM 5 – 85 AD

The Forum was the heart of Rome. Originally a market place, its grandeur grew over the decades.

17

CHAPTER I

JULIUS CAESAR

'I Am Not King, But Caesar'

A PURPLE toga was in shreds and thrown to a corner. Blood was congealing on the stone floor. The room was silent now, except for some distant sobbing, though only minutes before the scene had been one of confusion, distress and fear. The examining doctor had counted twenty-three stab wounds, most of which were superficial slashes and cuts. But one, to the chest, had struck especially deep. Death had not come painlessly. Yet it had come and now the man – who had woken this very morning with a head full of ideas and plans – lay waiting to be burnt in the time-honoured Roman way. Only a few hours earlier he had been perhaps the most powerful human of all the 300 million men and women on earth. Now Gaius Julius Caesar, Dictator and ruler of the Roman Empire, was dead.

In life, Gaius Julius Caesar had been a fortunate man. He had lived in a great city, seen much of the western world, loved a foreign queen, and accumulated enormous wealth. In a world where most rarely even left their villages and were always under the shadow of debt, famine or conquest, Julius Caesar was privileged. His fortune had brought him great power – so great that it has often been said that he was a man who changed the course of history, achieving miracles, accomplishing what had been thought impossible, helping to further the Roman Empire.

Yet, having survived countless battles on foreign soil, he was murdered in Rome, by Romans. Why was one of the greatest soldiers in all history, a

Gaius Julius Caesar (100–44 BC) one of the greatest soldiers in all history who personified Rome's rise to glory. Brutally assassinated, his name remains synonymous with strong and powerful leadership to the present day.

man who, more than any other, personified Rome's rise to glory, brutally stabbed to death?

❖

In the boiling height of summer in the year 100 BC, Aurelia, a young woman of Rome, gave birth. The other women present presumably tried to comfort her as she struggled to provide her husband with an heir. Aurelia's husband, Gaius, was an aristocrat and politician (a senator in Rome's governing body, the Senate). But Gaius's ancestry no longer counted for as much as it once had; the old-established nobility were being superseded by a growing number of astute senators from 'new money' families.

Though Aurelia and Gaius lived in the humble Roman district of the Subura, it was still a comparatively comfortable household into which the new child was born. Aurelia, as custom dictated, would have laid the healthy baby at her husband's feet. If he refused to pick up the baby, it would be taken to a public place and left either to the mercy of passers-by or to die. Aurelia's husband, however, did not hesitate to raise up his first-born son.

A woman delivers a baby using a birthing chair.

On the child's ninth day, the household gods would have been honoured, incense burnt and the baby ceremonially bathed. We can assume that friends and relatives stopped by, bringing gifts to the contented family. And the boy was named: his first name was, like his father, to be Gaius, followed by the clan name of Julius and the family name of Caesar.

Outside their home, a city of over half a million people hummed with traders and travellers. The metropolis was consuming on an ever-increasing scale. It was the most influential city in the western world. Great cities in the Middle and Near East had come and gone. Magnificent Assyrian, Persian and Macedonian states were no more. The age of the great Pharaohs had passed. Carthage was destroyed. Athens and Sparta were tired and politically inconsequential. Nothing compared to Rome, which now ruled over an empire stretching from Spain to Asia Minor and from southern France to northern Africa.

Merchants and messengers from all over this huge area walked and rode towards Rome along the specially built, straight, durable, well-maintained roads. Through Italy came carts and shiploads of wine, olive oil, building materials, fruit, vegetables, bronze and silverware, furniture and cloth.

Barges travelling up the River Tiber brought grain from Sicily, Sardinia and North Africa; slaves from Asia Minor, the Black Sea and southern Russia. From Greece came works of art, and rare types of marble for building. From the coast of Syria came pearls, purple-dyed cloth, rare woods for expensive furniture; spices arrived from South-East Asia; from North Africa one could purchase wild animals for the arena; and from Egypt fine linen and glass.

The stream of goods seemed never-ending. To cater for the merchants, roadside stalls sold cakes, drinks, fruit and meats, or offered places to stay, bargains to buy, sights to see. Other bystanders waited to take advantage of travellers who showed any signs of naivety – in the absence of a police force, crime was common.

The city was the largest in the western world. But Rome's rise to such prominence, fuelled by ambition and conquest, had taken centuries.

❖

The Romans themselves dated the birth of their city to 753 BC when a king called Romulus established a small settlement on a hill beside the River Tiber.

The area was known as Latium and its people were Latins. There were many such villages but Rome was lucky: its seven hills lay on one of the few fords across the Tiber, providing opportunities for trade. Latium was fortunate to be at the meeting point of the powerful Etruscan culture to the north and the cultured Greek-run cities to the south. The site had the further advantage of being far enough up river to avoid the numerous pirate fleets of the Mediterranean and yet near enough to the sea to exploit its commercial opportunities.

In the seventh century BC, the village was turned into a city when Etruscan kings took it over. Under the guidance of these kings, the Forum was drained and laid out, and markets, hostels and taverns were built. In 510 BC, however, 400 years before the birth of Gaius Julius Caesar, Rome's small aristocracy, resenting the rule of a single man, managed to evict the monarchy. In turn, they declared their city a Republic (*respublica* – a 'public concern'). The city was now governed annually by two men, called consuls, elected by an Assembly of citizens from the Senate which then contained approximately 100 men.

The system was strong, and the Romans ambitious. The city began to fight, defeat and incorporate its neighbours. Crucially, it did not crush those it defeated but offered them a share of the spoils. Romans had no racial singularity which prevented them incorporating non-Romans into their society. Within 250 years, most of central Italy was under their control.

Rome's ambitions spread and it challenged the North African city-state of Carthage for control of the western Mediterranean. Rome could have been crushed for good by the Carthaginians, under their leader Hannibal, but sheer determination and spirit, backed by political resilience and the reserves of a strong economy, saw them emerge victorious after decades of war. Rome had now become the greatest force in the Mediterranean. It was a critical moment in Roman history, for their first major victory outside Italy was so profitable that Romans were excused all taxes. This made them aware

of the rewards that warfare on an international scale could offer. Before long, Greece and Macedonia, both ancient centres of Mediterranean civilization, also succumbed to Roman assaults.

In this haphazard way, in pursuit of financial and military security, the Romans acquired their empire.

❖

A Roman boy's childhood would have been less haphazard. Feeding, crying, standing, walking, talking – all took place strictly under the protection of a different deity who had to be respected. Gaius Julius Caesar's day probably began early, with a light breakfast of fruit, bread, honey and olives. A nurse may then have watched over the child as he played in the garden, perhaps occupying himself with wooden toy ships or balls made from animal skin. When the nurse's patience had worn thin, she might have led the boy back inside and sung him lullabies and soft rhymes to put him to sleep. If all else

Goat carts were among the toys of an aristocratic child who could imagine himself a great general while he played.

23

failed, Gaius may have been warned that, if he did not rest, Lamia, an evil witch who sucked children's blood, would come and get him.

After his nap, Gaius would no doubt have run noisily from room to room, disturbing servant and family alike. As he grew, he perhaps began to demand that the family play games like Hide and Seek, Blind Man's Bluff, or marbles (using hazelnuts). On occasion he might have been allowed to drive a goat-cart and imagine himself a great general. Such childish enthusiasms would have been indulged so long as he never disobeyed his father, whose word was law.

These days of childish innocence did not last long. By the age of seven, his

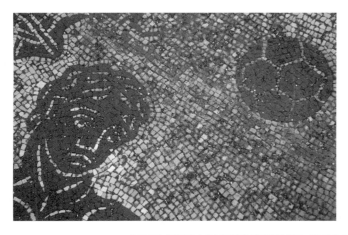

education began. His early schooling was undertaken by his family. His parents had a comparatively modest income and they were presumably determined that their only son should lead them back to their rightful place in society. His mother would have taken great pains to instruct him in reading and writing Latin and Greek as well as speaking with a good

Physical training – a game of ball and lifting weights – helped youths to build up the strength and skills they would use one day in battle.

accent. His father, when time permitted, evidently focused on more physical activities such as wrestling, javelin-throwing and swimming.

As Gaius grew, his formal education passed into the hands of a trusted slave. With this tutor he progressed to more difficult lessons, learning grammar and literature. Such lessons were attended at home, a daily routine of writing on his wax tablet, having his work checked and then smoothing the wax for a new lesson.

In the afternoons, Gaius and his friends may have idled down the busy streets towards the large open area of the Campus Martius. This field, named in honour of the war god Mars, was supposed to be used primarily for military parades and training, but most days it was available for sports and games. The geographer Strabo wrote: 'This is an admirably large field on which an enormous number of chariots and horses can race unimpeded and a host of people can daily play ball games and practise discus-throwing and wrestling.'

Caesar spent a great deal of time here. He is said to have become a highly accomplished rider who loved to show off by folding his hands behind his back and riding the stirrup-less, small horses as fast as possible. It was probably here, on the outskirts of the great city, that he began to build up the physical skills he would one day use in battle.

While dining each day in the late afternoon, Gaius would have heard from his father the latest tales from the Senate and Forum – the main meeting square outside the Senate House. How interested Gaius was in such political titbits is unknown. Perhaps he cared more for news of the next gladiatorial show or military Triumph (the great lavish processions of victorious generals through the streets of Rome). Nevertheless, at the age of fifteen, his father decided that Gaius was entitled to wear the *toga virilis* – the adult toga. Though a plain garment, it signified the arrival of adulthood. It was also the mark of a Roman citizen, the national costume by which he was distinguished wherever he went. Wearing it was a jealously guarded privilege – it was the accepted dress at all social functions and public engagements. Although the toga was simply a large piece of woollen cloth it was very difficult to hang correctly. Gaius would thus have been instructed, with the aid of a valet, in how to wear it with elegance, setting the folds and creases as expected of a young gentleman.

We can imagine that this would have been a big day for Gaius. It would have begun at home, with family, relatives and friends gathering in their finery to offer good wishes and presents. Then, with his father, he would have proudly walked the mile or so to the city centre to offer a sacrifice to Jupiter and be formally registered as a citizen.

Occasionally, perhaps, Gaius Julius Caesar would eavesdrop at the door of the Senate (which met usually twice a month) and hear the aristocracy within debating the Republic, which they considered their personal property. This was a time of change and discord in Rome and the senatorial debates were often heated. The Senate was a city government trying to rule a world empire, and the pressure was taking its toll. The senators, by this time numbering 300, were finding it increasingly difficult to restrain the provincial governors, who were also the army commanders. For an impressionable young man like Caesar, however, it must have seemed the height of excitement and privilege. Caesar was at the doors of what seemed the most powerful room in the world – and he wanted to enter.

The ladder of political hierarchy, however, was based on age and strictly enforced. Natural talent was a minor factor; family, experience and training were considered more important. Within a few years what had been happening for some time became law: you had to be aged thirty before being elected a *quaestor* with financial duties, aged thirty-nine to become a *praetor* with judicial duties, and to have reached forty-two before being elected a consul. For a teenager like Caesar, the wait ahead must have appeared endless.

❖

Death was ever-present in a world of disease, warfare, crime and hunger, and in 85 BC Caesar's father died. Caesar was now the head of the family. A year later, at the age of only sixteen, he took a further step towards adulthood by getting married. Showing uncommon ambition, the young man broke off one betrothal, to a girl called Cossutia, and accepted the much more politically useful hand of Cornelia, who was being offered by her father Cinna.

Rome was not a stable, secure place. It was racked with problems: above all,

Romans fighting Romans. The city's very success, and its considerable increase in wealth, had encouraged some of its own senators to bid for a bigger slice of that new money and power. For the previous fifty years, Rome had been suffering from great internal political disorder. Its commercial and financial expansion had led to real moral and political confusion, and the Senate was clearly finding it impossible to rule this expanding empire. The biggest problems were caused by aristocratic rivalry and ambition. These rivalries between Rome's leading families had once been fought out within the city but were now occurring across the Empire, since the opportunity to acquire fame, military kudos and wealth had become so much greater. The ambitions of these men were, on the one hand, a major stimulus for the continued expansion of Rome's empire – as Caesar was later to demonstrate better than anyone – but they also brought with them the danger of autocracy and dictatorship. Senators, whether in Rome or acting as military commanders and provincial governors abroad, began to fight among themselves.

There were a number of men struggling for prominence in the years of Caesar's youth – men like his new father-in-law Cinna, his uncle Marius, and their mutual enemy Sulla. Rome's political world was divided into two groupings – the *Optimates*, generally representing the aristocratic perspective, and the *Populares*, claiming to represent the people. Both groups continually attacked one another, alleging (with good cause) corruption and abuse of privilege. Caesar was a member of the *Populares*; and the claim to 'represent the people' was central to the way he presented himself to the public throughout his life. This grouping was dominated by Cinna and Marius. Sulla, their enemy, was a leading *Optimate*. Neither group was distinguished by any particular policies, other than the desire to secure and retain power. Certainly the idea of acting on behalf of the population was largely an irrelevance. Rome belonged to the Senate – the question was: which faction of the Senate?

Soon after Caesar's marriage, civil war broke out once again. Sulla won and took bloody revenge on his opponents' supporters. Caesar would have witnessed the awful carnage and was no doubt anxious when he was brought before Sulla. The victor demanded that Caesar divorce his wife and

remarry, thus abandoning Cinna's camp and joining Sulla's. Courageously Caesar refused and fortunately Sulla was reluctantly persuaded to release him. On his release, Sulla confiscated the whole of Caesar's inheritance. Caesar, penniless and very much a suspect outsider in the eyes of the ruling circle, decided this would be an appropriate time to leave Rome, and join the army.

The military was Rome's backbone. For centuries an annually raised body of citizens with property had provided their own armour and weapons. These heavily armed infantrymen were organized into legions which were versatile in their use of long- and short-range weapons, well-disciplined, and flexible in their tactics. They fought, as was common in antiquity, from the end of spring to the end of summer, until the need to harvest their crops brought them swiftly home.

Barbarian captives dragged before a victorious Roman general. Such scenes often adorned the burial sarcophagi of wealthy Romans.

By Caesar's time, the desire to conquer new provinces had taken Romans far beyond Italy's borders. The distances involved meant that troops could no longer travel home: year-round campaigning was often required. The army had gradually and reluctantly been opened up to any citizen, however landless or poor. These recruits received their equipment from the state, and entered an increasingly professional army for the duration of an assignment.

Over the centuries the Romans perfected techniques, tactics and equipment to create a highly mobile and disciplined military machine which could go practically anywhere and do practically anything.

The Romans were great imitators; they absorbed the best elements of other cultures (especially Greek), copying military equipment and techniques from their enemies. Rome defeated her great rival Carthage, for example, partly by copying and mass-producing just one captured Carthaginian ship. Furthermore, they frequently borrowed manpower as well, enrolling their former enemies' troops to fight alongside their own legions.

The Romans not only won the war, they also won the peace. Their policy towards the defeated was a vital part of their success. They decided early on that direct conquest in Italy was not the correct way to proceed. Instead they frequently made alliances with defeated neighbours, who became 'friends and allies' and agreed to supply troops to the Roman army. This policy was not new in antiquity but it was important in the early phase of Roman imperialism. What *was* new, and crucial, was the degree to which Rome granted full or partial citizenship to the conquered.

Roman imperialism was very slow but, as with most empires, there was a perceptible 'snowball' effect; the continued success and growing reputation of Roman armies undermined their opponents' military confidence. This was exacerbated by Rome's increasing reputation for brutality, far exceeding that in the 'civilized' (Greek) world. Once Rome had dispensed with the great powers of the Mediterranean, smaller states hurried to be included among the 'friends of Rome', rather than face its legions in battle.

At the age of eighteen, Caesar joined this army. Young aristocrats like him typically served for a year or two on a general's staff; the only difference in Caesar's case was that he had a particular reason for doing so – he had thought it wise to leave Sulla's Rome for a while. Caesar bade his family and friends farewell, perhaps made a final offering to the household gods, and left home, with baggage and servants, not knowing when he would return.

Little is known about Caesar's time in the army except that he further demonstrated his courage fighting in the front line. Having saved a comrade from death, he was apparently awarded the 'civic crown'. This wreath of oak leaves was highly respected: at public games people would have to stand if Caesar passed by wearing it.

In 78 BC, Sulla died, and having been in the army four years, possibly culminating in a short but exciting period fighting pirates on the Mediterranean, the twenty-two-year-old Caesar returned to his wife and young daughter, Julia, in Rome. The teenager who had gone to war returned a man, ready for a new but very different campaign.

❖

In his *Lives of the Caesars*, the Roman historian Suetonius describes Julius Caesar as of: 'imposing stature – white-skinned, slim-limbed, rather too full in the face, and with dark, lively eyes… He not only had his hair carefully cut and was clean shaven, but also removed his body hair with tweezers'.

The Greek biographer Plutarch, in his *Parallel Lives*, said that, 'though subject to epilepsy, his physical endurance was phenomenal. He was particular of his personal appearance and dress, was clean-shaven and was sensitive of his premature balding'.

As to his character, Suetonius claimed that, 'he greatly loved pleasure, spent much money in order to gratify his passions, and seduced very many ladies of quality'.

Yet pleasure alone did not satisfy Caesar – even as a young man he believed his greatest reward would come through entering the inner circle of the ruling class. It had everything he desired: wealth, power, influence.

Although the absence of the term 'politician' in Latin reflects the essentially amateur nature of politics in Rome, for aristocrats there were few alternatives to a political life. Politics was what happened in the *polis* (the city). Politicians were the city magistrates, who consisted almost entirely of the city's wealthy. There was no professional civil service, full-time religious hierarchy, or permanent military command structure. These offices existed but they were all legally informal and temporary. Social advancement went hand-in-hand with political promotion.

Like most young aristocrats, Caesar decided to improve his public position by bringing legal actions against political enemies. Trials were frequently undertaken for political rather than criminal reasons and hearings took place not in courtrooms but on platforms in the Forum, or indoors, in spaces large enough to admit an audience. The Roman legal system was based on the prosecution and defence putting their case in front of a judge, and a jury deciding the verdict. Trials were a form of entertainment and could attract huge audiences. It was an easy way, therefore, to get noticed and build up both public support and political contacts.

Caesar apparently impressed everyone with his performances – except the jurors. He lost his first two cases. Determined not to lose a third, he set off to Rhodes, intending to study under Apollonius Molo, the most respected teacher of oratory in the Roman world.

While sailing, however, he was captured by pirates and held for ransom.

As Plutarch tells us: 'When the pirates demanded a ransom of 20 talents Caesar burst out laughing. They did not know, he said, who it was that they had captured, and he volunteered to pay 50'.

While his few companions and slaves hurried off to collect money from the nearest ports, Caesar made himself comfortable among his captors. Plutarch again:

He treated them so high-handedly that, whenever he wanted to sleep, he would tell them to stop talking. For 38 days, with the greatest unconcern, he joined in all their games and exercises, just as if he were their leader instead of their prisoner. He also wrote poems and speeches which he read aloud to them, and if they failed to admire his work, he would call them to their faces illiterate savages, and would often laughingly threaten to have them all hanged. [1]

Once the ransom was paid and Caesar released, the pirates sailed away, not expecting to see the haughty young Roman again – but they were mistaken. Caesar rushed off, hired ships and men, captured the pirates, and had them crucified. Because he somewhat admired them, he slit their throats first. The message was clear: Caesar, like his city, was both arrogant and ruthless.

The Roman scholar Pliny the Elder summarized Caesar's qualities as: 'his energy and steadfastness… his sublime ability to comprehend everything under the sun… the vitality he possessed and the fiery quickness of his mind…'

Caesar carried on to Rhodes but soon after his arrival he heard that part of Asia Minor (modern Turkey) had been invaded again by a king called Mithridates. The twenty-six-year-old left his studies and, on his own initiative and quite illegally, raised a militia. He did not even ask the local governor's permission before turning up and driving the enemy troops out of the locality. Such audacity was virtually unparalleled. Caesar had again marked himself out as a distinctive young man.

❖

For the rest of his twenties, Caesar lived in Rome, building up his circle of contacts – and creditors. He continued to live with his wife and mother in the Subura, east of the Forum. Life here must have been busy and noisy. Unlike wealthier nobles who lived in the more peaceful surroundings of the Palatine Hill, Caesar lived among the noise and trade of the common people. This was not his choice – he was not rich. He certainly did not inherit great wealth from his father (whose own inheritance had been confiscated by Sulla). Notwithstanding this, he knew he had to spend – and spend excessively – to stand any chance of securing a position of real and effective power. This highly overdrawn but free-spending, fun-loving man worked hard to become popular.

As Plutarch put it: '…he was very much in the good graces of the ordinary citizen because of his easy manners and the friendly way in which

The Regia, where Caesar lived when he moved from Subura after being elected as Pontifex Maximus. *His house (behind the high walls) was just on the edge of the Forum.*

he mixed with people. Then there were his dinner parties and entertainments and a certain splendour about his whole way of life; all this made him gradually more and more important politically.'

Caesar spent hours and days persuading money lenders, senators and wealthy benefactors to provide him with funds. In return he promised that when he, Gaius Julius Caesar, rose through the political ranks, they could expect a healthy return on their investments.

This was the way Roman politics worked. Every citizen (those free, adult males born in Rome and, after 90 BC, in Italy) could vote but only if they were directly present at Assembly meetings. Most people had better things to do, so it was usually only the idle and the unemployed who turned out. These were the type of people whose votes were easily purchased. The system was corrupt.

Plutarch again: 'candidates for office quite shamelessly bribed the electorate… people who received the bribes went down to the Forum not so much to vote for their benefactors as to fight for them with bows and arrows and swords and slings. Often, before an election was over, the place where it had been held was stained with blood and defiled with dead bodies…'

Many senators – however corrupt – truly believed in the Roman Republic. The Senate and Assembly had led Rome to unthought-of power and wealth, and few dared suggest radical change. But the Empire was now so large that this small group of men was finding it increasingly hard to manage and control. Other groups wanted a greater share of the success: landless veterans, those nobles who were outside the charmed inner circle, knights (effectively the petit bourgeoisie of Roman life). The situation was moving towards a complete breakdown of law and order. Few had any idea of how to solve the problems. Those who had tried had failed. There was too much innate conservatism and too strong a desire within the nobility to protect their vested interests. The stage was therefore set for a Roman who possessed the typical Roman characteristics of ambition, aggression and energy to such an extent that he could, through sheer force of personality, seize control.

Caesar wanted the highest role – that of consul – but remained some distance from fulfilling his ambition. To gain power cost money – enormous amounts of money. Senators bought other senators and, more importantly perhaps, the general populace of Rome, who were primarily interested in free grain, cash and extravagant games.

Caesar understood the rules. According to Cassius Dio, the historian, writing in the third century AD, 'he showed himself perfectly ready to serve and flatter everybody, even ordinary persons... he did not mind temporarily grovelling'.

At the age of thirty, Caesar's expenditure and efforts brought their reward: he became a *quaestor*, a magistrate. Twenty were elected annually – eighteen of whom were sent to the provinces to assist governors with their financial and administrative affairs.

Caesar served his term in western Spain. On one occasion while he was there, according to Suetonius, Caesar saw a statue of Alexander the Great. It dawned on Caesar that by the time the great Macedonian general had reached thirty-one he had conquered most of the known world, whereas Caesar was still dealing with accounts and petitions. So overcome was the Roman by this comparison that he was said to have broken down in tears.

After his year's posting was completed, he returned to Rome. Election as *quaestor* carried with it automatic and life-long entry to the Senate. Caesar had become one of the now 600 members who could proudly wear a broad purple band down the front of their tunics.

Caesar's first wife had died before he had left for Spain and on his return he got married again – this time to Pompeia, the wealthy grand-daughter of Sulla. Although the nobility numbered relatively few families and the tangle of alliances between them was certainly very complex, Caesar's marriage to the daughter of the man who had once threatened his life showed that political and financial considerations came before everything else. Pompeia not only became a wife and stepmother but she also financed his career too. Nevertheless, Julius Caesar was spending so much that his debts continued to grow. In Plutarch's opinion: 'He was unsparing in his outlays of money, and was thought to be purchasing a transient and short-lived fame at a great price, though in reality he was buying things of the highest value at a small price.'

Now Caesar, aged thirty-four, progressed to a higher office; he became one of four annually appointed *aediles*. They had responsibility for the upkeep of Rome and its entertainments. Nothing could have suited him better. He spent enormous amounts of borrowed money on staging the most extravagant games ever seen at the specially erected wooden arenas; he is said to have dressed gladiators in silver armour, flooded one arena for a mock sea battle, and imported wild and exotic animals from Africa and the East.

The general public loved it, but Caesar was risking everything. If he didn't start earning a return on his investments soon his creditors would ensure that he either paid them back or was humiliated and exiled.

Caesar seems to have been deliberately nonchalant in the face of such pressures. It is said that he continued to fill his modest home with expensive furniture, pictures and imported vases. The historian Suetonius later wrote that Caesar was 'reported to have paid such immense prices for well-built slaves that he was ashamed and forbade the payments to be entered in the account books'.

His extravagance knew no limits. He reputedly gave a white pearl to his mistress which cost the equivalent of a year's pay for 13,000 soldiers! He is also said to have built a villa at great expense, then torn it down because he did not like it.

In 63 BC – aged thirty-six – he tried for election as *pontifex maximus* – supreme priest of Rome (the title the Pope still uses today). Caesar evidently spent lavishly on his campaign and, on the day of election, as he set out from home, we hear from Suetonius that he turned to his mother, saying, 'Today, Mother, you shall see your son either as *pontifex* or an exile'. He had presumably spent so much on bribes that, if he had not won and thus secured a position that he could exploit to pay back some of his debts, he would have been finished. It was a huge gamble but it paid off. He won, and the life-long post did indeed bring him wealth, prestige, privilege and even an official residence behind high walls in the Forum.

The average citizen of Rome, walking past the high walls of Caesar's new, very public home, would have been aware of the political intrigues of the senators but more concerned with finding bread and shelter. As Rome had grown over the centuries, so had its attraction for villagers and labourers from far afield. Many were peasant families who had lost their land while their bread-winners were away on extended military service. This situation had been worsened by the steady influx of slaves being brought back from successful campaigns or by travelling merchants. Many of these slaves were sent to work on huge landed estates – *latifundia* – and the locals were left with little alternative but to migrate to the capital in search of employment.

Rome was thus over-populated and bursting at the seams. Makeshift shelters sprang up alongside the walls and main roads of the city. The streets were often open sewers. Those that could afford to found accommodation in high-rise tenement blocks, some up to 25 or 30 metres (80 or 90 feet) high. Conditions in these rooms were dreadful, and the meagre space had to be shared with strangers, animals and insects. Fires were a common problem – often deliberately started by unscrupulous businessmen who would then buy the land at a reduced price. Crassus – who was to be one of Caesar's prime financial backers – apparently made a fortune in this way. As rents increased, so did the hardship. The wealth of the expanding Empire was not being evenly distributed and those at the lower end of this widening gap became easy prey for strong orators with deep pockets. The name Julius Caesar was heard in taverns and markets, and before long found its way on to the graffiti-strewn walls. For many of these under-privileged Romans, Caesar offered an alternative. As a conspicuous *Popularis*, the public expected certain things from him if he came to power: such as increasing the grain hand-outs, debt reform, even cancellation of debts, redistribution of land. These were standard populist measures.

In 61 BC, after a year as *praetor* carrying out judicial functions in Rome and Italy, Caesar became governor for a year with the authority (*imperium*) to command an army. At this time, Rome controlled fourteen provinces around the Mediterranean. Caesar's governorship was in western Spain (*Hispania Ulterior*). His debts having reached an enormous sum, he only just managed to leave Rome and escape his creditors, thanks to Crassus standing as his guarantor.

As governor for a year, Caesar automatically became commander-in-chief of the troops (including local levies) stationed in his province. And as soon as he arrived in Spain, he led his troops to battle against tribes in the north-west (in what is now Portugal). Apparently displaying legendary energy, combined with unwavering military determination, Caesar cut a swathe through the territories he attacked, stripping them of anything of value. Even towns and settlements which opened their gates and surrendered were rumoured to have been sacked and looted.

Rome's military strength – its legions – was also its political weakness. Stationed in the provinces, far from Italy, the soldiers (who owned nothing outside the army) relied on their commanders to make sure they were paid, fed, and given ample opportunity to secure the spoils of war. They were therefore happy to follow the lead of men like Caesar. They would benefit as much as he would from extensive military conquest. On completing their terms of service, they further required their commanders to ensure that they received the farms they had come to expect as reward from the state. Therefore it was their commanders, men like Caesar, who controlled the legions.

The dangers were obvious: a general with personal ambition could easily have legions whose first loyalty was to him rather than to Rome.

When Caesar's year as governor came to an end, the Senate awarded him a Triumph. These Triumphs were highly prized, allowing a victorious general on his return to Rome to dress in purple, and lead his army, its captives and booty through the streets.

Caesar, however, faced a dilemma. If he accepted the Triumph he could not enter Rome until the day of the march itself. But in the meantime the next elections for consul were to take place in the Assembly. Caesar wanted to be a candidate – but was prohibited if he remained outside the city walls. Though he desperately wanted the thrill and pride of the Triumph, he waived his right to it and announced his candidacy, preferring to sacrifice one day's glory for the sake of what could lie ahead.

Caesar made the right decision: within weeks, although legally two years

too young, he had been made consul. The year was 59 BC. The eyes of Rome were upon him.

Caesar and his co-consul Bibulus were the first men of Rome. But, again, it seemed that this was only the start of Caesar's ambition. For he now agreed a political pact with two men who had been frustrated by the Senate. The first was Pompey, aged forty-six, who was the greatest Roman general, having recently conquered much of the East. The second was Caesar's financial backer, Crassus, aged fifty-five, one of the richest men in Rome, and determined to become even richer. To cement this pact, Caesar gave his only daughter, Julia, to Pompey in marriage.

These three – known to history as the First Triumvirate – effectively ruled Rome. A pamphlet published at the time prophetically condemned them as a 'three-headed monster' which would devour the Republic. Bibulus, the second consul, was physically bullied into staying at home (he had dung thrown over his head), complaining of bad omens. A joke passed through the taverns of Rome to the effect that all new decrees were being signed not 'in the consular year of Bibulus and Caesar' but 'Julius and Caesar'.

Pompey demanded land for his veteran soldiers. Crassus demanded financial advantage. Caesar satisfied both. But his own ambition was over-riding. At the end of the year's consulship he would, as was normal, take up a provincial governorship. Caesar wanted one which offered plenty of opportunity for continued conquest. He could then earn enough to become both wealthy and powerful – with loyal legionaries behind him.

The Roman general Pompey who conquered much of the East and to whom Caesar gave his only daughter, Julia, in marriage.

The Senate was divided in its attitude towards Caesar. Some saw advantages in joining forces with him. Others despised the senator. Cicero believed 'the monstrosity of Caesar's nature' was 'concealed in his gay and friendly manner'. And Plutarch recorded that:

Cicero, who understood how powerful a character was hidden behind Caesar's agreeable, good-humoured manners, said that, in general, he could detect in everything that Caesar planned or undertook in politics a purpose that was aiming at absolute power. 'On the other hand,' he said, 'when I notice how carefully arranged his hair is and when I watch him adjusting the parting with one finger, I cannot imagine that this man could conceive of such a wicked crime as to destroy the Roman Republic...' [2]

Others pointedly declared their complete lack of interest in him. 'I am not remotely eager, Caesar, to please you. Nor to know the first thing about you,' claimed Catullus, a contemporary poet and wit.

Those who were becoming concerned about Caesar's behaviour had good reason to be so. Not only was he happy to engage in political bullying but he was increasingly resorting to physical intimidation and violence. Rome – like the entire ancient world – was used to violence. It was part of daily life. Nevertheless it was feared. For Caesar it was a tool – he had used it before and he used it now. He evidently had a very short fuse and disliked people who disagreed with him. Opposing his demands began to require courage.

The provinces that were assigned to the consuls at the end of their year in office were decided upon before their election. But everyone knew Caesar would win, so apparently a group of senators deliberately tried to frustrate his plans by announcing that Caesar's consular province would be 'Italian forests and cattle paths'. If this is true, Caesar would clearly not have been amused – what chance of booty and glory lay in local woods? He had so effectively bribed and intimidated the Assembly that he instead demanded, and had himself voted, the provinces of *Illyricum* (east of Rome as far as Greece) and *Gallia Cisalpina* (now northern Italy). Moreover, he was appointed for a five-year, rather than a one-year term. Then, by a quirk of fate, the governor of *Gallia Transalpina*

The Triumphs of Caesar *as imagined by Andrea Mantegna, in the late fifteenth century.*

41

(southern France) died, and Pompey persuaded the Senate to let Caesar have the third province too. Approximately 320,000 square kilometres (200,000 square miles) were his to do with, in his opinion at least, as he pleased.

❖

Caesar left Rome. Although his position as governor and commander-in-chief prevented his indictment, he remained under great threat from hostile senators. They wanted to prosecute him for allegedly replacing the gold bars in the treasury with gold-plated bronze bars, and forcing through a land bill for Pompey's veterans. In the end the charges were irrelevant; they just wanted to destroy him. Actually Caesar did not go very far: he put on his armour, made sacrifices to the appropriate gods, sounded the trumpets and marched outside the city boundary. There he stopped. Being outside the walls, and thus having taken up his command, he was legally safe.

For some months, he camped in sight of the city, biding his time, unsure of which of his provinces to travel to and, at the same time, keeping abreast of political events within the Senate. Then, in the early spring of 58 BC, news reached him that a large Celtic tribe called the Helvetii were leaving their homes in what is now Switzerland and heading west, to pass through Roman southern Gaul. This was just the opportunity Caesar had been waiting for. He could claim that such a tribe – numbering maybe tens, even hundreds of thousands – was too dangerous to allow near the Roman province.

Caesar deflected the Helvetii from the Roman province but then pursued them, even though it was illegal for a governor to lead his forces outside his province without the Senate's permission. Caesar, however, did not hesitate, claiming that he was pursuing an enemy passing through allied territory. It was even less acceptable that he was now turning an arguably defensive policing action into a general conquest and permanent occupation. The war to conquer all of Gaul was one that we can assume he decided upon for personal gain, regardless of the fact that it could bring the Empire into conflict with dozens of tribes on a much larger scale than ever before. Some claimed, on Caesar's behalf, that he was acting for the sake of Rome's greater glory. The truth was blunter. Caesar, aged forty-one, was acting to further his own glory.

Yet this is why Caesar so perfectly reflects Rome in its early days. His energy, determination and ruthlessness mirror the forces that propelled this small village to such prominence. As the city and then the Empire grew, success paved the way for more success. As the Empire expanded, the rewards of military expansion continued to increase, thus motivating the Romans to carry out further conquests. At the same time, the personal greed and ambition of Roman aristocrats like Caesar involved Rome in wars that it might not otherwise have attempted.

To succeed, Caesar had to be not only a brilliant and manipulative politician but also a great commander. He was apparently perfectly willing to travel thousands of miles on horseback or in a carriage, testing his own endurance, and that of all those around him.

According to Suetonius: 'Caesar was a most skilful swordsman and horseman, and showed surprising powers of endurance. He always led his army, more often on foot than in the saddle... If he reached an unfordable river he would either swim or propel himself across it on an inflated skin, and often arrived at his destination before his messengers whom he had sent ahead to announce his approach'.

Suetonius also mentions that: 'Caesar was accustomed to write or dictate and read at the same time, simultaneously dictating to his secretaries four letters on the most important subjects or, if he had nothing else to do, as many as seven'.

And Plutarch tells us that: 'he used warfare as a tonic to his health. By long hard journeys, simple diet, sleeping night after night in the open, and rough living he...made his body strong enough to resist all attacks'.

Such behaviour inspired his soldiers, as they slogged behind him carrying their weapons and equipment, three days' rations. saw, sickle, pickaxe, stakes for constructions, chain, wicker basket and rope.

When Caesar finally brought his army face to face with the Helvetii he is said to have addressed the soldiers, his words being passed back down the ranks. He evidently told them that they were fighting for Rome and for themselves. If victorious they would receive money and slaves. Caesar further told them that he had sent his own horse away so that he would stand in the front lines with them. He also issued a warning – any deserter, without exception, would be killed.

In the battle that followed, the Helvetii were crushed. Caesar now turned to unconquered Gaul.

To further his self-promotion, Caesar himself recorded his campaign in Gaul in his *Commentaries*, one of Latin literature's great texts. Referring to himself throughout as 'Caesar' (as if he were a dispassionate and objective observer), the *Commentaries* naturally portray him as a great and successful leader. This was a remarkable and highly effective piece of propaganda:

Caesar had to do everything at once – hoist the flag which was the call to arms, recall the men from their work on the camp, fetch back those who had gone far afield in search of material for the rampart, form the battle line, address the men, and sound the trumpet for going into action...

As the situation was critical and no reserves were available, Caesar snatched a shield from a soldier in the rear, made his way into the front line, addressing each centurion by name, and shouting encouragement to the rest of the troops... His coming raised men's hopes; each man wanted to do his best under the eyes of his commander-in-chief...
so ended the battle by which the tribe was almost annihilated and their name almost blotted out from the face of the earth...

Caesar sold all the inhabitants of the place by auction in one lot. The purchasers reported that the number of persons included in the sale was 53,000...
Caesar remained a few days in their territory, burning all the villages and cutting down the crops...

Caesar resolved to make an example of them in order to teach the natives to be more careful in future... he had all their councillors executed and the rest of the population sold as slaves... [3]

Dozens of large and small tribes were coerced to Caesar's will as he criss-crossed the countryside, inflicting what effectively amounted to a massacre of the Gallic peoples. Some of his actions in Gaul were carried out simply to impress his peers and the voters back in Rome. In 55 BC, he became the first man to bridge the Rhine. In 55 and 54 BC he became the first Roman to invade Britain. According to Plutarch: 'many…asserted that the place did not exist at all and that both its name and the reports about it were pure inventions. So, in his attempts to occupy it, Caesar was carrying the Roman Empire beyond the limits of the known world…'

In the *Commentaries* we read that:

Caesar made active preparations for an expedition to Britain… [but] although he interviewed traders from all parts, he could not ascertain anything about the size of the island, the character and strength of the tribes which inhabited it, [or] their manner of fighting…

most of the tribes in the interior do not grow corn but live or milk and meat, and wear skins. All the Britons dye their bodies with woad, which produces a blue colour, and shave the whole of their bodies except the head and upper lip… Wives are shared… by far the most civilized inhabitants are those living in Kent…

Caesar set sail about midnight… Caesar reached Britain with the first ships about nine o'clock in the morning, and saw the enemy's forces posted on all the hills… Caesar thought this a quite unsuitable place for landing…after proceeding about seven miles he ran his ships aground on an evenly sloping beach, free from obstacles..

The soldiers, weighed down by the heavy burden of their arms, had at the same time to jump down from the ships, get a footing in the waves, and fight the enemy…they did not show the same enthusiasm as they usually did in battles on dry land… [but] they charged the enemy and put them to flight… [4]

As always, Caesar was portrayed in heroic terms: 'Caesar prepared for anything that might happen', 'Caesar guessed the truth', 'Caesar came to the rescue', 'Caesar foresaw that what had happened before would happen again', until finally 'Caesar compelled [them] to make peace'.

Caesar did indeed secure a foothold and then return to the mainland. In reality, his two raids on Britain had actually resulted in the partial destruction of his fleets due to bad weather and his near defeat on land due to stiff resistance. In the words of the historian Cassius Dio, writing in the third century AD: 'Caesar gained nothing either to himself or his country but the glory of having fought in Britain'.

But it wasn't what actually happened that counted: it was what Romans were told had happened. Caesar knew the value of self-promotion and he knew how to get the results he wanted. The *Commentaries* tell us that: 'On the conclusion of these campaigns and the receipt of Caesar's dispatches, the Senate decreed a public thanksgiving of 20 days…'

In 52 BC, Caesar finally defeated the Gauls. At Alesia, he encircled an entire hill (and the army on top of it) with over 32 kilometres (20 miles) of fortifications. He then simultaneously fought both the besieged army and a massive relieving army at his rear – and won. The tribes of Gaul later agreed that further rebellion was pointless. Rome was their master.

After eight years of warfare, Gaul was conquered. Eight years of travelling along stone and dirt tracks, eating poor food and sleeping under leather tents or rough ceilings. Eight years of maps, tactics, discipline, courage, treaties, executions and sheer brutal, bloody battle. Thousands of Roman soldiers had died and hundreds of thousands of Gauls had been slaughtered. The fifty-year-old Caesar was much changed from the thirty-year-old who had cried before Alexander's statue. He had felt the thrill of victory and the sweet sense of absolute authority. In Gaul, he was omnipotent and it was a power he was reluctant to relinquish.

❖

During his long absence from Rome, Caesar appears to have relied on the remaining two members of the Triumvirate. Whenever he could – and especially during the winters – he had journeyed to the borders of Italy to meet colleagues or Pompey and Crassus themselves. In 56 BC, three years into Caesar's Gallic campaigns, the three men had met at Lucca (now in northern Italy). There it was agreed that Pompey and Crassus would support Caesar in his bid to gain another five years as governor of his three provinces. Soon after that, Caesar sent troops on leave to vote in Rome for Crassus and Pompey to be made consuls in 55 BC. The plan worked perfectly. However, the Triumvirate soon began to fragment. Caesar's daughter Julia died in childbirth in 54 BC and her husband Pompey was encouraged by some senators to abandon Caesar and set himself up in opposition. Then, in 53 BC, Crassus was killed while fighting the Parthians (rulers of what are today Iran and Iraq).

Seeing Caesar's weakness, this same small group of senators – at the conclusion of his Gallic wars – vowed to take him to court for his alleged abuses of power prior to his departure for Gaul a decade before. They couldn't face the prospect of Caesar becoming consul again.

From his province of Cisalpina, Caesar considered his options, and is alleged to have said: 'I would sooner be the first man in a barbarian village than the second in Rome'. He, Caesar, the mighty conqueror, was not going to face trial. To a man inflated with power and success, the very idea was abhorrent. Eventually, after months of negotiation and bargaining, he decided that the only course of action was to take his legions directly to Rome and declare himself the new authority. He refused a senatorial order to give up his legions and, in effect, declared war on Rome itself.

Cicero expressed the senators' collective sense of outrage in one of his letters: 'This insane, miserable fellow has never had the least inkling of the good! Yet he claims that he is doing everything for the sake of his honour! But where does honour reside, if not in honourable conduct? And can it be honourable to hold on to an army without the approval of the Senate? How can it be permissible to begin a civil war for the sake of one's own honour?'

Cicero – Rome's greatest orator and writer at the time of Caesar.

In his *Civil Wars*, Caesar claimed it was the Senate who was acting dishonourably – 'my prestige has always been of prime importance to me, even outweighing life itself'. The truth was that he was a rebellious general who had brilliantly and brutally conquered Gaul and was now attempting to overthrow the legitimate government of Rome. Caesar's alternative was nothing but his dominating rule. He, however, had no doubts: to protect his honour, to save himself from prosecution and exile, civil war was the only path he could take. He took the gamble and declaring 'the die is cast', crossed the north-eastern border of Italy – partially marked by the minor river Rubicon – and headed towards Rome.

Word presumably spread quickly through the fine villas and tenement flats, through the wine shops and the bakeries. Few had not heard about Caesar's actions in Gaul over the previous years. They knew of his cruel enslavements and executions – Romans could accept this treatment of foreigners but now they feared it would happen to them. Those with most to lose packed their most valuable possessions on to carts, left slaves in charge of their property, and headed south. The opposition too (accompanied by their military commander Pompey), were among those who left, decamping to Greece. Pompey, however, had a strategic reason for doing so; he knew Caesar would follow him and thus hoped to over-extend his supply lines.

As Caesar made his way south, his experienced soldiers easily demolished hastily organized city defences. However, he ordered that those who were caught should be released and simply asked not to take arms against Caesar again. Word of this unusual clemency circulated. Fears were calmed, city gates opened without a fight. Caesar soon won the heads, if not the hearts, of his fellow country-people.

Cicero lamented this turn of events – 'The country towns are treating him like a god… What ovations and honours these towns offer him!… They are delighted with the cunning kindness of Caesar' – but his words fell on deaf ears. Caesar entered Rome. Nevertheless he would not celebrate victory until Pompey and his legionaries were defeated in battle.

A war had to be won, the most remarkable civil war in history, for it was fought not only nationally but internationally – in Europe, North Africa and the Near East. The western world was the battleground for these two men.

Pompey had taken his legions to Greece. Caesar ignored them, turned his men around and marched to Spain to face legions loyal to Pompey. There, Roman soldier faced Roman soldier. Both armies were equally well trained and equipped. Both knew how the other would fight. Both thought they had right on their side.

Here, more than in Gaul, Caesar's motivational skills were vital. He told his troops that without him they would never receive the back pay, awards and farms they had been promised. Caesar's words of inspiration, though used often before, helped secure victory. Without celebrating, he hurried east, intent on confronting Pompey himself.

The *Optimate* senators, sitting out of harm's way in Greece, had appointed Pompey supreme commander and he had had a year to prepare for the forthcoming battle. He now had nine legions (with two more on the way) and many thousands of allied stone-slingers, horsemen and archers. Though approaching sixty, he impressed all the allied troops with his skill, energy and determination. Caesar landed in Greece, and offered to talk peace. Pompey refused and it was clear that this dispute would now only be decided on the battlefield.

After months of manoeuvring, the two armies met on the plain of Pharsalus. Caesar was outnumbered two to one: 45,000 men against his 22,000. Many in Pompey's camp regarded victory as certain and were already arguing over who would get Caesar's property. But once battle was joined, Caesar took control, anticipating all Pompey's actions and, by using his reserve at a crucial moment, crushed the over-confident enemy. A total of 15,000 were killed and 24,000 captured. It was a decisive victory.

Pompey, however, escaped and fled to Egypt. Caesar gave chase but, in his haste, became increasingly reckless. He crossed the Mediterranean with hardly enough men or supplies for a skirmish but the gods had been benevolent for so long that he probably could not believe this would change, now that he was so close to the ultimate victory.

In 48 BC, Caesar sailed into Egypt's capital, Alexandria, the biggest port in the Mediterranean. Ships arrived daily from Spain, Greece, Gaul and Italy. Egypt's glory was in the past, but the country, still an independent state, remained enormously wealthy. Its greatest resource was its grain which had brought the Romans here 200 years earlier and had made them frequent visitors to Alexandria's docks ever since.

When Caesar's ship arrived at the quayside there was something special waiting for him – Pompey's head. The thirteen-year-old Egyptian boy-king, Ptolemy XIII, thinking that Caesar would be the next ruler of Rome, had killed Pompey as a gift.

Caesar was enraged: not only was it appalling for a foreigner to behead a noble Roman but Caesar had been robbed of his honourable military victory, robbed of his chance to demonstrate once and for all that he was now the greatest Roman general.

In Rome, at taverns, bath-houses and markets, rumours spread that Pompey was dead and Caesar had taken himself an Egyptian mistress – the new queen of Egypt, a twenty-year-old called Cleopatra. She was clearly bewitching him in her desire to be queen of Rome. It was reported that they had sailed up the Nile together like young lovers.

The gossips and rumour-mongers were kept fully occupied. They talked of a battle in Alexandria against rebellious Egyptians, in which Caesar, then fifty-three, had to swim to safety. They recounted a subsequent victory when Caesar, journeying to Rome, had beaten Pharnaces, the son of King Mithridates of Pontus. The victory had been so swift that Caesar was supposed to have remarked: 'I came, I saw, I conquered'.

❖

In 46 BC, having returned to Rome once again, Caesar organized not one but four Triumphs (taking care to focus on his victories over non-Romans – Gaul, Egypt, Pontus, North Africa). Events lasting over a month were organized. Supporters and sycophants rushed to his side. Many others were war-weary and willing to give him a chance, provided his rule was temporary. Out of respect, idolatry or fear, Caesar was again made Dictator. He had first had this six-month designation in 49 BC but now he was appointed for an unprecedented ten years.

Caesar faced enormous problems, many caused by the civil war, others unsolved from previous years. The war had severely affected life in Rome – and throughout Italy. There had been no government, retired veterans had been called up from their farms, money had been spent on armies and weapons. It had been largely Caesar's fault; now it was entirely his responsibility. And Rome, tired of disorder and chaos, looked to him for a new start.

Caesar needed to work at his desk from before dawn till after dusk. His workload was enormous and no doubt there were rooms full of written petitions covering tables, chairs and floors. There were no civil servants to aid him, only his friends – especially his right-hand-man Mark Antony – slaves and ex-slaves (freedmen). Many of those senators who had opposed him he allowed to return in safety and without punishment. The Senate, however, he effectively continued to ignore. His first priority was to see his veteran soldiers settled in new towns or on confiscated lands. Caesar always knew – and declared – that power rested on soldiers and money, with the latter securing the former. In 49 BC he had illegally seized the contents of the State Treasury; now he confiscated the property of those he had recently defeated but not pardoned.

To facilitate the settlement of his veterans, he established up to twenty new Roman sites or 'colonies' around the Mediterranean. This sometimes involved the rebuilding of cities that Rome itself had destroyed, such as Carthage in North Africa and Corinth in Greece. These settlements were also set up to attract many of Rome's urban poor who had caused so many problems in the previous decades. It was brilliant: at a single stroke Caesar was able to rid himself and Rome of a problem and help further the Romanization of certain provinces.

Caesar's intellect was all-embracing: he rewrote laws, encouraged teachers and doctors to come to Rome, and laid down rules for funerary monuments. He replaced the lunar calendar (which had added extra days whenever necessary) with a solar year of 355 days, with added day

The Senate House before Caesar's reconstruction.

every fourth year. (The year 45 BC was thus 445 days long, so that the following year would start at the right point.)

After five months in Rome, Caesar was again forced to leave on campaign, travelling west to Spain where Pompey's sons had amassed a strong army and overthrown Caesar's appointed governor. Among Caesar's staff was a young relative, Octavius, who would later become Rome's first emperor, Augustus.

In 45 BC, at the Battle of Munda, in southern Spain, Roman once again faced Roman. It was a desperate fight and Caesar, though fifty-six years old, was seen in the front line encouraging his men to one last great effort. Spurred on, his armies were victorious. But it had been close. According to Plutarch: 'As he was going away after the battle he said to his friends that he had often fought for victory, but this was the first time he had fought for his life'.

Caesar returned to Rome. Did he have a long-term ambition, now that he had finally achieved power? Caesar's greatness lay in winning such conflicts; it did not apparently lie in establishing political stability. Rome seemed to bore him and his mind turned back to life with his soldiers. Perhaps he, like Alexander, could conquer as far as the borders of India? He decided to launch a huge assault on the Parthians, Rome's rival in the East. His deputies could look after Rome.

Before leaving for Parthia, Caesar increased the number of senators from 600 to 900 – showing favour to many of those who had helped him during the recent wars. He also gave senatorial status to men from Italian cities and, in a momentous step towards changing Rome from city-state to world empire, he even gave citizenship to some non-Italians, among them Gauls from *Gallia Transalpina*. Incorporating those who had been defeated into the central body politic was absolutely fundamental to the success of Roman imperialism, marked Rome out as very different from other ancient empires such as Sparta, and helped secure the Roman Empire for centuries to come. At the time, however, senior senators were appalled.

Caesar was apparently unconcerned about these elder statesmen. He concentrated instead on his campaign arrangements, and thinking up even more projects for Rome. He was planning to build a great library, to drain marshes, to build a canal, to improve roads and harbours. He even passed a law forbidding carts laden with goods, except those being used for building, to appear in the streets of Rome between sunrise and sunset. Though still not monarch in name, he had become one in deed. His birthday was declared a public holiday – and *Quinctilis*, the month of his birth, was later renamed 'Julius' (July). Moreover, he, unlike all other mortals, was to be allowed to have a burial plot within the city walls.

The title of 'king' was of little interest to him and he was astute enough to reject the offer of a crown. (In an anecdote recorded by Suetonius, he said: 'I am not king, but Caesar.') But only the foolish could fail to perceive what he had become. He had taken to sitting in a golden chair at Senate meetings. He still had his foreign mistress, Cleopatra, housed quietly on the other side of the Tiber and he no doubt offended some when he built a new Temple of Venus and put a statue of the Egyptian queen inside it.

Cleopatra, Caesar's Egyptian mistress, with Caesarion, her son by Caesar.

Power was clearly going to his head. He became the first Roman to wear an entirely purple toga as a sign of highest dignity (as opposed to its traditional use by successful commanders during a Triumph). The colour purple was highly expensive because it was so difficult to produce. (Crushed sea-shells gave off a yellowish-white pigment which, when exposed to sun and damp, became a deep violet.) After Caesar, it was to remain the imperial colour.

In February 44 BC, Caesar arranged for his appointment as Dictator to be open-ended, which effectively removed any accountability he may have had. He also decided which of his friends would hold offices of state for years ahead. These actions, however, were not likely to unify Rome. One of his friends, Gaius Matius, pointed out, in a letter to Cicero, that: 'for all his genius Caesar could not find a way out of the Republic's problems'. His power was based on many sections of the community but it threatened the self-interested ambitions of the nobility in the Senate. Caesar was convinced the only way forward for the Empire was strong one-man rule but the nobility simply could not accept this. Too many senators who had been excluded from the possibility of consulship or governorship, thus losing out in terms of both status and money, considered this a step too far. The Republic had, in effect, been suspended – and this was not to everyone's liking.

A plan to murder Caesar had been hatched and it now began to take shape. A group of fifty or sixty leading senators decided that enough was enough. Little thought seems to have been given to what would happen after his death. They could not really be sure whether the general public would support them or not. All that concerned them was removing Caesar. It was planned, as Cicero wrote, 'with the courage of men but the understanding of boys'.

The date of the assassination was set for the Senate meeting on 15 March, known as the Ides of March, three days before Caesar was to leave for Parthia.

The day arrived. Caesar had, by this time, dismissed his Spanish bodyguard, declaring that it was better to die once than constantly fear death. Ignoring his long-suffering wife's plea that, due to a bad dream, he ought to remain indoors, he left home for the last time. The Senate House was being rebuilt, so the senators were to meet on the Campus Martius at the grandiose theatre (the first stone theatre of Rome) built by Caesar's former arch-rival Pompey.

Plutarch writes of Caesar elbowing his way through the crowds and into the building. One man, who knew of the conspiracy, is said to have tried to hand Caesar a warning, but failed to make him read it. Another had prophesied that evil would occur on the Ides of March and, on seeing him in the doorway, Caesar smiled and said that the Ides had come and no misfortune with them. The fortune teller replied that the day had indeed come but had not yet ended.

Inside, Caesar walked along the colonnade and towards a large hall behind the stage. Some of the conspirators were waiting. As Caesar reached them, other senators crowded around him, as if to petition him before proceedings began. He refused and bade them return to their seats. Then, in an instant, his toga, the symbol of citizenship so lovingly awarded him fifty years before, was pulled down around his shoulders so he could not fight back, and the daggers of more than twenty men struck home.

Plutarch described the scene: 'whichever way he turned he met the blows of daggers and saw the cold steel aimed at his face and at his eyes. So he was driven this way and that, and like a wild beast in the toils, had to suffer from the hands of each one of them; for it had been agreed that they must all take part in this sacrifice and all flesh themselves with his blood'.

Many of the blows were feeble scratches and Caesar tried to struggle free. His supporters were too far away to help – this was the last place anyone expected Caesar to be attacked. But, amid a frenzy that caused many senators to injure one another, Caesar, fatally wounded in the chest, sank to the floor. With a last effort he is said to have pulled his toga over his head, so that no one should see him wounded, dying, powerless. As helpless as the baby born to Aurelia fifty-six years earlier, Gaius Julius Caesar died.

News reached the waiting senators – and chaos ensued. Some men fled, fearing for their own lives; others apparently sat motionless, unable to

comprehend the news; while others smiled and clapped their hands in relief. Meanwhile, almost unnoticed, the torn body of Caesar was taken away by servants. After five days, in front of a huge crowd of distraught Romans, it was ceremonially cremated.

❖

As he had hoped, Caesar's legacy survived, not only for a few decades or centuries, but even to the present day. His conquest of Gaul had given Rome a critical secondary centre focused on north-western Europe and the Atlantic. Under the emperors that followed, the Roman world survived for another 400 years in the West and even longer in the East. Roman – and with it Greek – culture was widely disseminated from the Atlantic to the Black

The Ides of March – the date of Caesar's assassination – as imagined by Vincenzo Camuccini (1773-1844). The Senate was the last place Caesar expected to be attacked, but the daggers of his enemies struck home and, fatally wounded in the chest, Caesar sank to the floor.

Sea. Never before or since have Europe and the Mediterranean world been so united – politically, economically, even culturally. It was in such conditions that ideas, religions (not least Christianity) and goods were exchanged, and modern Europe was born. The very name 'Caesar' became synonymous with strong and powerful leadership. The Tsars, the Kaisers, the emperors who followed all took what was originally simply a family name and made it a symbol of their power.

But at Caesar's death Rome was in turmoil. The Republic had collapsed. Civil war was breaking out again. Out of this upheaval, however, there was to arise a stronger Rome led by a man who would change the Roman Empire for ever – the first of the emperors, Augustus.

CHAPTER II

AUGUSTUS

First Among Equals

THE murder of Julius Caesar in 44 BC had brought the Roman Republic to its knees. Once again, civil war looked inevitable. No one seemed able to take control…

Until a teenager arrived, who, through the force of his ambition, personality and skill, proceeded to guide the city and Empire to unsurpassed power and prosperity.

He became the first Roman emperor. And he ruled for over forty years, during which time the Senate gave him the title 'Augustus'.

❖

Julius Caesar was assassinated on 15 March 44 BC. He was stabbed twenty-three times by men he considered colleagues, even friends.

The Republic of Rome had been through decades of sporadic civil war and many had hoped that Caesar, self-appointed Dictator for Life, could bring stability to both city and Empire. But there were a few powerful men who hated him and what he stood for. These men believed that Rome should never bow to the will of one man. They clung to the Republican ideal of annually elected consuls, and they considered Caesar a despot who had fought and manipulated his way to power in an un-Roman, un-Republican manner. It had cost Caesar dear.

❖

Octavius had been born in Rome in September 63 BC. The baby began life

Augustus (63 BC–AD 14), the first of the Roman emperors, who changed the Empire forever. He steadily formulated a system of government which was essentially a monarchy, but clothed in the trappings of a 'restored republic'.

with the same name as his father, Gaius Octavius, who was from a relatively modest background; the descendant, according to his enemies, of merchants rather than aristocrats. As the historian Suetonius put it: 'Cassius of Palma similarly sneers at [Octavius] as the grandson of a baker and a money-changer, writing in one of his letters: "Your mother's flour came from a miserable Arician bakery, and the coin-stained hands of a money-changer from Nerulum kneaded it."'

Though Octavius was born in Rome, his family were of rural Italian descent. His father was from Velitrae, a little town not far from Rome. Having successfully invested in agricultural estates, Octavius's family had for some time been among the town's wealthiest. Even the main street was named after them.

Octavius's father sought political and administrative posts in Rome, not for money, since there was no salary attached to them, but because such posts brought lucrative 'perks' and the opportunity to climb the political ladder.

Octavius was their third child, but their first son, and his proud parents clearly hoped that he would one day be able to improve the family's standing in Roman society. Atia, his mother, was related to some senators and ex-consuls but, most significantly, her uncle was the increasingly important politician, Julius Caesar. When Octavius was only four, his father died. Thereafter Octavius was brought up by his mother, who subsequently remarried.

At the age of twelve, death struck again. His beloved grandmother Julia (Julius Caesar's sister) died. Octavius seems to have been as close to her as to his own mother. On the day of her entombment in the family mausoleum, the young boy, despite being surrounded by senators and other dignitaries, evidently did not shy away from delivering the funeral oration. Indeed, it seems the strength of his tribute impressed the attending Caesar and perhaps for the first time he took note of the fair-haired boy.

Studies in rhetoric, philosophy, Greek and Latin continued, and his elderly Greek tutor, Apollodorus of Pergamum, accompanied the teenager everywhere. Octavius was a good student – and is said to have particularly enjoyed hearing anecdotes which demonstrated moral precepts, many of which he learnt by heart and later in life sent as reminders to his staff. Octavius' heart, however, was no longer in the classroom and, aged seventeen, he was offered the chance of something more exciting – a post on Caesar's staff, campaigning in Spain.

Suetonius described how: '[Octavius] followed with a very small escort, along roads held by the enemy, after a shipwreck too, and in a state of semi-convalescence from a serious illness. This action delighted Caesar who, moreover, soon formed a high estimate of [his] character quite apart from the energetic manner in which he had made the journey.'

After a time in Spain, Caesar sent Octavius east to the Adriatic, in preparation for a major new campaign against Rome's rivals, the Parthians. Octavius was to command the cavalry – a remarkable appointment for one so young. But it was not to be. It was here that Octavius heard that Caesar had been murdered and, to his great surprise, that Octavius himself had been declared, by Caesar, as his heir. This made him heir to both the wealth and the family name of 'Caesar'. Accepting the bequest, he was renamed Gaius Julius Caesar Octavianus – officially becoming head of the Caesar family. (From that moment on he was known to the Roman world as 'Caesar' but, for the sake of clarity, historians refer to him from this point as Octavian.)

Despite his mother's and stepfather's pleas not to get involved, Octavian rushed back to Rome.

❖

Caesar's assassins had not worked out how to deal with this situation; they presumably assumed the old system would automatically reassert itself. In the confusion that followed the assassination, Mark Antony (Caesar's right-hand man) continued as consul but many senators feared, probably unjustly, that he would be even more dictatorial than Caesar. Caesar's adoption of Octavian gave the Senate an alternative.

Octavian seemed ideal as a short-term figurehead, someone to rally around. As the leading senator Cicero wrote, once the traditional process of

Republican government had been reinstated, Octavian, a mere teenager, could be dispensed with. They could 'Praise him, honour him, then get rid of him'.

❖

Octavian promised that he would fight to save Rome from anarchy and dictatorship. Those senators wanting a counter-balance to Mark Antony were happy to give him their backing.

Caesar had been deified and so the youth could offer himself as the son of the divine Julius. Octavian could also use Caesar's name and money to call up his great-uncle's veterans from retirement. He could give the Senate an army to oppose Antony, which would give him credibility and force, if necessary. Although he was legally too young, he was made a senator and given official command. Together, he and much of the Senate immediately sought to undermine Mark Antony with accusations and slanders.

One of the most vocal was Cicero:

...let us speak of the vilest kind of vulgarity. You with that gorge of yours, with those lungs, with that gladiatorial strength of your whole body, had swallowed so much wine at Hippias' wedding that you were forced to vomit in the sight of the Roman people the next day. At an assembly of the Roman people, while in the conduct of public business, it would be disgraceful even to belch [but he] vomited and filled his own lap and the whole tribunal with morsels of food reeking of wine... [1]

Antony's brother Lucius loyally responded in like manner: 'Octavian sold his favours to Aulus Hirtius in Spain for 30,000 gold pieces, and used to soften the hair on his legs by singeing them with red-hot walnut shells'.

Such propaganda was typical and effective. Pamphlets and graffiti appealing to mobs and armies were frequently disseminated in order to gain support. There was no one to check accuracy, no way of suing for libel. There were few boundaries, few restrictions on taste. The war of words was vicious.

Mark Antony attacked Octavian by claiming that 'Julius Caesar made him submit to unnatural relations as the price of his adoption', while Cicero sprang to the young man's defence: 'How uncivilized! How crude! He has heaped on [Octavian] filthy charges drawn from memory of his own indecency and licentiousness. For who is more chaste than this young man? Who more modest? What brighter example have we among our youth of traditional purity? But who is more unchaste than that man who speaks ill of him?'

Mark Antony's year as consul concluded and, as was customary, he became a provincial governor for a year. He wasted no time and immediately set off for the province of Cisalpine Gaul, in northern Italy, to take up his new post and assume command of the province's legions.

Meanwhile Antony's opponents – the Senate and Octavian – quite illegally encouraged the existing governor not to step down. Antony, quite legally, besieged him. The Senate used this as an excuse to send an army against him. The army was led by the two new consuls and Octavian.

In the two battles that followed, Mark Antony was defeated but survived. Both the consuls, however, were killed. The victor therefore was the remarkably composed and clearly ambitious Octavian who then made a decision that would change the course of history.

The nineteen-year-old Octavian had no intention of passing on this victory to the Senate. Instead he turned the legions around and marched on Rome. Suetonius recorded that:

Mark Antony married Cleopatra, Egypt's queen, but the marriage was not recognized in Rome because he was still married to Augustus's sister Octavia.

...at the age of 19 he created himself consul, marched on Rome as though it were an enemy city, and sent messengers ahead in the name of his army to demand that the appointment should be confirmed. When the Senate hesitated to obey, one Cornelius, a centurion leading the deputation, opened his military cloak, displayed the hilt of his sword, and boldly said: 'If you do not make him consul, this will.' [2]

Having been outwitted by the teenager, the Senate granted his request. In only sixteen months Octavian had pulled off a remarkable *coup d'état*. Rome had traditionally been ruled by aristocrats well into middle age. Now it was ruled by a political outsider, not yet twenty.

❖

Although defeated in battle, Mark Antony remained a powerful man, and he was busy raising new legions in Gaul. Octavian also knew that power lay with control of Rome's legions. Instead of pursuing Antony, he sought an alliance with him and with Lepidus, the commander of the powerful Gallic legions, an important general and a former colleague of Caesar. Together, the three of them formed the Second Triumvirate, imitating the one established by Caesar, Pompey and Crassus over a decade earlier. This Triumvirate, however, was no private pressure group; it was sanctioned in law as a three-man dictatorship. Rome was being governed by three war lords.

These war lords now took revenge against those who had opposed them. Hundreds of senators and leading citizens were killed or forced into immediate exile and their property greedily confiscated. Antony made sure that the slanderous Cicero was among those who died. Octavian did nothing to help his former allies – indeed he co-signed their death warrants.

The young man's avowed desire to avenge Caesar's death was apparently only mentioned when it suited him. Sometimes he used it as an excuse to take punitive action against those he disliked or feared. As a result, he developed a widespread reputation for being bloodthirsty and merciless. But Rome had been built on violence; and death was politically acceptable to a man like Octavian. He had no qualms about ordering the execution of large numbers of prisoners, reputedly greeting pleas for mercy with three words: 'You must die'. The actual number of casualties, as so often, is unclear and may have been much less than the 300 senators and 2000 lesser nobility that was claimed. However, fear of death certainly seems to have removed any remaining opposition. It was a period of terror but Octavian no doubt believed that Caesar had made a fatal mistake when, during the civil war, he had offered clemency to his opponents – including those who would later assassinate him. Octavian was not going to make the same error: According to Suetonius: '…when a father and his son pleaded for their lives, [Octavian], it is said, told them to decide which of the two should be spared, by casting lots…The father sacrificed his life for the son; the son then committed suicide; [Octavian] watched them both die…'

Having crushed the opposition, the war lords, encouraged by Octavian, now prepared for war against those of Caesar's assassins who had fled Rome for Greece. Octavian, however, was not a great military commander. Perhaps he was too cautious and calculating by nature. Suetonius tells us that:

…he constantly quoted such Greek proverbs as 'More haste, less speed'. It was a principle of his that no campaign or battle should ever be fought unless the hope of victory was clearly greater than the fear of defeat; and he would compare those who took great risks in the hope of gaining some small advantage to a man who fishes with a golden hook, though aware that nothing he can catch will be valuable enough to justify its loss… [3]

At Philippi in Greece, he became ill and was forced to leave the fighting to Mark Antony who successfully saw to it that Caesar's assassins died and their armies surrendered.

The Triumvirate now divided up the Empire between them. Octavian took control of Italy and the West; Mark Antony took Greece and the East; while Lepidus was given North Africa. Antony was clearly the senior partner at this stage, and had taken the wealthiest and most advantageous territory with opportunity for eastward expansion. Octavian, on the other hand, had the huge problem of settling 130,000 demobilized soldiers. He was forced to confiscate large areas of land throughout Italy – an act which made him extremely unpopular with farmers and landowners who made up most of the population.

In the early forties BC, Octavian, to strengthen the always unstable pact, married Claudia, Antony's stepdaughter. But while Antony was away, Antony's wife Fulvia and his brother Lucius had tried (probably encouraged by Antony) to take advantage of the widespread unhappiness of those who had been evicted from their lands. (The only surviving example of Octavian/Augustus's poetry is from this period. Deliberately coarse in language, the poem bluntly concedes that, though Fulvia wants an affair with him, he would rather 'let trumpets sound' and fight than have sex with her.)

Fulvia's and Lucius's attempted revolt against Octavian failed, thanks to Octavian's friend and general, Agrippa, who successfully put it down. Antony rushed back from Egypt and the two war lords attempted to patch up their alliance. They succeeded, and signed the Treaty of Brundisium, which involved Octavian dissolving his unconsummated marriage to Claudia, and Antony (Fulvia having conveniently died) marrying Octavian's much-loved sister, Octavia. Behind the facade of unity, however, the hostility remained.

❖

Octavian seems to have been consumed with a desire to secure his position. After the Treaty of Brundisium, he married Scribonia but he grew to hate her nagging and divorced her soon after she had given birth to their daughter, Julia.

Then, in 38 BC, aged twenty-four, he married Livia. Though only nineteen, she already had one child (the future Emperor Tiberius), and was pregnant with another, but she found Octavian attractive. According to Suetonius:

[He] was remarkably handsome and very graceful...but negligent of his personal appearance... He always wore a serene expression... [His] eyes were clear and bright, and he liked to believe that they shone with a sort of divine radiance... His teeth were small, few and decayed; his hair, yellowish and rather curly; his eyebrows met above the nose;... [his] body and limbs [were] so beautifully proportioned, one did not realize how small a man he was, unless someone tall stood close to him. [4]

Octavian demanded that her husband divorce Livia so that he could marry her. This proved to be a vital alliance because Livia came from an important Republican family and brought with her the support of the highest nobility, something Julius Caesar had always lacked.

One of the key reasons Octavian had earlier married Scribonia was that she had previously been married to two ex-consuls and was related to Sextus Pompeius, who was proving to be a military thorn in Octavian's side.

The fight against Pompeius was, by Octavian's own admission, the longest and hardest of his life. Pompeius wanted to exploit the memory of his father Pompey (Caesar's great rival) and secure some status for himself. In pursuit of this aim, he was actively interfering with grain ships heading for Rome. The conflict was complex but Octavian, again reliant on Agrippa's great military skills, emerged triumphant. This proved a great propaganda success, as he could claim to have been looking after Italy's interests (restoring the grain supply and destroying the 'pirate' Pompeius) while Mark Antony was elsewhere squandering Roman manpower. The young war lord had another problem too: he had to eliminate Lepidus, who was becoming ambitious in North Africa. This proved easier to deal with, as Lepidus's legions willingly deserted to Octavian, vividly illustrating the power exercised over the legions by the name 'Caesar'. 'Now,' according to the historian Appian '[Octavian] and Antony divided the whole Roman Empire between them.'

The marriage of Augustus to Livia lasted for decades and, rarely for the Roman nobility, seems to have been a love-match.

❖

Mark Antony was unsettled. In 41 BC he had fallen in love with Egypt's Queen Cleopatra, descended from one of Alexander the Great's generals. She considered Mark Antony the new ruler of Rome and sought to seduce him, as she had Julius Caesar. She succeeded but this was the point at which Mark Antony had to return to Italy to shore up his relations with Octavian, and agree the treaty that involved marrying Octavian's sister, Octavia.

Mark Antony had then taken Octavia to his home in Athens. But in 37 BC

The elaborate decoration of a wealthy Roman home.

he made the fatal error of sending her back to Rome so that Cleopatra could join him. He not only preferred the Egyptian queen's company but he also needed her wealth to maintain his position against Octavian and to help finance a new campaign against Parthia. In return, she wanted Antony to help her create a new empire centred on Egypt. Mark Antony married Cleopatra – although it was not recognized because he was still married to Octavia, and a Roman marriage to a non-citizen had no legal status. In Rome, Octavian was incensed at this treatment of his sister but was also aware that he had been handed a powerful propaganda weapon – he could now present himself as the guardian of traditional Roman values while Antony was seen as the libertine being corrupted by the East. The rift between the two men could no longer be healed. Octavian claimed this was now a war for the integrity of Roman life itself.

Antony was singularly unfortunate in falling foul of Cicero and Octavian, the two greatest propagandists and perverters of the truth in the late Republic. The fact that Antony had rescued Rome from chaos following Caesar's assassination was forgotten in the flood of vitriol that was now directed towards him. The historian Cassius Dio later echoed their condemnations:

...who would not weep when he sees and hears what Antony has become?... now he has abandoned his whole ancestral way of life, has embraced alien and barbaric customs, has ceased to honour us, his fellow countrymen, or our laws, or his father's gods... He is either blind to reason or mad, for I have heard and believed that he has been bewitched by that accursed woman... Henceforth, let nobody consider him to be a Roman citizen, but rather an Egyptian... [5]

Octavian forged or illegally removed Mark Antony's will from its supposedly inviolable safe storage with the Vestal Virgins and read it out in public: in it Mark Antony apparently named his children by Cleopatra as his heirs. This horrified Romans. Rumours spread that he was even thinking of taking over Rome and then moving the capital to Alexandria.

In contrast, Octavian continued to portray himself as the defender of tradition, acting not for a foreign queen, but for the people of Italy – the townspeople, the farmers, the veterans.

Antony must have known he was losing the war of words with Octavian. He had hoped to score a major propaganda victory by defeating the Parthians in the East but had instead suffered the humiliating loss of legionary standards and was in no state to attempt their retrieval.

Octavian, meanwhile, realized that ultimately he would have to defeat Mark Antony in battle, and preferably not on Italian soil. For four years he laboured to build up a fleet until, in 31 BC, he prayed to the god Apollo, and headed east to bring this rivalry to a climax at the battle of Actium, on Greece's western coast.

The poet Virgil described the scene:

In the centre could be seen the fleets of bronze, the battle of Actium; you saw all Cape Leucas aglow with War's array, the waves ablaze with gold. On one side Augustus leading the Italians into battle, with the Senate and People, his household gods and the great gods... On the other side, with barbaric wealth and motley arms, Antony, victorious from the nations of the dawn and the Red Sea, brings with him Egypt, and the powers of the Orient ...and there follows – Oh shameful thing – his Egyptian wife... [6]

Octavian's friend, the great general Agrippa, won the sea battle. But it was at a cost. Many great men of Rome and Italy who – despite all the propaganda – had sided with Antony, died.

'Now a second generation is ground to pieces by civil wars,' asserted the poet Horace, while the philosopher-playwright Seneca lamented that 'Actium's waters had been stained with Roman blood'.

Mark Antony and Cleopatra fled in their ships to Egypt. But their reprieve was short-lived. When Octavian arrived overland the following year, both committed suicide: Mark Antony, in despair at having abandoned his fleet and the humiliation of his position, stabbed himself. Cleopatra, in fear of being dragged through Rome as a prisoner, took her life with the poisonous bite of an asp.

❖

Octavian returned to Rome and celebrated in triumph.

According to Macrobius's *Saturnalia*, written in the fourth century AD:

He returned to Rome with all the glory of the victory at Actium. Among those congratulating him was a man carrying a raven which he had taught to say 'Hail, Caesar, victor, commander!' Caesar was amazed. A friend of this person told Caesar that the man had a second raven and asked him to insist on its production. The bird was brought and spoke the words it had learned 'Hail, victor, commander, Antony!' [7]

Octavian had ordered that Caesarion, the child of Cleopatra and Julius

Caesar, be killed so that he would never challenge his position. Now, showing rather more compassion, he spared Antony and Cleopatra's two children and had them brought up, where he could keep watch on them, in his obliging sister Octavia's household.

Octavian made the deceased Cleopatra's nation his personal province and banned senators from going there. Apart from its vital grain, Egypt brought Octavian enormous wealth from the Queen's treasuries. He could now patronize all sections of the community, paying off his armies and making gifts to the people.

He later recorded that: '...about 500,000 Roman citizens were under military oath to me. Of these, when their term of service was complete, I settled in colonies or sent back to their own municipalities a little more than 300,000, and to all these I allotted land or made cash payments as a reward for military service'.

Some criticized his behaviour but they could do little. The historian Tacitus claimed that: 'He seduced the army by gifts, the common people by the provision of cheap food, and everyone by the blandishments of peace. Men of spirit had died on the battlefield. The remainder were rewarded by wealth and position in proportion to their readiness to accept servitude'.

At the age of thirty-three, Octavian was master of Rome and all its provinces. Rome, however, had experienced fourteen years of struggle and decades of bitter, costly civil war before that. Octavian could not afford to relax.

The great general Agrippa, Augustus's friend and right-hand man.

For many of Octavian's contemporaries, Actium was not the turning point that some have claimed. Day-to-day life was never that quick to change. But this was the moment at which Octavian seems to have decided to create a new era of peace and prosperity. As a tangible sign of the return to stability, Octavian – with much help from his friend and right-hand-man Agrippa – began a huge building campaign.

Aided by the opening of the local Carrara quarries, which provided a huge supply of fine white marble, Octavian began a process that was to occupy him for decades – the improvement of the capital city. 'I found Rome brick,' he said, 'and left it marble.'

In 28 BC alone he restored no fewer than eighty-two temples. And, according to Suetonius, he encouraged others to do the same: 'He urged leading citizens to embellish the city with new public monuments or to restore and improve ancient ones, according to their means. Many responded: thus the Temple of Hercules raised by Marcius Phillipus, the Hall of Liberty by Asinius Pollio, an amphitheatre by Statilius Taurus…'

Octavian portrayed himself as a patron, injecting money into the economy and elevating the splendour of the city. Though immensely rich, he, himself, lived frugally. In Rome, he evidently slept in the same bedroom for over forty years, even though the winter climate did not agree with his health. His bed was low and without frills. And his clothes were homespun and woven by his wife Livia, his daughter Julia and his granddaughter, also called Julia. He only wore 'good' clothes for official occasions. His office he called 'my little workshop'. He was determined to remain a pious, modest image of Italian virtue rather than espouse the royal pomp of Egyptian pharaohs and Oriental monarchs. His one noticeable vanity was the thick soles on his shoes to make him seem taller – he was apparently embarrassed about his height.

His house was neither particularly large nor elegant. He deliberately avoided living in a palace as part of his anti-monarchical image. Though he was busy cladding the rest of Rome in marble, his own living quarters were devoid of marbles and mosaics. There were few statues or paintings, though he loved landscaped gardens. Octavian was a man of enormous intellectual

curiosity. He loved 'rarities' and at his summer house on Capri he displayed the weapons of ancient warriors as well as a collection of gigantic skeletons of extinct land and sea animals.

Though, in some ways, he was acting in a way he thought appropriate, he was, by nature, a man of unpretentious habits. Not for him the elaborate Roman dinner. He actually preferred to eat simply. Suetonius tells us that: 'He was frugal and, as a rule, preferred the food of the common people, especially the coarser sort of bread, whitebait, fresh hand-pressed cheese, and green figs of the second crop; and would not wait for dinner, if he felt hungry, but would eat anywhere...'

Wall paintings from the House of Augustus, c. 30–25 BC. Augustus avoided living in a palace as part of his anti-monarchical image.

According to Suetonius, this regard for moderation and simplicity extended even to his speech:

[Octavian] cultivated a simple and easy oratorical style, avoiding purple passages, artfully contrived prose rhythms, and 'the stink of far-fetched phrases', as he called it; his main object being to say what he meant as plainly as possible...

All important statements made to individuals, and even to his wife Livia, were first committed to notebooks and then repeated aloud; he was haunted by the fear of saying either too much or too little if he spoke off-hand. [8]

Octavian worked very hard, even dictating while being shaved or having his hair cut. If awake at night, he would get slaves to read to him. When time allowed, his pleasures seem to have been as uncomplicated as his habits – he enjoyed conversation, playing with children, walking, running, handball. He also enjoyed a little light gambling. Suetonius says that: 'At some dinner parties he would auction tickets for prizes of most unequal value, and paintings with their faces turned to the wall, for which every guest present was expected to bid blindly, taking his chance like the rest: he might either pick up most satisfactory bargains, or throw away his money.'

Everything he did, all that he said, was part natural, part act. Octavian knew that he had to be an actor, playing the role most likely to appeal to a demanding Roman audience. After a century of brutal civil war and arrogant triumphant army commanders, the people of Rome and Italy wanted a man who appeared to respect Republican virtues. If that was what they wanted then that was what Octavian would give them. If it was a mask, if only a partial mask, then Octavian would wear it. But behind the mask there was always a ruthless and autocratic leader.

❖

Octavian recognized, as Julius Caesar had before him, that the worst offence he could commit as far as Roman aristocrats were concerned was to call himself 'king'. Romans had hated the very idea since living under a monarchy many centuries earlier. And Caesar had met his death partly because the Senate would not tolerate his monarchical behaviour.

Octavian knew he had to avoid the same mistake. It was to take him forty years of development and adaptation to find the right political formula, but right from the start he made sure his public declarations were appropriate: 'May it be my privilege to establish the Republic in a firm and secure position'.

Despite such rhetoric, he was actually seeking to increase his executive powers. Publicly, though, he had to be seen as devolving power back to 'the Senate and the People' – *Senatus Populusque Romanus*. Achieving this deception required enormous political skill.

Octavian could never completely relax because he could never forget the fate of his 'father' Caesar. There was always the threat of assassination: a dagger in the back, a poisoned meal, an unexplained fire. His success as a military leader had eventually brought peace and earned him popularity with the war-weary public but he had to maintain his position with the Senate – the official governing body of Rome and the Empire. In the period of confusion and civil war between 44 and 29 BC the Senate had swelled to 1000 men. These Octavian reduced to 600, and all of them, one way or another, needed manipulating, nurturing, watching. Octavian loved boxing and his approach to politics was often reminiscent of the sport: protecting the head, parrying, then unleashing body blows or knock-out punches. This was how he dealt with senators. He worked with them, socialized with them, promoted and rewarded them. At times, he punished them. Slowly, in this way, the ancient Republican dynasties and the newly wealthy families were reconciled to his regime.

In 27 BC, after careful negotiations and stage-management he made a pretence of surrendering his powers back to the Senate. Cassius Dio claims he spoke the following words: 'The fact that it is in my power to rule over you for life is evident… I am mild by nature and have no desire to dominate… [my father Julius Caesar] refused the monarchy when you offered it, and I, when I hold it, now lay it down… who could be found who is more magnanimous than I…who more nearly divine?…Allow me to live out my life in peace…'

Despite the apparent return of the legal sovereignty of the Republic, the Senate knew there was, in fact, no alternative to strong one-man rule except civil war. As Tacitus put it: 'A world exhausted by civil war passed into his control... How many were left who could have seen the Republic?... the State had been transformed and the old Roman character no longer existed... the rule of a single man was the only possible remedy for a country in turmoil...'

His only title, *princeps* (meaning 'first citizen' and later becoming 'prince' in medieval times), was a mask behind which he exercised unlimited authority. Throughout the rest of his life Octavian portrayed himself merely as the humble servant of the Senate and People of Rome, from whom he had constitutionally received all his powers. Rome would be neither a monarchy nor a dictatorship, but a principate.

He also styled himself *Imperator* – the title given to a conquering general. Octavian used it to signify that he was commander-in-chief of all the armed forces. It is this term which gives us the word 'emperor'.

Octavian remained consul, automatically elected every year. He had won the civil war, was a bringer of peace, a giver of wealth, a bestower of patronage and prestige and, above all, he commanded the legions. As a further sign of his power, he was happy to wear the 'crown' of state. The *corona triumphalis* was traditionally a crown of laurel, given to generals returning in triumph from a victorious campaign. Originally made of real leaves, by Caesar's time it was made of gold. (Caesar liked to wear the *corona* because it obscured his bald patch.) It became the crown of emperors.

There were now two types of Roman province: senatorial provinces where the governors were appointed, under Octavian's careful guidance, by the Senate; and imperial provinces where he alone appointed them. Octavian's provinces (Spain, Gaul, Cilicia, Syria, Egypt, with Galatia and Judaea) contained the legions – and thus the real power of the Empire.

According to Cassius Dio: 'The purpose of this decision, as he explained it, was that the Senate should enjoy without anxiety the fairest territories in the Empire, while he should confront the hardships and dangers. But the real

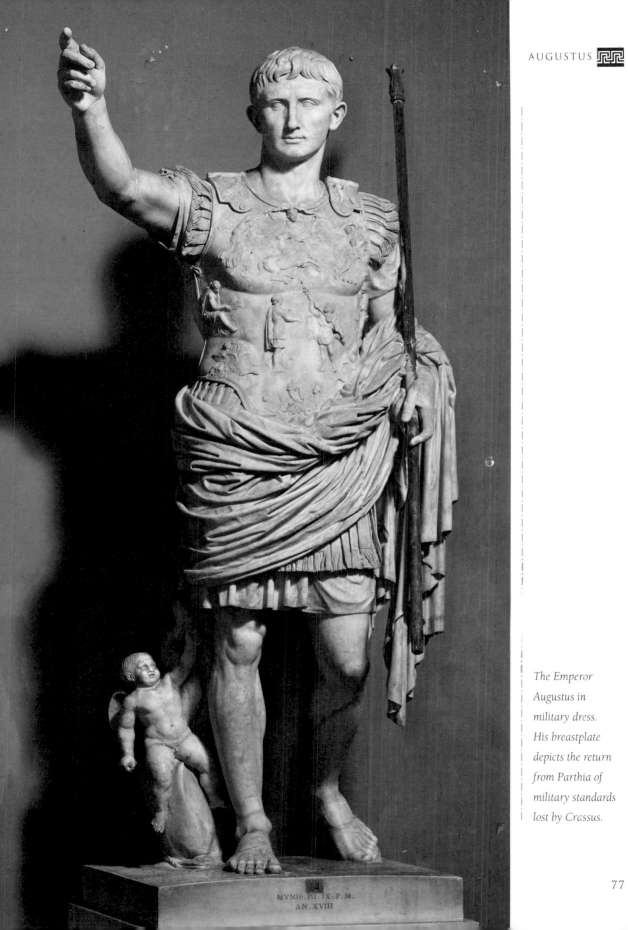

The Emperor
Augustus in
military dress.
His breastplate
depicts the return
from Parthia of
military standards
lost by Crassus.

MVNIF. PII. IX. P. M.
AN. XVIII

object of this arrangement was that the senators should be unarmed and unprepared for war, while he possessed arms and controlled the troops.'

The taxes from senatorial provinces went into one treasury and the taxes from imperial provinces went to another. Octavian supplemented both with his own large fortune.

After Actium he had over sixty legions. These he reduced and reorganized into twenty-eight legions, each with a number and a name, and established in garrisons in the frontier provinces of the Empire. These were the first permanent standing legions. They were recruited exclusively from citizens through voluntary enlistment. Each was commanded by a legate, who was of the senatorial order and, as often as possible, a friend or relative of Octavian's. The commands of these men were nearly always brief (two or three years) and varied. There was thus little danger of anyone building too close a relationship with a legion.

This essentially amateur nature of the Roman high command was compensated by the extreme professionalism of lower ranks within the legion, and in particular the senior centurions. The legions annually swore an oath of allegiance, not to the Senate or to the Republic but to Octavian.

He later established a military treasury, making the legions look to the state, and therefore the emperor, for funds, rather than to their immediate commanding officers. This addressed the key factor in the Republic's collapse: the lack of state provision for legionaries' pensions which had led to the creation of private armies at the disposal of ambitious politicians.

Almost half of the army was now made up of auxiliaries – much smaller units of non-citizens recruited in the provinces. In total their numbers were moving towards equity with the legionaries (about 150,000). Though auxiliary units had been employed before, they had never been in such numbers or on a permanent footing. This was partly an economic measure (since their pay was lower than that of legionaries), and partly a political measure (utilizing the available manpower of the provinces, thus making it unavailable for revolt, and giving provincials a conscious role in imperial defence). Octavian also felt that the particular skills of auxiliaries brought diversity to military tactics.

He frequently travelled to see his armies, rewarding those who had done well but brutally punishing those who had not. Suetonius tells us that:

If a cohort broke in battle, [Octavian] ordered the survivors to draw lots, then executed every tenth man... Centurions found absent from their posts were sentenced to death, like other ranks, and any lesser dereliction of duty earned them one of several degrading punishments – such as being made to stand all day long in front of general headquarters, sometimes wearing tunics without sword-belts, sometimes carrying 10-foot poles, or even sods of earth... [9]

As he slowly developed into the first emperor, Octavian was given a new name by the Senate: they debated various possibilities and finally decided on a word meaning 'revered' – *Augustus*. Octavian later recorded that: 'I received the title of Augustus by decree of the Senate and the doorposts of my house were publicly decked with laurels, the civic crown was fixed over my doorway, and a golden shield set up in the Senate House...in recognition of my valour, clemency, justice and devotion...'

Gaius Octavius had become Caesar Augustus.

The Senate later renamed his 'lucky' month – the month he had ended the war with Antony – 'Augustus' (August), directly following Julius Caesar's 'Julius' (July).

For the next four years, Augustus spent most of his time in Spain and Gaul on campaign or inspection. By remaining absent he hoped to demonstrate publicly that the Republic had apparently been restored and that the Senate was in charge.

Augustus now decided to seek a new arrangement which, once again, would appear to reduce his power within the Roman state, while effectively increasing it. The Settlement of 23 BC claimed to observe the correct constitutional procedures of the Republic; from now on Augustus was to hold no offices at all, not even the consulship.

Having been elected consul every year since his victory at Actium, Augustus decided that the post should now be fully reopened to the aristocracy. Strictly speaking, his repeated tenure as consul had been

LICENTIOSVS

PVRPVREVS SENTINVS ~ BA

illegal and a visible symbol of his dominance. It had also excluded the aristocracy from what remained a highly prestigious and potentially valuable position. It had been the ultimate goal of the nobility during the Republic and Julius Caesar's monopoly of the position had been a factor in his death. Augustus considered that his own authority was now so great that he didn't need any actual office. 'Although I possessed no more official power than others who were my colleagues, I excelled all in influence,' he commented.

The consulships, however, were still most likely to go to those whom Augustus favoured with his patronage. Throughout his life he retained a

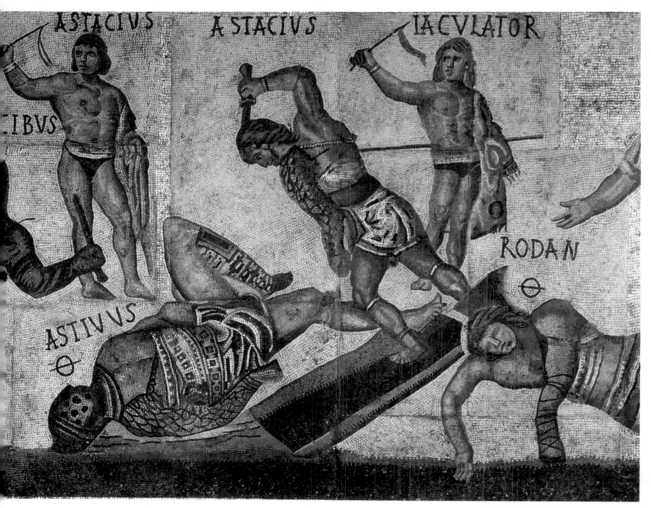

ASTACIVS   ASTACIVS   IACVLATOR

EIBVS

RODAN

ASTIVVS

great ability to manipulate events due to his position as Caesar's heir, the prestige gained from his military successes, and his wealth. He made the aristocracy feel grateful for an apparent return to normality and, with it, their ability to resume their old careers and ancestral ambitions – albeit under his patronage. Religion, too, could be manipulated to show that the gods favoured what Augustus was doing. Finally, but vitally, those who had survived the wars were only too glad of a period of peace and stability in which they could concentrate on their families, businesses and pleasures.

One privilege that was not returned to consuls and senators was the

The various types of gladiator to be seen in the arena. The Roman appetite for excitement and violence seemed limitless.

opportunity to gain Triumphs or to hold games in the arena – such sources of prestige and patronage were to be the exclusive preserve of Augustus. He initiated one set of games, in memory of Actium, which consisted of gymnastic and musical arts. But these Greek-style games were never very popular with Romans who preferred violence and excitement. Augustus gave them that too, though he limited gladiator fights to twice a year and only after the Senate had given its consent. He also limited the number of officially recognized gladiators to 120. Later, he flooded an entire amphitheatre and held a naval battle of thirty vessels between 'Persians' and 'Athenians'. Then he flooded a circus and had thirty-six crocodiles killed. The more extravagant the show, the more extravagant the next one had to be. The Roman appetite for excitement and violence seemed limitless. In sum, this new arrangement was an incredibly skilful act of political manipulation, slowly building what became the office of emperor through a gradual accumulation of powers. In effect, it amounted to a revolution.

To further safeguard his security, Augustus reorganized the Praetorian Guard which had begun to exist in the Republic as bodyguards to the very elite. Augustus expanded the Guard to 9000 men and posted them in and around Rome. They were, in effect, his personal, elite private force, answerable only to him. They ensured that what he could not achieve through political manipulation he could secure through force. It was a sign of his political skill, however, that he rarely required their assistance.

Augustus could apparently be equally harsh within his home. If any of his hundreds of slaves and servants disobeyed him or otherwise misbehaved, he would see to it they were punished. Suetonius mentions, for instance, that: 'Augustus sentenced Thallus, an imperial secretary, to have his legs broken for divulging the contents of a letter.'

Though life in the imperial household may have had its traumas, the atmosphere in the Empire was largely peaceful. There were no civil wars and, though there were rumours of plots against Augustus, most potential enemies had been killed in the civil wars or their immediate aftermath. Externally, however, the frontiers remained under constant threat. Many campaigns were fought in the Balkans and in Germany and these were among the largest Rome had ever undertaken.

❖

Augustus involved himself in everything: from complicated agreements with provincial governors and foreign kings to organizing night-watchmen to guard against fires. He improved the approaches to the city; he ordered that the images of the cross-road gods be crowned twice a year with wreaths of spring and summer flowers. He was equally particular in matters of justice, 'often remaining in court until nightfall …sometimes he even judged cases from his sick-bed in his house,' according to Suetonius.

Much of the work was done by his private household: his 'cabinet' was an intimate circle of friends and supporters. He seems to have been sensible enough to avoid too many supplicants and sycophants. He presumably recognized that the type of men he needed, noble or non-noble, would be fairly outspoken and he was willing to accept criticism; in fact, he preferred to hear it, believing that the occasional vocal attack would lessen the chances of a private physical assault. Those he befriended or took into his confidence could rely on his support indefinitely, so long as they remained trustworthy.

Even the humblest application could fall on Augustus's desk and he frequently spent hours on the humdrum business of Rome. For example, the inhabitants of the Balearic Islands applied to Augustus for military assistance to kill the rabbits that kept destroying their harvest. Once he had come to a decision, he communicated it as fast as possible, using a system he had devised – of horse-riders who took messages and orders by relay throughout the Empire.

The Greek geographer Strabo was among those who acknowledged his administrative skill: 'The Romans and their allies have never enjoyed such peace and prosperity as that provided by Caesar Augustus from the point when he acquired absolute dominion'.

Of course, in Rome, most of Augustus's subjects did not spend much time thinking or worrying about their emperor, except when his actions directly touched their often troubled lives. Virtually all of Rome's citizens lived in

The Senate House, as reconstructed by Augustus. In a time of stability he was able to improve many public services and introduced important changes to building regulations that, for example, ensured the use of more durable and fire-resistant materials and limited the height of tenement flats.

buildings made not of marble but of brick. Many lived in tenement buildings, freestanding 'high-rise' blocks known as *insulae* ('islands'). Some had brick-faced walls hiding a concrete core and timber frame. The ground floor was usually occupied by shops, between which stairways ascended from the street up to the corridors which linked the separate apartments. A citizen would be lucky to have more than one room.

The building's owner frequently lived on the whole ground floor or first floor above the shops while everyone else shared the often cramped building with animals (not just cats and dogs, but chickens, goats and cows – even on the roof).

The single window of each room was fairly small. They were occasionally glazed but, more often, wooden shutters were fastened over them tightly to try and keep the winter winds out. In the corner of some rooms was a charcoal brazier on which the women did all the cooking. The charcoal had to be purchased from a merchant and hauled up the stairs. It was smoky and in these communal buildings there was a constant risk of fire. With no fire escape, only the owner below stood a chance of survival. In fact, these braziers were officially banned because they were such a fire risk; many people lived on 'take-away' food, such as soup, instead.

At night, light was provided by small terracotta oil lamps, which added more unpleasant fumes to the poorly ventilated rooms. If water was needed, the eldest child went down into the street to fill a pitcher at a public fountain or rainwater cistern. Only a few homes had drainage systems; it was much more common to simply fill a pot, then throw it out of the window, giving a suitable warning cry to those below. Not surprisingly, epidemics were frequent, with the dead being buried in mass graves.

Everyone over fifty remembered the street warfare and gang violence of the years before Caesar's dictatorship, the death of Caesar, and the fourteen years of civil war that had followed. Now, in a time of stability, public services could be improved. There was, for example, the construction of a great new aqueduct, which Augustus's friend Agrippa was building to service the north of the city. This was Rome's sixth aqueduct, and vital for the needs of its inhabitants who now numbered nearly a million.

Like all such structures this aqueduct had its own name, Virgo. It was planned to be over 20 kilometres (12 miles) long, and said to carry over 100,000 cubic metres (3,500,000 cubic feet) of water every day. About its great arches, masons directed gangs of slaves, hauling great loads of bricks to the work face, mixing thick mortar for the lining, and manoeuvring the large stone slabs which capped the conduit. Engineers used their instruments to ensure that the gradient was right – no more than 2.5 centimetres every 30 metres (1 inch every 100 feet). Any more would cause spillage or even collapse. In the street below, cart-loads of the whitest marble from the new 'super-quarry' at Luna in Etruria wound their way to the bath complex under construction at the aqueduct's terminus.

Rome's River Tiber, dirty and polluted, was put under the direction of new magistrates, whose duty it was to dredge it of silt and urban rubbish. Perhaps the threat of spring floods could be averted for good.

Talk about Augustus focused not only on the improved water supply but also on his introduction of important changes to building regulations. These laid down that new buildings and conversions of old ones must use more durable and fire-resistant materials – less wood; more brick and concrete. Further safety regulations set a limit of 21 metres (70 feet) in height for any building. Augustus also divided Rome into fourteen districts. In each one he installed a body of 'watchmen' – a cross between policemen and firemen. These squads ensured, first, that the streets were clear of muggers and rival gangs. Second, they saw to it that, if a fire broke out in the crowded tenements, leather hoses and lines of buckets were organized as quickly as possible to try to contain it.

The increasing numbers of unemployed migrants living in Rome had been a major problem for over a century. Caesar had embarked on a policy of colonization and relocation, transferring some of the city's poor to new towns (colonies) around Italy and beyond. Still, between one-third and half of the urban population were reliant on state welfare. Regular measures of grain were distributed from the immense new warehouses built in the very centre of Rome. (The state grain dole went to heads of households, rather than to the homeless or vagrants.) Augustus followed his predecessor's example and eventually founded seventy-five colonies throughout the entire Empire.

In the census of 28 BC, 4,063,000 citizens were accounted for within the Roman Empire. Most would never see Augustus in person, so he made sure that youthful, attractive images of himself were sent throughout the Empire. Hundreds of statues, paintings and reliefs were packaged up and delivered to town councils in all the provinces. The legions also took new statues with them on campaigns and set them up in new towns or conquered territories. These statues were highly respected, even idolized. It became the custom that a man could claim sanctuary by clinging to the emperor's statue. Augustan portraiture turned away from the extreme anatomical realism of the Republic to a more idealized image, harking back to Classical Greek styles. The image of Augustus most frequently seen by people was that on coins – on which he was portrayed as the young, imperial, benevolent Augustus, the man who had brought the people of Rome, Italy and the Empire peace and stability. Many were persuaded that Augustus was quasi-immortal.

Augustus, like his fellow Romans, was only concerned about the provinces in order to preserve the wealth and security of Rome. The Romans not only regarded their own rural neighbours as simpletons and country bumpkins, but regarded all others with even greater disdain. Suetonius tells us that: 'Augustus thought it most important not to let native Roman stock be tainted with foreign or servile blood'.

Not just foreigners ('barbarians') but almost anyone outside Italy was deemed racially and morally inferior to the Romans. Roman literature and art is packed with racial stereotypes – eastern peoples were innately dishonest, whereas Romans always kept their word; northerners were stupid and primitive; even Greeks, from whom the Romans borrowed so much, were seen as cowardly, effeminate and cunning.

Nevertheless, the provinces were of great material benefit to the Romans. The key to running an empire, Augustus believed, was balance. He wanted to maintain imperial control of the provinces while keeping down the cost and difficulty of doing so. His solution was to devolve responsibility as much as possible to the governors of the provinces, now numbering twenty-two in total. Some former tribal states, like those in Gaul, were allowed a degree of self-government, with 'capital' cities developing as administrative centres. All self-governing communities had a council of about 100 men and, as long as their taxes made their way back to Rome along the Empire's sophisticated road network, the councils could govern themselves.

While the provinces operated efficiently, expansion could continue. In the East, however, things were different. For years the eastern provinces had suffered through Rome's wars with the Parthians but Augustus, to much acclaim, had concluded peace with Parthia in 20 BC and managed to persuade them to return the standards they had captured from Crassus and Antony. This achievement matched perfectly with Augustus's image as the man who ended the civil wars. Augustus as 'Peace-bringer' was an important part of imperial propaganda.

A new cult was created – the cult of the emperor. The son of the divine Julius was himself now seen as a god. Temples were built in his honour. Each of the allied kings who enjoyed his friendship founded a city called 'Caesarea'. Whether sincere or not, these public expressions of reverence continued to elevate him above ordinary mortals. He was particularly considered as a divine figure in the eastern provinces. Similarly, in Egypt, he was perceived, as the pharaohs had been, as a living god. Unlike some of his successors (such as Caligula, Claudius and Nero), he did not actively encourage this; in fact he prohibited it in Italy (where it was seen as 'un-Roman'). But he did not ban it in the East or Gaul. There he astutely asked that dedications be jointly offered to 'Augustus and Rome'. The well-being of Augustus and the well-being of the state became synonymous.

Augustus in the dress of Pontifex Maximus *(chief priest of Rome. The term is still used today by the Pope).*

The many conservatives who dominated the Roman aristocracy and political class greatly appreciated the external evidence of a return to traditional Republican morality. Augustus went further than building new temples; he introduced morality laws. Political renewal is often associated with moral reform and Augustus's rule was no exception. According to Suetonius: '[He] was exceedingly strict in checking the licentious behaviour of stage-players. [He] expelled Pylades not only from Rome, but from Italy too, because when a spectator began to hiss, he called the attention of the whole audience to him with an obscene movement of his middle finger.'

Starting in 18 BC, he attempted to restrict, by law, spending on luxuries, to make divorce more difficult, to impose heavy penalties for adultery and seduction, and to give Romans financial incentives to marry and have children. Cassius Dio imagines Augustus explaining his rationale as follows: 'it is through men who live their lives in this way that the Romans of future years will become a mighty people... How excellent, and how imperative it is, if cities and peoples are to exist, and if you are to rule others and the rest of the world is to obey you, that there should be a flourishing race of ours.'

Some deliberately had three or more children to make them eligible for new state benefits – Augustus wanted everyone to have large families to increase Italian manpower. Many children were, of course, accidents. Contraception was the responsibility of the woman, though animal gut condoms may have existed. (Among the most common female preventative measures was the use of vaginal wool anointed with oils, resins, vinegar, minerals and honey.) Abortions were recognized as being extremely dangerous, though not immoral.

Augustus wanted Rome to be well-run, decent and moral. To assist him in this, he asked an old friend, Maecenas, to engage leading poets and writers. Men like Virgil and Horace wrote of the beauties of Italy and the nobility of rural life. They spoke of the enduring miracle of the Roman Empire. And they credited the peace and tranquillity of daily life to Augustus. Horace was particularly effusive: 'Thy age, O Caesar, has restored to farms their plenteous crops and to Jove the standards stripped from proud Parthian columns…has banished crime and recalled the ancient ways whereby the Latin name and men of Italy waxed great, and the fame and majesty of our dominions were spread from the Sun's western bed to his arising…

Publius Vergilius Maro (Virgil is the anglicization). Originally from an obscure village near Mantua in Cisalpine Gaul (and thus not technically Italian when he was born), he lived through the same period of civil war as Augustus himself. Virgil had always planned to write a great epic, but when he finally began his composition it was not a eulogy of Augustus but of Rome itself.

He chose as his chief character Aeneas, the legendary Trojan prince who escaped the Greek sack of Troy and, after many trials and tribulations, arrived in Italy. His descendants were Remus and Romulus (the legendary founder of Rome). By choosing this character, Virgil linked the foundation of Rome with a mythical past and the Greek epic cycles of Homer, which gave Rome a culturally acceptable heritage in the eyes of Greek civilization. Virgil was also able to make Aeneas foresee all that Rome would become – Aeneas's jilting of the North African princess, Dido, became the mythical explanation for the long-standing enmity between Rome and Carthage; on a visit to the Underworld, Aeneas is shown all the great figures of Roman future; on arriving in Italy he visits the site which will become Rome, and sees a hill which will one day be the Capitol. Through this poem, the contemporary reader was able to perceive contemporary events and personalities.

Augustus waited impatiently for the completion of the work, and begged to see an advance copy of some of its sections. In 19 BC, as Virgil lay dying, Augustus perhaps heard that the poet, still dissatisfied with his work and realizing he would not live to complete its revision, had ordered it to be consigned to the flames. Augustus sent two officers to rescue it and bring it to him, thus preserving the *Aeneid* for posterity. Despite the fact that the epic was not directly about him, it did trace Caesar's and Augustus's lineage back to the gods and further portray Augustus as the defender of Roman tradition. Augustus was apparently delighted with it. It was yet another tool that he could use to maintain the stability and success of the Empire.

❖

Though on the one hand attempting to be seen as the keeper of the Republican flame, Augustus was equally intent on creating what was effectively a 'royal family'. He wanted his children and young relatives to be royal 'princes' and 'princesses' sitting at home weaving or drawing. They were forbidden to do anything that could not 'decently figure in the imperial day-book'. They were to model their handwriting on Augustus's own. They were to speak and behave like him.

To his regret, he and Livia had produced only one child but it had been born prematurely and died. His only living child was therefore Julia, born of his second wife Scribonia in 39 BC. Augustus was ambitious for a royal family of Julian blood (i.e. like himself, descended from Julius Caesar). And Julia became the key to fulfilling this wish.

He first married her to Marcellus, his sister Octavia's son, which placed Marcellus in a very strong position. But he was only a teenager and when

Augustus fell ill and thought he was dying, in 23 BC, he had passed his signet ring to his old friend Agrippa instead. Marcellus died later that year.

Julia (who had borne no children with Marcellus) was then married to Agrippa. Together they had five children, two of whom – Gaius born in 20 BC and Lucius born in 17 BC – were adopted by Augustus. He brought them up in the palace and groomed them as his heirs, even naming them 'Princes of Youth'.

Augustus was confident that his Empire was secure and the issue of succession settled. In 13 BC, Augustus unveiled perhaps his greatest monument: the *Ara Pacis* (Altar of Peace). The whole frieze suggests the harmony created by Augustus and his nobility but it also represents his ideal family life. On it Augustus and his family are shown on the way to a sacrifice. Augustus and Livia represent the decorum and tradition of the present, with the children symbolizing a glorious future.

However, a series of disasters now began to affect Augustus's reign. In 12 BC Agrippa died. Livia's son Tiberius (Augustus's stepson) was forced to desert the wife he loved very much and marry Julia instead. This was not only to prevent others from marrying her but to establish Tiberius as the guardian of Gaius and Lucius. Such a task would not have been easy, for, having been brought up in the palace, the two boys were extremely spoilt and they did not take easily to Tiberius's gruff military style. Tiberius could eventually take no more and went into self-imposed exile on Rhodes, where he sulked and read horoscopes. As Suetonius put it: 'At the height of [Augustus's] happiness and confidence in his family, Fortune deserted him.'

Julia, now effectively without a husband, rebelled. Seneca says:

his daughter was shameless beyond the indictment of shamelessness – she had been accessible to scores of lovers, she had roamed about the city in nocturnal revels, that the very Forum and the rostrum, from which her father had proposed a law against adultery, had been chosen by the daughter for her debaucheries, that she had daily resorted to the life of a courtesan and, laying aside the role of adulteress, sold her favours, and sought the right to every indulgence... [10]

The Imperial family,
as depicted on the
Ara Pacis. The frieze
suggests the harmony
created by Augustus
and his nobility, and
represents idealized
family life. Considered
Augustus's greatest
monument, it was
first unveiled in 13 BC.

When Augustus finally found out, he was ruthless and sent her into exile on an island where she was kept under guard and forbidden contact with men and wine. A delegation of the people came to see him, begging that she be recalled but he was unmoved.

He tried to continue in his attempts to cultivate the image of himself as genial father and grandfather – of his own family and, by inference, the nation. But it was an image which markedly differed from the reality. In private, Augustus referred to his daughter Julia and his two grandchildren as his 'three running sores'.

His granddaughter, also called Julia, had a pet dwarf called Canopas who was only 60 centimetres (2 feet) tall. She revelled in showing him off. Her behaviour, too, appalled Augustus and he tore down her home because it was too luxurious. He was finally forced to exile her as well for a similar sexual scandal to that of her mother. The 'royal family' could not live up to the demands Augustus placed upon it. According to Suetonius: 'When members of his family died Augustus bore his loss with far more resignation than when they disgraced themselves.' It was the familiar story of the public face being contradicted by the private reality. It was also an early indication of the difficulties that the Empire would face by becoming a hereditary monarchy.

Behind the scenes, even Augustus himself may not have been beyond reproach. Again, Suetonius tells us that: '…not even his friends could deny that he often committed adultery, though of course they said in justification, that he did so for reasons of state, not simply through passion – he wanted to discover what his enemies were up to by getting intimate with their wives and daughters…'

Augustus, on whom fortune had so often smiled, suffered badly as he persisted in his attempts to prepare for his successor. His grandsons Gaius and Lucius both died (in AD 2 and AD 4). Some wondered whether Livia had a hand in their deaths for the only beneficiary was her son Tiberius, who was now adopted as Augustus's son and likely heir.

❖

In 2 BC, aged sixty-one years of age, Augustus had been proclaimed *pater patriae* ('father of the fatherland'). The 'father', however, was aging. Suetonius gives us this vivid picture of the elderly emperor: '…sometimes the forefinger of his right hand would be so numbed and shrunken by cold that it hardly served to guide a pen, even when strengthened with a horn finger-stall… In winter he wore no fewer than four tunics and a heavy woollen gown above his undershirt… He could not bear the rays even of the winter sun…'

Augustus nevertheless continued to work. The Empire was largely at peace, though it was a peace underpinned by legionary force. Despite Augustus's ailments, he continued to command his lieutenants, and in the North he bought Roman expansion up to the River Danube – a natural frontier and a communications highway – and sought a similar border in Germany. He decided this should not be the River Rhine, but the River Elbe further east.

Then, in 9 AD, disaster struck. Three legions, the XVII, XVIII and XIX, led by Quinctilius Varus, had entered the dense Teutoburg Forest in Germany during their campaign to consolidate the Roman frontier from the River Rhine to the River Elbe. In the gloom and damp of a vast woodland, all three were attacked by local tribes and annihilated.

It was a bitter blow to Augustus, from which he never really recovered. Suetonius says: 'He was in such consternation at this event, that he let his hair on his head and beard grow for several months, and sometimes knocked his head against the door-posts, crying out, "O, Quinctilius Varus Give me back my legions!" And ever after he observed the anniversary of this calamity as a day of sorrow and mourning.'

He was unused to such failure – and, for the moment at least, it marked the end of all plans for further expansion. Indeed, this was a key point in Roman history, for the Empire was effectively beginning to reach its limits. Perhaps Rome was beginning to realize that the world (whatever its extent) was tougher than it had first seemed and that global conquest was not possible. Augustus felt Rome should push no more, but build up its frontiers and maintain the *pax Romana* ('Roman peace') that existed from the Atlantic to the Euphrates, from the Black Sea to the Nile.

Augustus was still concerned about the succession and made Tiberius his heir. A quasi-monarchy had now been established. Augustus's thoughts turned to posterity. He completed a public account of his life's work, called the *Res Gestae et Impensae* ('Things Done and Spent'). It was, naturally, a glowing epitaph.

In 14 AD, while travelling back to Rome from a trip south, Augustus was taken ill. By a remarkable coincidence, he was near a house his natural father had once owned. He was now mortally ill and was taken to the same room in which his father had died seventy years earlier. There Augustus apparently asked those present: 'Since well I have played my part, all clap your hands… And from the stage dismiss me with applause…'

Augustus died at the age of seventy-six. He had died in bed, an old man. That in itself was a great achievement. Many of the ninety or so emperors who followed him failed to manage it. Indeed, Augustus's longevity was a key element not only in his success but in the subsequent success of the emperors. For when Augustus died it had been over fifty years since he had taken control and few could remember what life had been like under the Republic, without an emperor.

Augustus had revitalized the Roman Empire. Its frontiers were strong, its cities were flourishing, its culture and trade were spreading and establishing ever more extensive routes to Africa, India, and, through middlemen, China. Augustus had created a new system of hereditary monarchy and it was Tiberius, though Augustus disliked the fact that he was a relation on his wife's side only, who would succeed. By adopting Tiberius, Livia's Claudian blood-line joined the Julian line and Tiberius would become the first Julio-Claudian emperor, a line that would last half a century.

Without Augustus, the death of Julius Caesar could perhaps have caused the Empire to fragment into a host of small states and warring kingdoms. But his force of personality, and his brilliance as an administrator, governor, manipulator, had not only held the Empire together but so strengthened it that it would last for another five centuries in the West and even longer in the East.

Augustus's funeral was unlike any previously seen. As flames licked the pyre, an eagle was released, symbolizing his soul ascending to the gods. Augustus's remains were then taken to the mausoleum that he had built beside the Tiber.

The gods had been kind – Rome was strong. It had to be. The winter Horace predicted saw a downward spiral ahead: 'Our parents, whose generation was worse than their parents', have brought forth us who are worse still; we shall produce descendants in whom vice is even deeper ingrained.'

Although Augustus, the first emperor, had bequeathed a strong and united empire to his successors, the words of Horace were to ring horribly true in the years ahead.

CHAPTER III

NERO

The Power and the Madness

ALTHOUGH Nero Claudius Caesar Augustus Germanicus took the names of his illustrious forebears Caesar and Augustus, this youthful emperor was a very different character. Despite initially promising much, he became synonymous with evil itself. While the Roman Empire was still moving towards its peak, its extraordinary wealth was sowing the seeds of a corruption that would one day encourage its decline.

❖

The future Emperor Nero was born Lucius Domitius Ahenobarbus on 15 December AD 37 at Antium (Anzio), a fashionable seaside resort to the south of Rome.

Nero was both the great-great-grandson and great-great-nephew of Augustus. His father, Gnaeus Domitius Ahenobarbus, was descended from a leading family of the Republic but had a terrible reputation: he never repaid debts, had gouged out a man's eyes in a drunken brawl, and had run his chariot over a child on the Appian Way into Rome. The name Ahenobarbus meant 'bronze beard' but it was said that, though the family's beards might be bronze, their hearts were lead.

The Ahenobarbus family had fought against both Caesar and Octavian. When Octavian became emperor, however, he pardoned the family in a rare example of political clemency, and married one of them to his niece.

Octavian's great-granddaughter and later Nero's mother, Agrippina, was

Nero (AD 37–68). Although his early years as emperor were a period of moderation, efficient administration and economic stability, Nero is best known for his licentious behaviour and debauchery.

an imperial princess, sister of the eccentric Caligula. Her youth had been traumatic. The Emperor Tiberius who succeeded Augustus tried hard to match his predecessor's skills but was unable to do so. Augustus had created a system of inherited monarchy that brought with it ambition and scheming. Tiberius feared that other members of the imperial court were plotting against him; members of Agrippina's family were among those forced into exile, starved to death, or forced to commit suicide.

Tiberius died and Caligula became emperor in AD 37, the year Nero was born. (According to Suetonius, Nero's father had said: 'Nothing that was not abominable and a public evil could be born of myself and Agrippina.') Agrippina once again found favour at the imperial court of her brother and she began to plan her son's assault on the imperial throne.

❖

Caligula (*caliga* meant 'soldier's boot', hence his name meant 'bootkins' given to him on a childhood visit to the legions in Germany) was initially welcomed by Rome. On his accession he spent lavishly on games, which were gratefully accepted by the people. Closely associated with his regime were his three sisters, including Agrippina, who were depicted on coinage as the epitome of virtue.

Agrippina, the mother of Nero, is seen here symbolically crowning her son.

Agrippina and her two other sisters, Drusilla and Julia Livilla, were made honorary Vestal Virgins. The 'Vestals' were a college of priestesses who served for thirty years (ten spent learning, ten serving, then ten teaching). Their chief function was to keep the flame of Vesta burning, for if it went out a terrible misfortune would befall Rome. The temple in the Forum was one of the oldest in Rome. Next to it was the House of the Vestals where many, including the emperor himself, deposited their wills for safe-keeping. If a Vestal broke her vow of chastity the man responsible was whipped through the Forum and she was buried alive. Agrippina enjoyed the honorary title of Vestal Virgin without the responsibility; thus she was allowed to marry. Indeed Nero was born within a year of her receiving the title.

Caligula's goodwill did not last. In AD 39 Nero's father died. Nero was only three, and Caligula had no hesitation in depriving him of the third of the estate that was his inheritance. Caligula, like Tiberius, soon feared domestic plotting and he was convinced that his sisters were conspiring against him. Agrippina was accused of attempting to replace Caligula with her lover (her sister Drusilla's husband) and was banished. With his father dead and his mother exiled, Nero was brought up in the house of his father's sister, Domitia Lepida. Unusually, she chose a dancer and a barber to be his tutors.

Caligula had come to power in AD 37 when he was twenty-four. He ruled Rome as an absolute monarch along the lines of the Hellenistic Kingdoms of the East. Any pretence of imitating Augustus's stance as 'First Among Equals', sharing power with the Senate, was abandoned.

Despite an enormous legacy left to him by Tiberius, extravagant games and performances soon left Caligula near bankruptcy. It was rumoured (and apparently much exaggerated) that madness had gripped him, and that he even wished to appoint his favourite horse consul. After less than four years in power he became the first emperor to be assassinated, and was replaced by his uncle Claudius.

Caligula, emperor when Nero was born, was the brother of Nero's mother.

101

Claudius, a shy and intellectual man, had been overlooked in imperial circles, possibly because he was slightly disabled and had a stutter. Yet, as emperor, he showed unexpected strengths. He had a good head for the complexities of administration and an eye for further expansion: Britain was added to the Empire in AD 43. Claudius recalled his niece, Agrippina, from exile and the young Nero was reunited with his mother.

Through the forties, Nero grew up in privileged and luxurious imperial surroundings. On her return from exile, his mother had immediately dedicated herself to promoting her son as the next emperor. This was her ambition and *raison d'être*. She dominated, protected and moulded him into the form that she thought most appropriate. In AD 47, aged nine, he made a successful first public appearance alongside Claudius's own six-year-old son Britannicus, so-named because of the recent conquest of Britain. Together they took part in the 'Troy Games', a martial display performed by young aristocrats. These games were part of the celebrations arranged by Claudius to mark what was considered to be the eight hundredth anniversary of the founding of Rome.

The following year, 48, Rome was rocked by the great scandal of Messalina, Nero's cousin, who after years of being unfaithful to her husband, the Emperor Claudius, had gone as far as publicly marrying her lover, with whom she planned to replace the Emperor. Messalina was forced to commit suicide and the devastated Claudius swore he would never marry again.

Now Agrippina saw her chance. Using all her powers of seduction, she won Claudius over, and persuaded him to retract his vow and take her as his fourth wife. Claudius succumbed, even though the marriage was technically incestuous and required a special senatorial dispensation.

❖

Agrippina, still only thirty-four years old, had positioned herself at the very heart of power. She now had one aim in life – to see her son become the next emperor. Tacitus commented: '…she holds her dignity, her modesty, her body, everything, cheaper than a throne…'.

Her main obstacles were Claudius's existing children by Messalina, namely Britannicus and his nine-year-old sister Octavia, both younger than Nero. Agrippina began by arranging for Nero to be betrothed to his nine-year-old stepsister Octavia. Shortly after this, in February 50, Agrippina persuaded Claudius to adopt her son as his own; the boy, hitherto known as Lucius Domitius Ahenobarbus, became Nero Claudius Caesar. His stepbrother Britannicus still insisted on calling him Ahenobarbus. Later that year Agrippina herself received the title *Augusta*, the first wife of an emperor to bear this title during her husband's reign.

Nero came of age in March 51 when he was thirteen, and assumed the *toga virilis*. In addition he received the honorary title *princeps iuventutis*, 'Leader of Youth', signifying his status as a role model for his own generation. In public, Nero, an attractive curly-haired youth, allowed to wear a purple robe, cut a fine figure compared to Britannicus, who was still in children's clothing. In this year Nero made his first speech to the Senate, a thanksgiving to Claudius for these honours. This and later speeches, several in Greek, were written by his tutor, the famous philosopher Seneca, whom Agrippina had employed to ensure that her son received the finest education available. All the time Agrippina furthered her plans, striking down any potential rivals with accusations of treason or black magic. Her victims included Nero's aunt (Agrippina's husband's sister) who had sheltered him during Agrippina's exile. Nero was even persuaded to testify against her. Agrippina also secured many appointments for her supporters, including her alleged lover Burrus, who gained the crucial office of Praetorian Prefect, commander-in-chief of the Praetorian Guard. The Guard were now becoming extremely influential and Burrus's new post was of great value to Agrippina.

In 53, the marriage of the fifteen-year-old Nero and Octavia was celebrated. Agrippina, however, remained unsure whether Claudius intended to re-establish Britannicus as heir as soon as he came of age in February 55. Furthermore, Britannicus was popular with the people as the natural son of the existing emperor.

Now Agrippina's murderous ambition reached its height. At a lavish banquet on 12 October AD 54, Claudius slipped into a coma and died.

The marriage of Claudius and Nero's mother, Agrippina, who persuaded Claudius to adopt Nero as his own.

Rumours immediately circulated that Agrippina was responsible and that the deed had been committed by poisoning Claudius's favourite food. According to Cassius Dio: '[Agrippina] sent for a famous dealer in poisons, a woman named Lucusta, …and preparing with her aid a poison whose effect was sure, she put it on a mushroom…'

Years later, Cassius Dio recorded a comment of Nero's which indicated that he knew of his mother's plot: 'Nero declared mushrooms to be the food of the gods, since Claudius by means of a mushroom had become a god.'

At noon on the day following Claudius's death, the sixteen-year-old Nero appeared outside the palace, accompanied by Agrippina and Burrus. Claudius's will was never read out. They then went to the Praetorian Guard's barracks and promised them each 15,000 sesterces (seven years' wages) if they hailed Nero as emperor. Some initially called for Britannicus, but ceased to do so after the promise of money. Now, it was not only clear that emperors could be assassinated, but that succession could be bought. On the day of Nero's accession the password for the Praetorian Guard at the palace was 'best of mothers'.

Claudius was promptly deified by the Senate, the first emperor since Augustus to receive such an honour, and a temple was constructed to him with Agrippina as his high priestess. Tacitus described how Nero praised the virtues of the late emperor in a funeral oration written by Seneca:

The praise of his graceful accomplishments and the remark that during his reign no disaster had befallen Rome from the foreigner, were heard with favour... The speech, which was composed by Seneca, exhibited much elegance, as indeed that famous man had an attractive genius which suited the popular ear of the time. Elderly men observed that Nero was the first emperor who needed another man's eloquence... [1]

❖

The character of Roman society was changing. Largely because of the civil wars and a declining birthrate, Nero's Senate was no longer the exclusive preserve of the haughty and arrogant Roman aristocracy as it had been in the time of Caesar and Augustus. Nowadays it was dominated by rich Italians and provincials who were often the first in their families to become senators. In practice, the Senate had lost much of its power. During his four decades of rule, Augustus had established a new political order. His 'Roman peace' had proved to many that an empire needed an emperor. It seemed to show that the only alternative to destructive civil wars was strong one-man rule. Nevertheless, the Senate still contained many experienced and influential men who filled all the senior official and military posts. Nero was aware that, if provoked, the Senate could cause trouble, even rebellion. Encouraged by Seneca, Nero declared his desire to take senatorial opinion into account.

The young Nero told the senators that he would respect the great practices of the Republic, would govern like Augustus, would treat them with honour and hear their views. In his first speech as emperor he promised to maintain the Augustan principle of a 'partnership' between *princeps* and Senate.

This augured well but the real power clearly lay behind the scenes. A battle was being waged in the imperial council for control of the adolescent emperor. Most of the council were shadowy figures, many of whom were also senators, but the victors of this contest, outplaying even Agrippina, were Nero's tutor, Seneca, and the Praetorian Prefect, Burrus. Seneca was from Spain and Burrus was from southern Gaul; two provincials now essentially controlled the Roman emperor. According to Tacitus: 'These two men, with a unanimity rare among partners in power, were, by different methods, equally influential. Burrus's strength lay in soldierly efficiency and seriousness of character, Seneca's in amiable high principles and his tuition of Nero in public speaking...'

On his accession, Nero was given almost unlimited flattery which he enjoyed and encouraged. Indeed, on the rare occasions when flattery was not forthcoming, he was known to throw childish tantrums. All the while, Seneca continued to exert a profound influence on the eighteen-year-old emperor and tried to guide Nero in how he should rule. In his work *On Clemency*, which was addressed to Nero, he pointed out that the only restraint on the young *princeps* was self-restraint: 'Happiness is vouchsafing safety to many, calling back to life from the brink of death, deserving a civic crown for clemency. No decoration is fairer or worthier a prince's eminence than this crown awarded for saving the lives of fellow citizens – not trophies torn from the vanquished, not chariots blooded with barbarian gore, not spoils in war.'

Seneca's philosophical view of the world influenced Nero in other ways. For example, Seneca abhorred gladiators because they contravened his concept of the unity of mankind. Augustus had not admired the fights either and had reduced them to two a year, but Nero went further. He would not abandon the circuses, for they were too popular. However, he encouraged games that were ingenious spectacle rather than gladiatorial murder. One day, for example, he had the arena flooded with sea water and filled with ocean creatures, which bears were then sent in to kill. Such shows amazed visitors to the city, one of whom, the poet Calpurnius Siculus, recorded his impressions:

Passing up the steps and slopes of gentle incline, we came to the seats, where in dingy garments the baser sort viewed the show close to the women's benches. For the uncovered parts, exposed beneath the open sky, were thronged by knights and white-roped tribunes... Rooted to the spot, I stood with mouth agape and marvelled at all... a man advanced in years...said to me: 'Why wonder, country cousin, that you are spellbound in the face of such magnificence? ...we rate all cheap we saw in former years, and shabby every show we one day watched.' ...Why narrate each sigh in order? Beasts of every kind I saw; here I saw snow-white hares and horned boars, here I saw the elk... Bulls too...sea calves also I beheld with bears pitted against them and the unshapely herd called [Hippopotamus]... Oh, how we quaked, whenever we saw the arena part asunder and its soil upturned and beasts plunge out from the chasm cleft in the earth... Oh would that I had not been clad in peasant garb! Else should I have gained a nearer sight of my deity, our worshipful Emperor-God... [2]

Seneca also encouraged Nero to be inquisitive about the world, prompting him to send explorers north and south. One group went to the Baltic and Jutland (modern Denmark) and came back laden with valuable amber. Another group went in search of the source of the Nile but were stopped by marshes in the Sudan.

Guided by Agrippina, Seneca and Burrus, Nero's early years were a period of moderation, efficient administration, financial prudence and economic stability. Rome was approaching its economic and strategic zenith. The frontiers were relatively stable; vitally the army was content and Nero was reasonably safe while they remained so; and there was a constant exchange of goods flowing throughout the Empire.

Naturally there were those who grumbled about the effects of these imports and developments. The Roman historian Tacitus, for example, decried what he saw as a loss of traditional Roman decorum:

...everything potentially corrupting and corruptible flow[s] into the capital – foreign influences demoralize our young men into shirkers, gymnasts and perverts... Roman morals had long become impure, but never was there so favourable an environment for debauchery as among this filthy crowd... Here every form of immorality competed for attention, and no chastity, modesty or vestige of decency could survive... [3]

The eighteen-year-old emperor lived in a luxurious palace on the Palatine Hill (from which we get the word 'palace'). This was the same building in which he had spent his childhood years. Constructed by Tiberius, it was the first purpose-built imperial palace and it was essentially a much-enlarged version of the luxurious homes that were built here during the Republic. The much more modest house of Augustus was swallowed up by this maze of private chambers, reception rooms and gardens. It was a remarkable home for a teenager. Spoilt by the luxury and sycophancy that surrounded him and uninterested in the arduous task of government, Nero began to indulge in the excesses for which he became infamous. According to Cassius Dio: 'whereas at first Nero was comparatively moderate in the dinners he gave, in the revels he conducted, and in his drinking and his amours, yet later, as no one reproved him for this conduct and the public business was handled none the worse for it, he came to believe that such conduct was really not bad and that he could carry it even further.'

Unlike men such as Julius Caesar or Augustus, Nero had had no military experience, no real political experience – in fact, virtually no experience of life. He was immature, a 'mother's boy', hardly out of the schoolroom, and now 'ruler of the world'. In the words of Aurelius Victor, who wrote his *Book of the Caesars* in the fourth century AD: 'Nero, in fact, spent the rest of his life so disgracefully, that it is disgusting and shameful to record the existence of anyone of this kind, let alone that he was ruler of the world'.

Although the first emperor, Augustus, had established a hereditary monarchy the Senate still believed it played a major role. However the army, the Roman masses and the provincial ruling classes all felt a much deeper loyalty to the families of Caesar and Augustus. The army, in particular, was

becoming a caste of its own which recognized the value of fathers passing their livelihoods on to their sons. This system worked if the Empire was led by strong, wise and prudent men, but men or boys of no experience, talent or suitability could also become emperor. In the days of the Republic, consuls were, at least, usually answerable for their actions and could be prosecuted. An emperor or *princeps* was under no such restraint.

In Nero's Rome, nakedness, debauchery and immorality were commonplace.

109

In such circumstances, it fell to the palace staff, the council of advisers, the Senate, or the well-intentioned to cushion the city and the Empire from the worst excesses of its emperor.

Nero took little part in political activities. His 'guardians', Seneca and Burrus, appear to have encouraged him to follow other pursuits so that his youth and inexperience would not wreak havoc in administration. Nero was not, however, completely unaware of events; he suggested abolishing all indirect taxation which would, he hoped, free up trade and make more people wealthy. The government, he believed, would not lose because it would enjoy an increase in direct tax (as people became richer) and the measure would have led to more people in the provinces fulfilling the wealth qualifications they required for many local offices.

Sadly, Nero lacked the energy to see his own idea through. Instead, rumours spread that he had chosen to exercise his powers in less productive ways, indulging himself in licentious behaviour, ignoring his wife while working his way through women, boys, slaves and imperial freedmen. Whatever the truth – and many of these slanders were written by senators, often decades later, with good reason to hate or denigrate Nero – it is clear that the young emperor was becoming progressively out of control. The historian Suetonius detailed some of his worst excesses:

Gradually Nero's vices gained the upper hand: he no longer tried to laugh them off, or hide, or deny them, but openly broke into more serious crime. His feasts now lasted from noon till midnight... Whenever he floated down the Tiber to Ostia...he had a row of temporary brothels erected along the shore, where married women, pretending to be inn-keepers, solicited him to come ashore...

Nero practised every kind of obscenity, and after defiling almost every part of his body finally invented a novel game: he was released from a cage dressed in the skins of wild animals, and attacked the private parts of men and women who stood bound to stakes. After working up sufficient excitement by this means, he was dispatched by his freedman...[4]

The truth may now lay buried deep within such slanders and abuse but, unlike

Augustus, Nero does not seem to have worried about his public image. As far as he was concerned, he was emperor and free to act as he pleased, even if it was not as bad as gossip would have us believe.

Such gossip revealed that his favourite companions were ballet dancers and actresses. He apparently became particularly enamoured of a freedwoman called Acte, who was said to look just like his mother, and to whom he gave several villas and a large staff of her own. Nero was also accused of being very fond of prowling the streets of Rome at night in disguise, together with a gang of friends, smashing up shops, groping women and assaulting passers-by.

Suetonius relates how: 'As soon as night fell he would snatch a cap or a wig and make a round of the taverns, or prowl the streets in search of mischief – and not always innocent mischief either, because one of his games was to attack men on their way home from dinner stab them if they offered resistance, and then drop their bodies in the sewer...'

According to Tacitus, several of his subjects began to follow their emperor's example: 'When it became known that the waylayer was the emperor, attacks on distinguished men and women multiplied. For, since disorderliness was tolerated, pseudo-Neros mobilized gangs and behaved similarly, with impunity. Rome by night came to resemble a conquered city.'

Nevertheless Seneca and Burrus were both men of great experience. Under their care and despite their young charge's excesses, the Roman Empire continued to enjoy a period of economic stability.

Rome was approaching the height of its expansion by the time Nero became emperor. During Claudius's reign there had been the conquest of Britain, citizenship granted to many Gauls and some new acquisitions in Thrace and North Africa. The frontiers were relatively stable, guarded by an apparently contented army. The city of Rome, above all, exploited its relationship with the increasingly wealthy provinces, being the largest single market for their luxury goods.

Such extensive importation, however, was having detrimental effects on Italy's domestic industry and, in particular, its agriculture. Tacitus pinpointed

The Circus Maximus at the time of Nero. The Imperial Palace is on the Palatine Hill overlooking the race track.

the problem: 'The trouble is not infertile soil. The fact is that we prefer to cultivate Africa and Egypt – thereby staking Rome's survival on the hazards of navigation.'

Much of the daily work dealing with such problems was done by imperial staff who were, in effect, Nero's ministers. Though they worked according to the dictates of the imperial council (especially Seneca, Burrus and – decreasingly, due to Seneca's efforts – Agrippina), they were able to operate largely independently.

The imperial bureaucracy was essentially 'household government'. Even in the Republic, powerful senators had employed secretaries and clerks to manage their affairs. Augustus used the slaves and freedmen of his household, the *domus Caesaris*, in this way. Under Claudius, specialized departments were created, each like a 'ministry', headed by a freedman secretary. The staff tended to be low-born non-Italians who directly owed their jobs to the emperor; they were his men, with no alternative loyalties.

These departments, formalized by Claudius, were called *scrinia*, after the *scrinium*, a portable chest used by the clerks. There were four main departments: one dealing with official correspondence; one a financial office; another for petitions and probably judicial matters; and the last department was a form of library and archive. It may not have been perfect but it was certainly functional.

Meanwhile, free of all responsibility, and surrounded by flatterers, Nero's abuses of power grew ever more glaring. Cassius Dio summed up the situation: 'Since Nero did not hear a word of truth from anybody and saw none but those who approved of his actions, he thought that his past deeds had not been found out, or even, perhaps, that there was nothing wrong in them. Hence he became much worse...'

Nero's thoughts turned to murder within the imperial household. The main threat to his position was posed by his neglected stepbrother Britannicus. Agrippina, aware that her influence with Nero was declining, may have chosen to develop her relations with Britannicus. Nero made sure her efforts came to nought. He allegedly engaged the services of the same female poisoner Agrippina had used to kill Claudius.

At a lavish banquet Britannicus suddenly went into convulsions and died. Nero, unperturbed, continued dining, claiming his stepbrother had suffered an epileptic fit. As they ate, however, Britannicus's body was being burnt.

Agrippina, who had controlled Nero for so long, was indeed losing favour with her ever more assertive son. Coins issued up to AD 55 depict her fall from grace, as she is first taken off the front (which she shared with Nero) and relegated to the reverse side, then removed altogether.

Suetonius believed that:

The over-watchful, over-critical eye that Agrippina kept on whatever Nero said or did proved more than he could stand... he refused to have her living with him and expelled her from his palace; after which he did everything possible to annoy her, sending people to pester her...disturbing her with jeers and cat calls. In the end her threats and violent behaviour terrified him into deciding that she must die...[5]

Nero decided to murder the woman to whom he owed everything. The catalogue of failed assaults is almost comical, including attempts at poisoning and having her bedroom ceiling fall on her. Eventually, in March 59, he employed an architect to design a boat that would collapse and kill her. Above her apartment in the boat were placed lead weights which, when released, were to fall and crush her, sinking the boat at the same time.

Nero invited her to dine with him at a villa near the Bay of Naples. Afterwards, he presented her with the specially prepared boat for her return journey, and said farewell, he thought forever. That evening he was horrified to learn that, by a bizarre twist of fate, she had survived the wreck. The high sides of her couch had saved her and, though shocked and injured, she had managed to swim to safety. Nero now abandoned any pretence of subtlety and dispatched some naval officers to her villa to simply stab her to death.

According to Tacitus: 'The murderers closed around her bed. First the captain hit her on the head with a truncheon. Then, as the lieutenant was drawing his sword to finish her off, she cried out, "Strike here!", pointing to her womb. Blow after blow fell, and she died…'

One account records that Nero, perhaps finding it hard to believe that she was really dead, came to see for himself. He inspected her naked body and, between sips of wine, passed comments on the good and bad points of her physique. The corpse was burned that night. Nero then explained away the murder by claiming that his mother had been plotting to assassinate him, and he announced a public thanksgiving for the emperor's 'deliverance' from this danger. Agrippina's birthday was declared a day of ill-omen. The irony of her fate did not escape Cassius Dio: 'Thus was Agrippina, descendant of Augustus, slain by the very son to whom she had given the sovereignty and for whose sake she had killed her uncle and others'.

❖

Free from his mother's interference, Nero could devote his time and energy to personal pursuits. His ambition was not, like Augustus, to bequeath a strong Rome to his successors, but to be the best artist in the world. According to Suetonius, Nero not only had his lack of artistic ability to overcome but also a rather unfortunate appearance: 'Physical characteristics of Nero: Height: average. Body: pustular and malodorous. Hair: light blond. Features: pretty, rather than handsome. Eyes: blue and rather weak. Neck: squat. Belly: protuberant. Legs: spindling.' It was little wonder that he craved praise.

He had grown up in a stable empire, had never had to fight for it, and so took it for granted and did not value it. He was surrounded by sycophants and he had no sense of worth. Perhaps he felt that only by the public recognizing and applauding his talents as an artist could he gain real self-esteem. To his credit, Nero worked hard at his chosen craft. Suetonius tells us that: '...little by little, he began to study and practise, and conscientiously undertook all the usual exercises for strengthening and developing the voice. He would lie on his back with a slab of lead on his chest, use enemas and emetics to keep down his weight, and refrain from eating apples and every other food considered damaging to the vocal cords.'

Yet he was not mature enough to accept failure as part of the path to triumph. He was too spoiled; he wanted instant success and could not accept the slightest criticism or setback. Judging from Suetonius's comments, fair play was an alien concept to Nero: 'To destroy every trace of previous winners in these contests he ordered all their statues and busts to be taken down, dragged away with hooks, and hurled into public lavatories'.

Though he wanted to perform poetry and songs, and to stage plays in which he was the principal actor, his greatest passion was reserved for the lyre, by this time the usual accompaniment to songs and plays.

At first Seneca and the other members of the council managed to keep these embarrassments private. The theatrical profession was wholly unsuitable for a man of Nero's station and public appearances would have been considered a disgrace. In the Vatican Gardens on the other side of the Tiber they organized a festival to the god *Iuventas* ('Youth'), called the *Iuvenalia*, and they hand-picked the guests who would see the performing emperor. Here Nero formed a personal retinue of young aristocrats called the *Augustiani*, who ensured that his 'divine voice' always received rapturous applause.

A Roman banquet. Nero was renowned for indulging himself in pleasure and licenticus behaviour.

Cassius Dio described the scene: 'so there stood this Caesar on the stage wearing the garb of a lyre-player…while many soldiers stood by and all the people that the seats would hold sat watching… Besides him stood Burrus and Seneca, like teachers, prompting him; and they would wave their arms and togas at every utterance of his and lead others to do the same.'

Seneca also had to restrict the emperor's other passion – for chariot racing. According to Suetonius: 'Every day he used to play with model ivory chariots on a board – and, despite all efforts to the contrary, his chatter about chariot races at the Circus could not be stopped…'.

It was not so much his love of chariot races that concerned Nero's aides and advisers but the fact that he sometimes took part in them himself. Traditionally, charioteers were specially trained slaves – Nero was acting in a manner demeaning to his class, and deeply offending senatorial *dignitas*. Once again, Seneca made sure that Nero used a race track that Caligula had built on the other side of the River Tiber.

By the time of Nero, nearly a hundred days a year were public holidays – although, as there were no weekends, this is not dissimilar to western societies today. However, some of the entertainments staged by Nero on these public holidays were becoming extreme, apparently including chariots drawn by camels and an elephant walking down a sloping tightrope.

The people of Rome loved such games but the senatorial class were more critical. To some extent, this was a case of sour grapes. Since the time of Augustus, senators themselves had been forbidden to put on such shows to prevent them 'buying' public support. The only person Nero wanted buying public loyalty was Nero; and he was more than generous, if Suetonius is to be believed: '...all kinds of gifts were scattered to the people – 1000 assorted birds daily, and quantities of food parcels; besides vouchers for grain, clothes, gold, silver, precious stones, pearls, paintings, slaves, transport animals, and even trained wild beasts...'

In AD 60 Nero inaugurated a new series of games in his own name, the *Neronia*. These were loosely based on the Olympic Games, since Nero held Greek culture in the highest esteem, and comprised competitions in athletics and gymnastics, chariot racing, poetry, music and oratory.

A scene from the arena. Nero was not fond of gladiatorial displays and preferred more unusual events, especially using exotic animals.

Nero never tired of gladiatorial displays and mock combats, for which he built a new wooden arena on the Campus Martius, but, perhaps still influenced by Seneca, he tried – not very successfully – to ban combats to the death as something 'un-Hellenic'. He brought ever more exotic animals to the public, and constructed an artificial saltwater lake, filled with 'sea monsters', on which to stage 'naval battles'. His enthusiasm for wrestling matches was so great that he could be witnessed acting as referee, down on all fours and giving the count. He also encouraged athletics, building a new gymnasium on the Campus Martius. Attached to this was a magnificent bath-house, the Neronian Baths, the first of the great bathing complexes of imperial Rome. Here Romans could come to get clean – only a tiny minority had piped water at home – and gossip. The baths were open to almost all social classes – there were no separate sections (except between sexes) as there were in the arenas. Most popular topic of conversation, with those you trusted, would almost certainly have been Nero's debauchery. According to Cassius Dio: '…people paid him reverence in public, but in private, so long at least as any could speak their minds with safety, they tore his character to shreds.'

Meanwhile, his imperial staff and, above all, his legions kept a firm grip on events in the Empire as a whole. The army remained remarkably loyal – provincial commanders keeping order in Nero's name. In the province of Britannia in AD 60 there was a bloody uprising, partly caused by over-zealous Roman tax collectors publicly flogging the recently widowed queen of the Iceni, Boudicca, and raping her teenage daughters. Boudicca raised the East Anglian tribes in a major rebellion. Three Roman towns were destroyed and perhaps 70,000 civilians killed in a bloody massacre and destruction of all things Roman.

The revolt was eventually suppressed with much bloodshed and Boudicca took her own life with poison rather than be paraded as part of a Roman Triumph. Nero's government instituted an inquiry into these affairs and replaced the governor of Britain.

❖

In AD 62, Burrus died, possibly poisoned by the twenty-four-year-old Nero, and Seneca was forced into retirement. Nero had finally dispensed with all the restraining influences of his youth. From now on he sought the company of those who flattered his vanity and pandered to his lusts.

In the words of Cassius Dio, 'he came to despise good advice, since he was always hearing from his associates, "Do you not know you are Caesar and that you have authority over them rather than they over you?".'

Burrus's position as Praetorian Prefect was taken by Tigellinus, a low-born and vicious Sicilian, who thereafter became Nero's chief henchman. In the same year Nero decided to rid himself of Octavia, his wife and stepsister, whom he had never liked and who had produced no children.

Nero wanted to marry his long-term lover, the nineteen-year-old Poppaea, who was already pregnant with his child. This would be difficult, as Octavia was popular with the masses as the natural daughter of the divine Claudius and as a woman of virtue. His first attempt to besmirch her name and banish her from Rome only resulted in disturbances. Her maid is said to have spat in the face of an interrogator and cried: 'The private parts of my mistress are cleaner than your mouth!'

After further groundless accusations of adultery and treason, Nero confined Octavia to an island where, soon after her arrival, he had her murdered. The head of the twenty-year-old Octavia was brought for Poppaea to gloat over; twelve days later she married the emperor. According to Tacitus, the couple were well matched: 'Poppaea had every asset except goodness… She seemed respectable. But her life was depraved. Her public appearances

Poppaea the beautiful and vain woman who, having been Nero's lover, became his wife.

were few; at them, she would half-veil her face to stimulate curiosity... To her, married men or bachelor were all the same...'

She was beautiful and vain – famous for developing a face cream made from dough and ass's milk and for keeping a herd of 500 donkeys which accompanied her on her travels so that she could always bathe in their milk. In January 63, to Nero's immense delight, she gave birth to a daughter, Claudia. By March, however, his daughter was dead and Nero was left to console himself by declaring her a goddess.

A year passed. Nero seems to have spent more and more time at his birthplace Antium, and it was there that, on 18 July AD 64, a messenger arrived with the news that Rome was ablaze.

Tacitus recorded the progress of the disaster:

Now started the most terrible and destructive fire... Breaking out in shops selling inflammable goods, and fanned by the wind, the conflagration instantly grew... There were no walled mansions or temples, or any other obstructions, which could arrest it... it climbed the hills – but returned to ravage the lower ground again. It outstripped every counter-measure. The ancient city's narrow winding streets and irregular blocks encouraged its progress. [6]

It burned for over a week, destroying perhaps three-quarters of the city, especially the centre where many important aristocratic families had their palatial houses and gardens. Cassius Dio gives a vivid description of the chaos that ensued:

There was shouting and wailing without end, of children, women, men, and the aged all together, so that no one could see anything or understand what was said by reason of the smoke and the shouting; and for this reason some might be standing speechless, as if they were dumb. Meanwhile many who were carrying out their goods and many, too, who were stealing the property of others, kept running into one another and falling over their burdens... Many were suffocated, many were trampled underfoot... [7]

Nero hurried back from Antium when he heard the news in order to direct the fire-fighting and to help the homeless. Even the historian Tacitus, who is often so scathing of him, gives Nero due credit for his response to the fire: 'Nero constructed emergency accommodation for the many destitute. Food was brought from Ostia and neighbouring towns, and the price of corn was cut... Yet these measures, for all their popular character, earned no gratitude.'

Amid the destruction, Nero saw a great opportunity. To prevent looting (or, rather, to prevent anyone but him looting) he cordoned off the burned areas, and had the rubble cleared. Then, without compensating those who had lost their property, he seized a vast area of central Rome and began to build, according to his own ideas of civic architecture. Tacitus described the results:

Street-fronts were of regulated alignment, streets were broad, and houses built round courtyards. Their height was restricted, and their frontages protected by colonnades. Rubbish was to be dumped in the Ostian marshes by corn ships returning down the Tiber... house-holders were obliged to keep fire-fighting apparatus in an accessible place; and semi-detached houses were forbidden – they must have their own walls... Some, however, believed that the old town's configuration had been healthier, since its narrow streets and high houses had provided protection against burning sun, whereas now the shadowless open spaces radiated a fiercer heat. [8]

Some of the rebuilding was a marked improvement on the slums of pre-fire Rome. But public sympathy waned when Nero's own new home began to emerge from behind its wooden scaffolding. This immense new palace was known as the Golden House and the people of Rome were aghast at a villa (considered fit for the countryside only) being built in the city. The extravagance, too, was shocking: it was an extensive complex of buildings, colonnades, parks and gardens, filled with works of art, mostly looted from Greece.

The design of the Golden House was ingenious, and no expense was spared, once the land had been cleared and plans drawn up. Only half a century had passed, but the Emperor Nero's new palace could not have been more different from Augustus's frugal home. Suetonius detailed some of the most striking features of the Golden House

The entrance hall was large enough to contain a huge statue of himself, 120 feet high; and the pillared arcade ran for a whole mile. An enormous pool, like a sea, was surrounded by buildings made to resemble cities, and by a landscaped garden consisting of ploughed fields, vineyards, pastures and woodlands – where every variety of domestic and wild animal roamed about. Parts of the house were overlaid with gold and studded with precious stones and mother-of-pearl. All the dining-rooms had ceilings of fretted ivory, the panels of which could slide back and let a rain of flowers, or of perfume from hidden sprinklers, shower upon his guests. The main dining-room was circular, and its roof revolved, by day and night, in time with the sky...

When the palace had been decorated throughout in this lavish style, Nero dedicated it, and condescended to remark: 'Good, now I can at last begin to live like a human being!' [9]

The project was so obscenely expensive that Nero was forced to increase taxation in the provinces. It is perhaps more than coincidence that around this time, Nero confiscated the property of the six richest landowners in Africa, who collectively owned over half the province. Nero, like most emperors, was always keen to acquire more property. The majority of people included him in their wills as a beneficiary, in the hope that he would allow their descendants to keep the rest. Sometimes, though, he could not wait and was reputed to have killed his aged aunt with an overdose of laxatives so that he could immediately acquire her extensive Italian estates.

Discontent with Nero spread. Reports circulated that Nero himself had started the fire deliberately so that he could build his vast home, and had played his lyre while watching Rome burn. This must be considered untrue but, to distract from these accusations, Nero sought a scapegoat. He settled on a religious sect known as the Christians, at the time a harmless and obscure Jewish sect. Secretive and little understood, the Christians were an easy target. They were rounded up and, according to Tacitus, executed in a number of horrific ways: 'Nero substituted as culprits, and punished with the utmost refinements of cruelty, a class of men, loathed for their vices, whom the crowd styled Christians... Vast numbers were convicted... And derision accompanied their end: they were covered with wild beasts' skins and torn to death by dogs; or they were fastened on crosses, and when daylight failed were burned to serve as lamps by night...'

However, the impact of these executions was not as Nero had hoped. Although the Christians were unpopular as antisocial blasphemers, there was widespread sympathy for their terrible fate. Rather than diverting blame from the emperor, these horrific executions simply added to a growing list of grievances that were held against him.

So far Nero's theatrical performances had been held privately, but an exaggerated opinion of his own talents now caused him to seek a wider audience. His appearances were no longer to be restricted to private, stage-managed shows. He began to give public recitals of his poetry and songs, and to appear on stage at public theatres. His first public appearance was at Naples, which was much more of a Greek-influenced city than Rome.

Many aristocrats, including Cassius Dio, regarded Nero's antics as an embarrassment and a disgrace: 'How could one endure even to hear about, let alone behold a Roman, a senator, a patrician, a Caesar, an emperor, named on the programme among the contestants, training his voice, practising various songs, wearing long hair... In putting on the mask [he] threw off the dignity of his sovereignty'.

Nero sensed the disapproval of the aristocracy and became increasingly sensitive to criticism. He surrounded himself with flatterers and sycophants. He even imported official clappers for his performances, though provincials, who were often trying to be more 'Roman than the Romans', sometimes found it hard to make the grade. According to Tacitus:

People from remote country towns of austere, old-fashioned Italy, or visitors from distant provinces on official or private business, had no experience of outrageous behaviour; they found the spectacle intolerable. Their unpractised hands tired easily and proved unequal to the degrading task, thereby disorganizing the expert applauders and earning many cuffs from the Guardsmen who, to prevent any momentary disharmony or silence, were stationed along the benches... [10]

The Roman Theatre at Bosra, in modern Jordan. To the embarrassment of the aristocracy, Nero began to give public recitals of his poetry and songs, and to appear on stage at public theatres.

It was said that the exits were barred during his long performances, and Suetonius described the suffering endured by the audiences: 'No one was allowed to leave the theatre during his recitals, however pressing the reason. We read of women in the audience giving birth, and of men being so bored with listening and applauding that they furtively dropped down from the wall at the rear, since the gates were kept barred, or shammed dead and were carried away for burial…'

Resentment against Nero was coming to a head. In AD 65, he discovered a confused plot to overthrow him and to replace him with Calpurnius Piso, who had a distant claim to the Principate. In his rage and fear, Nero executed more than fifty senators and army officers. One, named Flavius, asked by Nero why he had abandoned his military oath, replied: 'Because I hated you! I was as loyal as any of your soldiers as long as you deserved affection. I began hating you when you murdered your mother and wife and became a charioteer, actor and fire-starter.'

In addition to these senators and officers, Nero's old tutor Seneca, retired for three years, was implicated and forced to commit suicide. Tacitus gives this description of his death: '…by one and the same stroke [he sliced] with a dagger the arteries of [his] arms. Seneca – as his aged frame, attenuated by a frugal diet, allowed the blood to escape but slowly – severed also the veins of his legs and knees.'

Even Poppaea, for whom Nero had banished and executed Octavia, did not survive this period. Angry at being criticized one night for coming home late from the races, Nero kicked her while she was pregnant. As a result, she died. Full of remorse he gave her the most magnificent of funerals and declared her divine.

Discontent increased, and Nero began to sense plotting all around him. During an obscure period in 66, other arrests followed: aristocrats, courtiers, 'Republican' philosophers, poets – all were killed or banished and their property confiscated. One story records that, before he died, the court poet Petronius, implicated in a plot, took particular pleasure in deliberately smashing a vase which he knew Nero loved. The eminent philosopher

Chariot racing in the Circus Maximus. The two groups of triple columns mark the turning posts of the race track. Nero himself 'won' the ten-horse chariot race at the Olympic Games, even though his wheel fell off and he finished last.

Thrasea Paetus was condemned ostensibly on the charge of 'setting a bad example', because he refused to applaud Nero's performances.

An atmosphere of fear and suspicion pervaded the whole of Rome. Informers were everywhere – in brothels, in taverns, in public lavatories. Tigellinus dragged off any opponents for interrogation and secret trial. Anyone linked in any way to the imperial house was in particular danger; by the end of his reign Nero was the last man left alive with a blood connection to Julius Caesar or Augustus. He was thus responsible for the extinction of the Julio-Claudian dynasty. Nero became the last person who could genuinely be called 'Caesar' as a family name. From now on, it was solely an indication of rank and prestige.

The vast majority of these trials and murders were in Rome and Italy; the provinces were largely unaffected. As long as the army kept the provinces under control, and paying increased taxes to fund his projects, then Nero was relatively safe.

For the time being, the army could be relied upon to do just that. Nero had some ambitious military plans but they remained fantasies: he dreamt of campaigning in the Caucasus; of making the Black Sea another 'Roman lake' like the Mediterranean; and of emulating the conquests of Alexander, which caused him to begin to raise a new legion, 'the Phalanx of Alexander', every man over 180 centimetres (6 feet) tall.

Hoping once again to bolster his public support, Nero ordered a major Triumph to celebrate a settlement with the Parthians, concerning Armenia, achieved under his general, Corbulo, three years earlier. Nero presumably thought that a display of military extravagance and Roman might would elevate his own standing. The Armenian king Tiridates was told to come to Rome and Cassius Dio gives us this description of the scene that awaited him:

The entire city had been decorated with lights and garlands, and great crowds of people were to be seen everywhere, the Forum, however, being especially full. The centre was occupied by the civilians, arranged according to rank, clad in white and carrying laurel branches; everywhere else were the soldiers, arrayed in shining armour, their weapons and standards flashing like lightning. The very roof-tiles of all the buildings in the vicinity were completely hidden from view by the spectators who had climbed on to the roofs... At daybreak, Nero, wearing the triumphal garb and accompanied by the Senate and the Praetorians, entered the Forum. He ascended the rostra and seated himself upon a chair of state... [The King of Armenia] spoke...these were his words: 'Master, I am...your slave'... By special decree there was also a celebration in the theatre. Not merely the stage but the whole interior of the theatre round about had been gilded, and all the properties that were brought in had been adorned with gold... The curtains stretched overhead to keep off the sun were of purple and in the centre of them was an embroidered figure of Nero driving a chariot, with golden stars gleaming all about him... [11]

It was a great day, but it still would not save Nero's reign.

❖

There was only one province that Nero respected – Greece. 'The Greeks are the only people with an ear for music,' he said. 'They alone are worthy of my [artistic] efforts.' In late 66, Nero went there on a great tour. On arrival, although accompanied by a new wife, he appears to have gone through a bizarre marriage ceremony with a beautiful eunuch called Sporus, whom he subsequently also treated as a wife.

Nero had clearly become a megalomaniac – April was renamed Neroneus (unlike July and August, the name did not endure), and it was rumoured that Rome was to become Neropolis. Nero sensed that the elite were thinking of revolt. In 66, the emperor's suspicions fell on General Corbulo. Nero summoned him into his presence and ordered him put on trial. The highly experienced and respected general killed himself first. If the most famous living Roman general could be dispensed with in this fashion, no one was safe, even military commanders. Having spent his entire life within the palace, Nero had clearly failed to appreciate that even the legions, the ultimate source of his power, could be pushed too far. He had no rapport with the armies; he had never shared in their campaigns, never visited their camps, paid no attention to their conditions in the provinces, and had recently taken to giving senior army appointments to people he trusted, whatever their qualities or suitability for the post. The disaffected

Nero portrayed on an Egyptian temple as Pharaoh.

aristocracy who, as the remaining military commanders, had been pushed too far. Nero had made a fatal mistake – alienating the military doomed his reign.

Still in Greece, Nero ignored this developing situation. He was more interested in enjoying himself, entering competitions as a charioteer, singer and actor. He entered all the ancient games of Greece, and the many new events specially created so that Nero could win them. In fact he won everything, amassing a total of 1808 first prizes. He even won the ten-horse chariot race at the Olympic Games, despite having fallen from his chariot and failing to finish the race. Elated by his own success, he proclaimed the 'freedom of the Greeks', giving them immunity from taxation and increased self-government:

Unexpected is the gift with which I present you – though perhaps nothing can be thought unexpected from munificence such as mine... Not through pity, however, but through goodwill I now make you this benefaction, and I thank the gods whose watchful providence I have always experienced both on sea and land, that they afforded me the opportunity of so great a benefaction. Other emperors have freed cities; Nero alone a whole province...

Imperator Caesar declares: For its goodwill and piety towards me I wish to give something in exchange to noble-minded Greece... Freedom from Taxation! [12]

Nero also began work on a major engineering project – a canal through the Isthmus of Corinth to connect the Ionian and Aegean seas, thereby avoiding the need to sail around the dangerous Peloponnese. It was an ambitious project, attempting to carve out a depth of 90 metres (300 feet) of solid rock for over 5 kilometres (3 miles). Nero made the first cut himself with a golden trowel, but only a fifth of the distance was ever completed before the end of Nero's reign and the abandonment of the project. It would be more than 1800 years before the job was finished.

Nero was not only running out of money – he was also running out of luck and time. Back in Rome, he was universally loathed by the Senate, and there was growing discontent among the populace due to grain shortages. In the provinces, legionary commanders, already disillusioned with their emperor, were increasingly restless because of pay arrears. To make matters worse, Judaea was in open revolt. Nero's few remaining advisers suggested he return to Rome immediately.

❖

Nero did return to Rome, but at a stately pace. Not for him the 160-kilometre (100-mile) horseback rides of Caesar or the high-speed carriage rides through enemy territory of Augustus. Nero preferred to pass through Italy slowly, in a great procession, which culminated in a triumphal entry into Rome like a victorious general of old. On display for public admiration were his 1808 gold awards.

According to Suetonius: 'For his processional entry into Rome he…wore a Greek mantle spangled with gold stars over a purple robe… Victims were sacrificed in his honour all along the route, which was sprinkled from time to time with perfume.'

His old tutor Seneca had tried to teach Nero that, 'Excessive power seeks power beyond its power… A violent power no ruler wields for long. A moderate lasts and lives'. Unable to grasp this lesson, or the problems of his people, Nero did what he did best, producing a lavish but empty

The army general Vespasian who took control and established a new dynasty after Nero's death.

spectacle of his own vanity. The crowds may have called out, 'Hail victor of Olympia, Hail Pythian victor! Augustus, Augustus, Nero!' But they were hollow cheers. He had missed the last chance to rescue his position as emperor. Hardly had he returned than he set off to rest in Naples.

Nero had ignored the situation in the provinces for too long and a localized rebellion now broke out in Gaul. A new phenomenon had developed which Nero was oblivious to: rivalries had emerged between army groups which were to plague the Empire. Although legions had fought each

other in the past under ambitious men like Caesar and Pompey, these provincial legions were now flexing their muscles against other provincial forces. Nero reluctantly returned from Naples to organize his response to the Gallic legions' uprising, but the revolt quickly spread to the legions in Spain, which renounced their allegiance to Nero and proclaimed their commander, Galba, as emperor. Nero's enemies were far from Rome and the armies on the Rhine were still loyal, but Nero had become distrustful of everyone around him. In particular, the Praetorian Guard seemed restless. Even his faithful henchman, Tigellinus, abandoned him.

Suetonius tells us that, 'Nero was so universally loathed that no bad enough abuse could be found for him… A sack was draped around the neck of [a] statue, with a note reading, "you deserve the sack" ' – referring to the practice of putting those who killed their parents in a sack and throwing them into the Tiber.

Nero was not sure what to do. He thought about fleeing but had few supporters to aid him. On 9 June 68, Nero, hiding in a villa in the Roman suburbs, heard that the Senate had declared him a public enemy. It was the final straw and, in despair, he ordered his servant to stab him since he lacked the courage to kill himself. Apparently his dying words were, 'What an artist I die!' He was thirty years old.

Nero was the last direct descendant of Augustus – and his death brought to an end what had been, overall, a century of internal peace. Though the last of the Augustan bloodline had perished, the name Caesar lived on. The following year, as Rome again descended into civil war, there were four Caesars, emperors made and destroyed as provincial armies each raised their candidates in turn. Finally a general called Vespasian managed to take control and establish a new dynasty.

Nero had alienated most of the Senate, and from its ranks came the army commanders. These commanders, situated in the provinces, were increasingly aware that they had the power to decide who ruled Rome. As Tacitus wrote, 'the secret of Empire was out, that an Emperor could be made elsewhere than at Rome'.

A Roman boxer. The practice of weighting the 'gloves' with metal would be frowned upon today.

CHAPTER IV

HADRIAN

Within These Walls

THE entourage of self-important men swept down the provincial town's main street. Crowds lined both sides, pushing and shouting. Hawkers exploited the emperor's visit by selling pastries, nuts, fruit and wine to bystanders. Finally, preceded by a small bodyguard, the Emperor Hadrian appeared and began to make his way towards the Forum. One old lady shouted out that she had a petition for him to read but the bearded, muscular emperor continued to stride forward. 'I'm too busy,' he called to her over his shoulder. 'Then don't be emperor,' she shouted back. Hadrian stopped, turned and went to read her petition.

❖

The rule of Hadrian represents an important stage in the history and fortunes of Rome. Men like Julius Caesar and Augustus were born in Rome; and all the emperors who followed them were Italian. But Hadrian – and his predecessor Trajan – were provincials. Both were from the settlement of Italica (near modern Seville) in Spain. They were men from and of the provinces. Unlike Nero, who was Roman to the core and barely travelled out of Italy, Hadrian was a man of the Empire not the capital. At a time when the Empire itself was being forced to change from one based on military expansion to one based on territorial stability, the changing style and character of its emperors was a vital factor. Under increasing pressures, Rome was having to fight to keep its empire intact. Hadrian

Hadrian (AD 76–138). His reign marked the consolidation of the Empire and the stabilization of its frontiers.

would prove to be the most successful emperor during this time of transition.

❖

Publius Aelius Hadrianus (Hadrian) was born in Italica on 24 January AD 76. Some would later claim that he was born at Rome, but only when seeking to hide his true provincial origins. His ancestors took their family name from the town of Hadria in Picenum (on the eastern coast of central Italy), from where they had emigrated over 250 years earlier. They were settled by the great Roman general, Scipio, in a new town he called Italica in southern Spain. Scipio had recently taken this province from the Carthaginians and this was the initial garrisoning of new, 'barbarian' territory.

After a province like Spain had been conquered and pacified, a rate of tribute would be established, either in cash (which was the case in this metal-rich province) or in kind (grain, timber, hides, salt). This usually coincided with the creation or reorganization of settlements to create 'urban' centres which would serve as collection points for both tax and goods. From an early date, Rome had begun a policy of establishing military strongholds and communities in newly acquired provinces. These were often populated not by locals but by Romans and Italians, especially soldiers discharged as a result of the conclusion of hostilities. The settlements were frequently established at strategic points controlling important road junctions or river crossings. Italica was such a settlement; sited near a major river as it approached the Atlantic Ocean.

These settlements proved to be vitally important. They rid Rome and Italy of both discharged veterans (who could be troublemakers) and excess population. These inhabitants then created a nucleus of loyalty in the provinces, and in an emergency could be called to arms.

Ultimately, as these settlements grew, they became centres of local government. An extensive road network followed, markets, tax-collection points and crossroads of the agricultural and mineral exploitation of the countryside, bringing more land under the plough and opening up mines. Such urbanization was central to Roman life; most of the institutions and

features of Roman culture were specifically city-orientated. Indeed, to a great extent, the Empire consisted of a collection of locally autonomous cities, each responsible for running and exploiting a certain territory, with the central government playing only a supervisory role. This meant that the founding of cities was much more common in the West – in places like Spain – because in the eastern provinces an urban structure already existed which was often many centuries older than Rome itself.

In Italica, as the decades passed, Hadrian's ancestors had become part of the local elite, serving as magistrates. Hadrian's great-great-great-grandfather had become a senator late in the career of Julius Caesar, and was certainly one of the Dictator's supporters. Hadrian's father and Hadrian's mother, who was from Gades (modern Cadiz), were jealously proud of both their Italian origins and their place in their home-town's society.

Hunting was the most popular pastime for the aristocracy.

Consequently Hadrian and his younger sister Paulina grew up feeling as Roman as any Italian. Nevertheless, they probably would have remained provincials had fortune not taken a hand.

❖

In the year 85, when Hadrian was nine, his father died and he became the joint ward of Acilius Attianus and Marcus Ulpius Trajanus (Trajan), his second cousin. Trajan, a soldier, received orders to travel to Rome; Hadrian went with him. The boy would have heard stories about the imperial capital, but now he could see it for himself. Seventy years after the death of the first emperor and great builder Augustus, Rome remained the heart of a vibrant, exceedingly powerful empire.

It was only seventeen years since Nero's death but much had happened in that short period of time. The historian Tacitus commented that Galba's revolt in Spain, which had led to Nero's downfall, had set a new trend, that 'emperors could be made elsewhere than Rome'. Nero's death was followed by a year of intensive civil war and 69 is often referred to as 'The Year of the Four Emperors'. This was a destructive time, which once again brought home the fact that civil war was the result of disputed rule. Finally, however, there had arisen a new emperor, Vespasian. Born in central Italy, he had the humblest origins of any emperor thus far, being the son of a tax-collector. Originally hailed emperor by the legions of Syria that he had commanded, he managed to establish a new dynasty, the Flavians. He was strict and down-to-earth and, perhaps partly because of his own background, believed that promotions should be based upon merit rather than birth.

His rule was solid but, after only ten years, in AD 79, just before the infamous eruption of Mount Vesuvius 190 kilometres (120 miles) south of Rome, he died and was succeeded in turn by his two sons, first Titus and then Domitian. Hadrian arrived in Rome a few years into Domitian's reign.

After studying in the city for four or five years, Hadrian, aged fourteen, returned to Italica for his military service. Nothing is known of these teenage years in the army, but it is alleged that he spent a good deal of the time in the

southern Spanish hills engaged in the more enjoyable military exercise, which had become his favourite activity – hunting.

After three years, his cousin Trajan, who had recently been consul, recalled Hadrian to Rome. The Emperor Domitian, having made a promising start, had become uneasy. Considering himself threatened, he began to execute senators and officials. It was in this troubled environment that Hadrian began his career. In AD 94, aged eighteen, he became one of ten judges deciding upon contested wills.

He held the post successfully and was promoted to various other minor posts, until he was eventually appointed tribune (assisting the legion's commander) of the 2nd Legion (*Legio II Adiutrix*) in Lower Pannonia (roughly modern Hungary, south and west of the Danube). Then, in AD 96, he was appointed tribune of the 5th Legion (*Legio V Macedonica*) in Lower Moesia (roughly modern Bulgaria).

On 18 September 96, while Hadrian was abroad, the increasingly tyrannical Domitian was stabbed to death in a plot organized by his wife and the Senate. An aged senator called Nerva, replaced him. The Senate felt it had finally broken free from many years of oppression. Nerva's position, however remained weak. He had been supported because he was ailing and not a serious threat; simply a stop-gap solution while the real 'players' fought for supremacy. Although the senators felt they had triumphed in performing their 'ancient function' in electing one of their own, they had ignored one key factor – the army. History's largely unfavourable opinion of Domitian is based upon the writings of senators, as most of history and letters were written by such men. However, Domitian, no stranger to the camps on the Danube, had been popular with the armies, not least because he had campaigned with them, visited them and sizeably increased their pay. Their reaction to the coup was unfavourable.

Nerva and the Senate tried to secure the regime by passing a stream of popularist measures including tax exemptions and a form of child benefit. These proved insufficient. Nerva was forced to form an alliance with a popular and influential senator and, more importantly, a respected commander of the legions along the Rhine. This ally was Trajan. For the first time since the Republic two men were jointly in control.

On 27 January 98, Nerva died and Trajan, who was in Germany with his legions, was named Emperor. Hadrian, temporarily in Rome, heard the news and hurried to Cologne to be the first to inform his cousin. Hadrian's brother-in-law, Servianus, who also desired this honour, sabotaged the wheels of his carriage but Hadrian continued on foot, just managing to beat his rival's envoy.

Trajan had become the first non-Italian emperor. Some senators may have had reservations about his provincial origins but, to some extent, it depended on how 'Spanish' they considered him to be. An important feature of the Roman Empire was that it effectively imposed on a vast area a single, standard concept of what Roman 'culture' and 'civilization' were. Although the aspirations of the majority were rarely more than local, the educated elite from one end of the Empire to the other had more similarities than differences, and a senatorial gentleman from Spain would know how to behave and what to expect in the houses of social equals throughout the Empire.

Each province may well have had a distinctive accent but, since everyone in the higher middle class was striving to be as Roman as possible, a certain cultural uniformity existed. It was a sign of political maturity that the way Trajan acted towards the Senate was considered more important than his origins. Needless to say, he went out of his way to behave respectfully and defer to the Senate whenever possible. In return, they rewarded him with their complete loyalty.

Before long, a whole crowd of family and friends was seeking Trajan's favour, hoping for high office and promotion. Hadrian was more astute; he concentrated his attention on Trajan's wife, Plotina, instead. It was she who persuaded Trajan to give his great-niece, Sabina, to Hadrian in marriage. This was a coup; Hadrian was further tied to Trajan and had prevented anyone else successfully trying the same ploy. At the time the political marriage had little chance of becoming a love match: Hadrian, an energetic twenty-four-year-old, had married a girl of little more than twelve.

Under Trajan's wing, Hadrian made rapid progress. In 101, he became a
senator, years ahead of the strict career structure. The Senate traditionally
represented the opinions of Rome's upper class. As the Empire changed, so the
composition of the Senate changed with it. Up to half the senators were
provincials. Nevertheless, in Hadrian's first address to the Senate, he overheard
some of those listening sniggering at him. *The Augustan Histories* relate how, 'he
read a speech of the emperor to the Senate and provoked a laugh by his

*Trajan's Column:
Trajan, the first
provincial emperor,
watches his troops
beat off a Dacian
attack.*

141

somewhat provincial accent. He thereupon gave attention to the study of Latin until he attained the utmost proficiency and fluency…'

In 101–102, Trajan, wanting both to secure part of his northern border and to popularize his regime with a resounding military conquest, invaded Dacia, north of the Danube. This river was a firm Roman border but the increasing strength of the Dacians on its northern banks was becoming threatening. Hadrian was appointed to Trajan's staff.

The first Dacian war was inconclusive. In 105, a Second Dacian War was launched. Hadrian bravely led the 1st Legion (*Legio I Minerva*) to victory and helped make the war vastly beneficial by securing Dacia's gold and silver mines. As a reward, Hadrian was given the governorship of Lower Pannonia, where he continued to fight and gain victories. In 108, eleven years earlier than the usual minimum age, he became one of the two consuls. There were some, especially among the older overlooked senators, who began to resent Trajan's upstart relative. *The Augustan Histories* noted this sour reaction, '…that he was bribing Trajan's freedmen and courting and corrupting his favourites all the while that he was in close attendance at court, was told and generally believed'.

Trajan, significantly, rewarded Hadrian's bravery in the Dacian campaigns with the very same diamond that Nerva had given him as a sign of succession.

Success fuelled the ambitions of the aggressive Trajan. In 113, confident in officers like Hadrian, he attacked Parthia. Trajan's aims in this war are not entirely clear: certainly he was brutal, callous and enjoyed military campaigning. Possibly he was attempting to stabilize the Roman Empire's long eastern frontier once and for all by destroying the Parthians, the only real power bordering the Empire.

Whatever his motives, his successes were phenomenal; in just three campaigning seasons he annexed the Kingdom of Armenia and conquered the whole of Mesopotamia, creating four new provinces. Roman troops captured the Parthian capital at Ctesiphon and for the first (and last) time bathed on the shores of the Persian Gulf. We know nothing of Hadrian's role in this but he clearly saw that Trajan was overstretching the Empire's

resources. The Parthians had not been defeated; they had just withdrawn to regroup. In addition, the Jews throughout the Roman Empire (except in Judaea) took this opportunity to rebel against imperial rule, with widespread massacres in North Africa, Egypt, Cyprus and Mesopotamia. Provincial governors led their legions against them but Trajan decided to return to Rome to make sure that order was successfully restored. In the meantime, he left Hadrian at Antioch to govern the East.

In Cilicia, on the return journey to Rome, the sixty-four-year-old Trajan suffered a severe stroke and died. With no natural or adopted son, the question was: who would succeed him and become emperor?

❖

On 9 August 117, Trajan's widow Plotina and the chief of the Praetorian Guard, Attianus (who, with Trajan, had brought Hadrian up in Italica) declared that, on his death-bed, Trajan had formally 'adopted' his second cousin Hadrian and named him as his successor. The truth will never be known, but it was popularly believed that Plotina had engineered this accession. According to the *Augustan Histories*, it was even said that, 'it was not until after Trajan's death that Hadrian was declared adopted, and then only by means of a trick of Plotina's; for she smuggled in someone who impersonated the emperor and spoke in a feeble voice'.

Hadrian was informed of his succession and two days later, on 11 August, the army of the East, in part due to the promise of a large cash payment, acclaimed him emperor. We do not know why the childless Trajan had not adopted Hadrian before but, as Trajan's nearest male relative, an experienced soldier known to the troops, and with first-hand experience of most of the European and Asian provinces of the Empire, the forty-one-year-old Hadrian was the natural choice as successor. He inherited an empire 4000 kilometres (2500 miles) from east to west, and 3700 kilometres (2300 miles) from north to south, with a population of 50–60 million.

Hadrian had already spent many years as a soldier, politician and administrator. This gave him a marked advantage over an emperor like Nero who acceded in his teens. Hadrian's experiences had prepared him to deal with the three key groups he would have to manage: the Senate, the public and the army.

Although Hadrian had been proclaimed emperor by the army, he was immediately concerned to obtain the Senate's approval. Remaining at Antioch, he wrote to the Senate apologizing for the fact that it had not been consulted on the 'adoption'. He humbly requested that Trajan receive divine honours and that his own position as emperor be confirmed. He undertook to be a servant of the state and promised that he would *never* put a senator to death. The Senate, knowing the eastern army had already approved Hadrian, had little choice if it wished to avoid civil war but to hope he would keep his word.

News reached Hadrian, however, from Attianus that there had been a senatorial plot against him. Hadrian rushed to the capital to deal with the matter but, on arrival in July 118, he found that his supporters had already taken it upon themselves to execute the 'ringleaders'. These were four distinguished senators, all former consuls and friends of Trajan, who had probably resented Hadrian's adoption. Hadrian claimed the executions were nothing to do with him and removed Attianus from office (although his 'punishment' later included elevation to senatorial rank). Thereafter, whatever Hadrian might achieve, much of the Senate never stopped hating him for so quickly breaking his initial promises.

Whether Hadrian was involved in the murder of the four senators or not is conjecture – but he certainly did eliminate people during his reign – as most emperors did. It seemed inevitable that emperors had to 'get rid of' opponents. But, under Hadrian, such political deaths were relatively few. Generally those who had been his enemies before his accession he tended simply to ignore or release: on becoming emperor he said to one particular foe, 'You have escaped' and he remained reasonably confident throughout his reign that his rule was secure.

Hadrian's deference to the Senate was more than just a constitutional fiction. In Hadrian's youth Domitian had tried to rule without the Senate, eventually almost declaring war on it. As a result his reign had become increasingly fraught, culminating in his assassination. Hadrian realized that an emperor had to be more than a military autocrat. He followed the example of Trajan who, mindful of the Augustan model, had always shown respect to the Senate and involved its members in decision-making. In return, the Senate had given Trajan a high degree of loyalty, and after his death proclaimed him a god. The Senate never seem to have grown to like Hadrian but they did learn to appreciate him and approve of his rule.

Hadrian, who had taken over Trajan's enormous wealth and moved into his vast palace in Rome, also had to concern himself with placating the general public. For most of the populace, as long as they had enough food to eat and entertainments to enjoy, it made little difference who was emperor but they could still cause enormous trouble.

It was customary for new emperors to mark the start of their reign with extravagant popular measures. Hadrian was no exception: he held lavish games, including a hunt of a hundred lions. *The Augustan Histories* claim that: 'In Rome, in addition to popular entertainments of unbounded extravagance, he gave spices to the people in honour of his mother-in-law, and in honour of Trajan he had essences of balsam and saffron poured over the seats in the theatre…'

Hadrian also cancelled all private debts to the State Treasury, making a public bonfire in the Forum of the lists of debts and debtors, and thus writing off 900,000,000 sesterces of bad debts. (This was a huge amount; the annual wage of a legionary was 900 sesterces.)

❖

Though his relationship with the Senate and the people was never based on great affection, Hadrian felt confident enough to spend long periods away from Rome without fear of conspiracy. He knew where the real power lay – with the military. So it was on them that Hadrian concentrated his initial efforts.

He left Rome in late 120 to tour the provinces and the legions who safeguarded them. It would be five years before he returned. He was already well known to the legions in the East so he travelled to Gaul, Upper Germany, the Upper Danube, Lower Germany, Spain and Britain.

Hadrian felt that the Empire should not – perhaps could not – expand any further. Trajan's conquests, which were proving temporary, had convinced him of this. He felt sure the Empire should now focus on strengthening its boundaries.

Four centuries of overseas expansion were ending. The engine of empire – military conquest, looting, economic exploitation – had run out of steam. Rome had, in effect, run out of peoples it could safely conquer and turn into provincials. The distances and terrains involved would simply be too taxing. Hadrian's reign therefore marks this vital phase in the internal consolidation of the Empire and the stabilization of its frontiers. Emperors like Nero had exploited the success of the Empire for their own ends. Emperors like Trajan had ignored Augustus's maxim on maintaining existing frontiers and had pushed the borders to an even greater extent, crossing both the Danube and the Euphrates. Hadrian, although he knew that military expansion was popular, was convinced that he had to do the opposite. Trajan's Dacian campaigns would prove to be Rome's last great conquest.

Almost immediately after becoming emperor, Hadrian withdrew all Roman troops from the recently conquered eastern provinces, leaving them in the hands of client kings, a standard Roman tactic. This effectively moved the Roman frontier back to the Euphrates, where it had been prior to Trajan's campaigns. He was persuaded to retain Dacia as a Roman province, since abandoning the Roman settlers there would not have been tolerated by public opinion. But he insisted on destroying the only bridge over the Danube to prevent possible attack.

Hadrian wanted the frontiers firmly positioned at such natural barriers. Where there weren't any, he built his own, for example, reinforcing the defences along the relatively recent road through the Black Forest that linked the Danube and Rhine. There he ordered new fortifications, comprising a palisade of split oak trunks, 3 metres (10 feet) high, embedded in a ditch and fastened together on the inside by planking. These defences, intended to mark the frontier and prevent small-scale raids, stretched 320 kilometres (200 miles) and, for the first time, linked these two key border rivers.

Hadrian's policy of withdrawing to secure Rome's frontiers did not suit everyone. Some of the army officers questioned his decision. To them it seemed like an admission of weakness. Hadrian tried to mollify them by claiming that his actions were in accordance with secret instructions received from the much-respected Trajan. More successfully, he sent them gifts of money. Hadrian's greater concern, however, was long-term: if he followed a policy of border control rather than conquest, where would the military gain the new victories and booty that would keep them content? Similarly, if they were not on campaign, how could he keep them 'fighting fit' and occupied?

Having left Rome, he travelled first to Gaul and Germany. There he began making a series of personal morale-boosting inspections of the frontier camps and defences. Cassius Dio tells us that he:

...travelled through one province after another, visiting the various regions and cities and inspecting all the garrisons and forts. Some of these he removed to more desirable places, some he abolished, and he also established some new ones. He personally viewed and investigated absolutely everything...such as weapons, engines, trenches, ramparts and palisades, but also the private affairs of every one, both of the men serving in the ranks and of the officers themselves – their lives, their quarters and their habits – and he reformed and corrected in many cases practices and arrangements for living that had become too luxurious. He drilled the men for every kind of battle, honouring some and reproving others, and he taught them all what should be done. And in order that they should be benefitted by observing him, he everywhere led a rigorous life and either walked or rode on horseback on all occasions...[1]

According to the *Augustan Histories*, he placated his soldiers as best he could:

Though more desirous of peace than of war, he kept the soldiers in training just as if war were imminent, inspired them by proofs of his own powers of endurance, actually led a soldier's life, cheerfully ate out of doors such camp-fare as bacon, cheese and vinegar. And, that the troops might submit more willingly to the increased harshness of his orders, he bestowed gifts on many and honours on a few.. He wore the commonest clothing, would have no gold ornaments on his sword-belt or jewels on the clasp...visited the sick soldiers in their quarters...banished luxuries on every hand...improved the soldiers' arms and

equipment...strove to have an accurate knowledge of the military stores, and the receipts
from the provinces he examined with care in order to make good any deficit... [2]

Hadrian used any method he could; even introducing a new cult: *discipulina* ('discipline' personified in a divine form).

In sum, these efforts made him highly respected by the military and served the desired purpose of keeping the legions loyal, fit and well-trained. The Jewish historian Josephus recorded: 'They do not wait for war to begin before handling their arms, nor do they sit idle in peacetime, but as if born ready-armed, they never have a break from training... It would not be far from the truth to call their drills bloodless battles... their battles bloody drills'.

❖

Wherever Hadrian was, there was the centre of empire. The provincial camp, house or villa were his home, his headquarters. In these residences Hadrian was more than a soldier. According to the *Augustan Histories*: 'In poetry and in letters Hadrian was greatly interested. In arithmetic, geometry, and painting he was very expert. Of his knowledge of lute-playing and singing he boasted openly. He ran to excess in the gratification of his desires, and wrote much verse about the subjects of his passion. He composed love poems too.'

He was a man of high culture and very wide interests. He had a vast memory and did not require the services of the imperial *nomenclator*, whose job it was to announce guests; Hadrian always knew the names better. He could apparently write and dictate simultaneously. He was also remembered as being very witty: for example, a grey-haired man brought a request before Hadrian but was refused. Undaunted, the man disguised himself, chiefly by dying his hair black, and again came to the emperor with the request. Hadrian, recognizing the man and amused by the lengths to which he had gone, replied, 'I have already refused this to your father'.

He wrote a now lost autobiography, which was published under the name of one of his freedmen to disguise its true authorship (it was very favourable to him). But, on the negative side, he was often accused of being pedantic

and dilettantish, and could not endure anyone outshining him in anything. He was never slow to give his opinion on a performance or work of art or literature. His poetry was sometimes of a deliberately obscure and archaic style. He liked to debate on all subjects with professors and philosophers, either by means of exchanged pamphlets and poems, or in person. He even had poetic 'slanging matches' with other poets. In fact he seems to have entertained famous scholars and orators at his court just so that he could enjoy scoring academic points over them.

Some of these adversaries seem to have decided that discretion was the better part of valour. For example, a famous scholar, Favorinus, was forced to bow to Hadrian on a minor linguistic issue. When his friends condemned him for backing down when he was actually correct, Favorinus is said to have replied: 'You are urging the wrong course, my friends, when you do not

Trajan's Column: legionaries building fortifications.

allow me to regard as the most learned of men the one who has 30 legions…'

Hadrian's youthful passion for hunting never abated and whenever possible he sought out boar, deer or lion. He even founded a city called Hadrianutherae ('Hadrian's hunts') on the site where he had killed a bear. He loved his horses and dogs as individuals, giving them formal burials and personally composing poetic epitaphs for them, such as:

Borysthenes the Alan
Was mighty Caesar's steed:
O'er marshland and o'er level,
O'er Tuscan hills, with speed
He used to fly, and never
Could any rushing boar
Amid Pannonian boar-hunt
Make bold his flank to gore [3]

Although a 'provincial', Hadrian was the very embodiment of Classical tradition. Since boyhood Hadrian 'the Greekling' had been a great admirer of Hellenic civilization. He cultivated a Hellenic appearance, with a carefully groomed beard and a hairstyle created with curling tongs. According to the *Augustan Histories*: 'He was tall of stature and elegant in appearance; his hair was curled on a comb, and he wore a full beard to cover up the natural blemishes on his face'. In this he set the imperial style for some generations to come, as courtiers and nobility followed his example.

❖

Tacitus wrote: 'Britain is the largest island known to Romans… The sky is overcast with continual rain and cloud, but the cold is not severe.' When Hadrian made his visit to Britain in 122 he had decided that the northern frontier, only established a few decades earlier, was inadequate. Previous attempts to subdue the Caledonian tribes to the north had proved only partially successful, the terrain as much of a hindrance as the natives. Hadrian now ordered the construction of a vast symbolic 'wall' to cover the 117 kilometres (73 miles) from sea to sea.

An inscription excavated in Jarrow, north-east England, reads: 'Son of all the deified emperors, Imperator Caesar Trajanus Hadrianus Augustus, when the necessity of keeping the Empire within its borders had been imposed upon him by divine instruction... having routed the barbarians, added a fortified boundary line between each ocean's shore...'

Julius Caesar had been the first Roman to visit Britain almost 180 years earlier and

Hadrian cultivated an Hellenic appearance, with a carefully groomed beard and a hairstyle created with curling tongs.

the Emperor Claudius had begun its conquest in AD 43. The legions had been dispatched into lands about which they knew little, with frequently inaccurate maps. All this made the lives of the soldiers and officers that much more difficult and nerve-racking.

Their only information came from travellers or merchants, whose accounts would be compiled and distributed. Frequently, such accounts deliberately served to convince the soldiers of the weakness of the opposition rather than giving them an accurate idea of what they were up against. The Britons north of the border were portrayed as typical barbarians.

The historian Herodian, who lived in the late second and early third century AD, wrote: 'They tattoo their bodies with various patterns and pictures of all sorts of animals... They are very fierce and dangerous fighters... Because of the thick mist which rises from the marshes, the atmosphere in this region is always gloomy'.

Cassius Dio, meanwhile, said the British tribes, '...inhabit wild and waterless mountains and desolate and swampy plains, and possess neither walls, cities, nor tilled fields, but live on their flocks, wild game, and certain fruits… They dwell in tents, naked and unshod… they are very fond of plundering; consequently they choose their boldest men as rulers. They go into battle in chariots, and have small, swift horses.'

By Hadrian's era much of Britain had been conquered and its tribes absorbed into the Roman world. The island had been considered peripheral but useful and Hadrian saw no reason to disagree. He did feel, however, that defences to the north were required.

The wall's final design in Hadrian's lifetime consisted of three lines: to the north was a V-shaped ditch, about 9 metres (30 feet) wide and 3 metres (10 feet) deep. In central sections the ditch was unnecessary because the wall was built on a steep volcanic ridge. About 6 metres (20 feet) south of the ditch was the wall, averaging 4.5–6 metres (15–20 feet) in height and 2.4–2.7 (8–9 feet) thick. To the east, this was stone, and to the west, where stone was in

When Hadrian visited Britain he ordered the construction of a vast wall to divide the Roman south from the barbarian north.

short supply, this was of turf. The wall was probably crenellated on its
northern face, with a walkway along its top. To the south of the wall was a
parallel deep and wide trench.

It took about six years for the line
of the wall to become continuous. It
was built by legionaries, each unit
being responsible for a certain
section, and thus served a further
purpose: building it kept the troops
busy and out of trouble.

Once completed, it was manned
by 15,000 auxiliaries from various
parts of the Empire. Every mile

there was a small fort with a garrison of a few men. In addition there were
eventually seventeen auxiliary forts, the walls of which were built into the
main wall. Within these forts were carefully laid out barracks, administrative
buildings, granaries, and hospitals. Outside were sometimes bath-houses and
a great variety of temples to cater for the different religions and cults of
soldiers from all over the Empire. Parallel to the wall ran a road, an equally
important part of the system. Communications were vital for subduing,
administering and defending any province.

A funerary relief erected in northern Britain by a Syrian trader from Palmyra for his British wife.

'Hadrian's Wall' was more than a visible statement of Roman authority and
a barrier against small-scale northern raids. It also prevented or regulated
north–south movement, thus isolating the Romanized province to the south
from the influence of the native tribes to the north.

The permanent camps along such frontiers were the mainstay of the *pax
Romana* and the principal agents of Romanization in border areas. These
camps – and the civilian communities around them – rapidly developed
many of the amenities of Roman towns, and gave rise to Romanized
townships outside their walls, which in turn promoted trade and, later,
intermarriage between Romans and provincials.

Though military units, predominantly auxiliaries, were occasionally moved to different provinces, they generally stayed put and became part of the local, increasingly Romanized, communities. From these communities, they recruited their new soldiers. Their duties changed from offensive to defensive: internal policing; supporting tax-collectors; guarding courts, prisons, mints, mines; manning customs posts; building and surveying forts, bridges, roads, aqueducts and canals.

Local tribes had little say in these events. Some may have even been physically displaced by such frontiers – their rough houses demolished because they sat within a military zone. Defences had cut some tribes in half, allowing them only restricted communication; stopping some reaching fields or religious sanctuaries on the other side. In addition, from the viewpoint of these tribal people, there were suddenly hundreds of foreigners about. Everything about them was different: the way they looked, behaved, dressed, ate, talked and smelt.

With these new arrivals initially came taxation, forced labour, forced recruitment, occasional beatings and rapes, new diseases. They took over land and called it theirs; many natives may not have understood private land ownership but they understood private land loss.

Throughout the Empire, however, the key to successful long-term occupation was to share the benefits of Roman life with the local people. While some hated this oppressive, foreign force, there were many who stood to gain from its arrival. Traders, craftsmen and merchants were engaged to assist in the construction of good roads, buildings, bridges, irrigation, sanitation and bath-houses.

Rome focused on incorporating the existing ruling class by offering it these benefits and the status of a new provincial Roman aristocracy. Most existing elites were only too eager to adopt the conqueror's culture, and were soon wearing the toga, and aping Roman social etiquette, dress and appearance, even down to hairstyle. Eventually many tribesmen and women became more 'Roman' in their behaviour than the Romans.

Roman gods were worshipped, but local religions were also permitted. Rome did not try to eradicate traditional beliefs but practised syncretism,

whereby a Roman god would be identified with a local equivalent (for instance, Mars would be identified with a local war god), and both would be worshipped under both names.

The use of Latin spread and a Roman education became necessary for the sons of tribal rulers. The historian Tacitus wrote an account of his father-in-law's actions as governor of Britannia half a century before Hadrian:

In order that a population scattered and uncivilized, and proportionately ready for war, might be habituated by comfort to peace and quiet, he [the governor of Britain] would encourage individuals, and communities to erect temples, market-places, houses... he began to train the sons of the chieftains in a liberal education. As a result, the nation which used to reject the Latin language began to aspire to rhetoric: further, the wearing of our dress became a distinction, and the toga came into fashion, and little by little the Britons were seduced into alluring vices: to the lounge, the bath, the well-laid dinner table. [4]

Hadrian was also always keen to exploit and incorporate 'foreign' fighting skills into the army. According to Arrian, a very successful Greek politician and author, and a personal friend of Hadrian's, '...the Emperor has also introduced the practice of barbarian manoeuvres, such as the Parthian and Armenian horse-archers carry out, together with the turns and feigned retreats of the Sarmatian and Celtic stave-bearers, with cavalry taking turns to charge and varieties of skirmishing, useful in battle; and they also use war cries native to each race, Celtic...Getic...Rhaetic'.

By Hadrian's time, auxiliaries were recruited from provincial non-citizens, and not always placed under Roman officers, as Caesar had done, but sometimes under their own native officers. Armed and equipped much like the legions, they were also deployed as permanent garrisons on the frontiers. However, Hadrian was careful to deploy troops far from their place of origin, so that their loyalty to Rome would always outweigh their loyalty to home.

One such unit of troops on Hadrian's Wall was the Syrian 1st Cohort of Hamian Archers. This 500-strong unit, recruited from Syria for their specialist archery skills, was based at the fort at modern Carvoran, a little way south of the wall itself. About 5 kilometres (3 miles) east there was a similar-sized unit of Nervii from

Gaul, and to the west there were 1000 more men from the Gallic Tungri tribe. There were also Germans, Spanish, Frisians and Dacians. Each auxiliary unit worshipped their own native gods. The Hamians, for example, brought with them the worship of Dea Syria, Hammia and Jupiter Heliopolitanus.

After twenty-five years' service an auxiliary would be discharged and receive citizenship. This gradual extension of citizenship to its subjects was what made Rome different, indeed unique, among ancient empires, such as Athens or Sparta, who would have found enfranchizing their 'subjects' unthinkable. The Romans offered a 'carrot' as well as using the 'stick'.

For Hadrian, such native units were vital for, when given a greater share in the defence of the Empire, they developed a deeper sense of Roman identity. Hadrian also raised the length of legionary service from twenty to twenty-five years, making it equal to that of auxiliaries. Even within the legions, Hadrian encouraged the appointment of non-Italian officers, like himself, for all but the very high commands. The armed forces (with the exception of the Praetorian Guard which remained mostly Italian) thus came to be more representative of the Empire as a whole.

❖

Hadrian had established a strong position in Rome because he was popular with the legions for looking after their welfare, and popular with the general population for cancelling their debts. He was also fortunate because, with hindsight, we can see that this was a relatively slack period between Rome's earlier military expansionism and the internal trouble which followed. In addition, Hadrian was a man of proven ability who seemed to have no rivals. The time and energy he devoted to the provinces were crucial to his reign. This was his answer to the problem of how the Empire could survive without the dynamic of expansion. In his view, Rome itself was only a small part of the whole. No emperor had given more time to the provinces – thirteen of Hadrian's twenty-one years in power were spent outside Italy. As Cassius Dio noted: 'He saw many cities, more in fact than any other emperor.'

Hadrian's travels were marked by the issue of special coins, each inscribed with the name of the province in which he had just arrived. From these it is

clear that he journeyed to the very extremities of the Empire, from the advanced urban culture of the Greek-speaking East to the Atlantic coast of Spain, and from the grain-rich forts of North Africa to the towns growing in Britain. On these journeys, Hadrian passed through an almost infinite variety of peoples and cultures, languages and religions, all within the embracing rule of Rome, all enjoying (in Hadrian's opinion) the benefits of Roman civilization. The *pax Romana* ensured safer travel and Roman law offered better security under a single, empire-wide legal system. Thriving urban centres arose where before there had been none, with all the associated modern amenities – aqueducts, roads, bridges, drains, baths, theatres.

Wherever Hadrian was, that was the effective hub of the Roman world. Rome and the Senate were secondary. Hadrian had left his civil service and his Council of State (senators chosen to advise the emperor) with executive powers for use in any emergency in his absence.

He had also made changes to this bureaucracy. The principal posts, most importantly the secretaries in charge of departments were given to knights (who were one class lower than senators). Administrators were no longer part of the emperor's personal household staff but, rather, public servants. This separation of the administration from the emperor's household professionalized it and improved its efficiency.

Hadrian's own daily business fell into two main categories: first, his role as supreme judge, whether in Rome or while travelling. People would come to the emperor from all parts of the Empire with appeals or petitions. Second, there was his 'foreign policy'. The emperor received foreign ambassadors to discuss disputed borders or trading arrangements. As long as they could find him, they could meet him.

During these travels, he had also ordered that Roman laws be codified properly for the first time. Hitherto they had been a combination of statute laws and accumulated interpretations and precedents by individual magistrates (not unlike modern English law). Hadrian asked the jurist Salvius Julianus, one of his legal advisers, to establish one set of laws that was to be both universal and permanent. Thereafter, when disputes still could not be settled, it was up to the emperor to decide. This increased the emperor's control over the legal system and removed from judges the power to alter or add to the law. Hadrian's codification was a major influence on the development of Roman law and also began a long tradition of legal studies. He further improved the administration of justice by establishing four circuit judges for Italy. These eased congestion at the imperial court and removed the cost of having to go to the emperor for a decision. These laws were not, however, equitable. As Roman citizenship had spread and consequently devalued a once exclusive privilege, a new class-based hierarchy had developed in Rome, with the creation of wealthy *honestiores* and the poorer *humiliores*. A key difference between the two was that the former were exempt from capital punishment.

Hadrian's predecessor, Trajan, had spent a great deal on military expansion, and the state finances (dependent on taxation) had been stretched. Hadrian had opened his reign by cancelling all debts but his policy of peace thereafter meant that the treasuries soon replenished their stocks. Throughout his reign his coins maintained their weight and value. But there was still massive expenditure on entertainments and building projects both in Italy and the provinces. All this was achieved by financial prudence, rather than by illegal confiscations. According to the *Augustan Histories*: 'He had as complete a knowledge of the state budget in all its details as any careful householder has of his own household'.

Hadrian established an audit for the state accounts every fifteen years, particularly aimed at preventing a reaccumulation of bad debts. He also abolished the last vestiges of the highly corrupt 'tax-farming' system (by which private companies collected taxes on behalf of the government), so that all tax was now collected by government officials. He established new financial officers, most importantly a *procurator* to oversee the efficiency of the *saltus* or 'crown land' (estates personally owned by the emperor). But, to prevent exploitation of the peasants, he allowed them, in theory at least, direct appeal to the emperor and also permitted a kind of 'squatters' rights' on imperial estates where the land was marginal or derelict.

In 122–123, after leaving Britannia, he went to Spain. En route, he travelled to his home town of Italica and ordered the construction of a magnificent amphitheatre. Then he sailed towards the Greek-speaking East that he loved. Associated with his affection for Greek life was the fact that his wife Sabina took second place to Hadrian's young male lover, Antinous, from Bithynia (north-west Turkey). The relationship was no secret and seems to have been easily accepted by both courtiers and soldiers. At that time homosexuality carried with it much less stigma than it does today.

When travelling, Hadrian was very careful not to burden the provinces with the expense of his upkeep. His entourage was modest and he insisted on a lack of pomp and ceremony. The emperor's protection was entrusted to a handful of guards, but they were outnumbered by engineers and artisans, who advised Hadrian on the impovements that could be made in the provinces. Due to their efforts, there were almost always visible benefits as a result of the emperor's visits.

In the words of Cassius Dio: 'He visited more cities than any other ruler, and to all he was benevolent; he gave aqueducts and harbours, corn and gold, buildings and honours of many kinds'.

At the same time as Roman influences (including art, architecture, literature, language, warfare, finance) were spreading to the provinces, there was a counter-current of provincial culture being adopted by Rome. By far the most important and obvious influence was that of the Hellenistic East. Many features of 'Roman' culture were greatly influenced by Greece. The poet Horace even claimed that: 'Captive Greece hath conquered her captor Rome…'

When the Romans had first conquered Greece over 300 years before Hadrian, they had regarded the literary and artistic culture of Greece as far superior to their own. It became quite common for campaigns to end with hundreds of works of art coming to Rome as booty. Such works of art – sculpture, painting, literature and architecture – were adopted, imitated and, in Roman eyes, improved upon. Greek-speaking artists, architects, poets, historians, doctors and entertainers from all over the East migrated to Italy to find patrons.

Sabina, the wife of Hadrian, took second place to Hadrian's male lover, Antinous.

The Pantheon (opposite), the largest unsupported dome until the twentieth century.

Hadrian spent the winter of 124–125 in Athens. There he commissioned a new aqueduct, completed the temple of Olympian Zeus (begun 650 years earlier), an immense new library, a whole new quarter to the town called Hadrianopolis (linked to the old city through a great arch), and a codification of ancient Athenian laws. In the stadium he held a wild beast hunt of a thousand animals. He also instituted the Panhellenic Games to rival the ancient games of Greece.

After six months in Athens, and a total absence of over five years, Hadrian returned to Rome where he immediately began indulging another of his loves – architecture. Here he worked on the construction of several new buildings, including magnificent temples of Hellenic inspiration (amongst them, the Temple of Venus and Rome). But he was no slavish copier of Hellenic models, and his most impressive creation was a complete innovation. The Pantheon, a massive temple to Roman gods, is not only a remarkable architectural achievement, and still one of the most famous buildings in Rome, but it may have been designed by Hadrian himself.

In Rome, Hadrian was (as Augustus had been) a stickler for correct Roman manners. Even though the toga was becoming an antique mode of dress, the *Augustan Histories* tell us that:

He ordered senators and knights to wear the toga whenever they appeared in public except when they were returning from a banquet, and he himself, when in Italy, always appeared thus clad. At banquets, when senators came, he received them standing, and he always reclined at table dressed either in a Greek cloak or in a toga. [5]

He was careful that at such banquets everyone was well treated. He apparently even went so far as to have dishes from the lowest tables set before him to ensure that his cooks had taken equal care with less important people's fare. His own favourite dish was *tetrapharmacum* (pheasant, ham and sow's udders in pastry). He had a healthy appetite and was known to eat meals even while judging trials.

Hadrian stayed in Rome just over a year and then continued his tours of the provinces. In 127 he toured Sicily, then North Africa.

In 128–130 he travelled through Greece and Asia Minor. Then he travelled to Syria and the stretch of the Euphrates that marked the border with Parthia. Roman influence in the region had been consolidated in the previous decades, especially after the conquest of the new province of 'Arabia' in 106. This was marked by a road Trajan had built from the Red Sea, via the provincial capital at Petra, to Syria. (In 107 a soldier had written home to his family: 'I give thanks…that, while all are labouring the whole day through cutting stones, I as [an officer] go about all day doing nothing'.)

Imperial visits continued to confer widespread benefits: a new aqueduct at Corinth; a new harbour at Ephesus; many new roads and bridges, especially in Spain and the Danubian provinces. Sometimes these were paid for by Hadrian and the Treasury in Rome; at other times the city councils were expected to provide the necessary finance. Wherever disaster had struck, Hadrian stepped in; rebuilding areas devastated by earthquakes, providing famine relief, and sending assistants to reorganize the mismanaged finances of provincial cities. In return, the grateful cities showered him with honours – calling him 'Restorer', 'Benefactor', 'Liberator', 'Redeemer of the Universe'; 'Zeus', 'Divine Saviour of the World'.

In his wake he founded or rebuilt cities – several called Hadrianopolis (the largest of which is modern Edirne in European Turkey); Forum Hadrianeia in Lower Germany; Colonia Julia Hadriana Avenio (which became Avignon in France), Hadrianutherae, Hadrianiea.

Although the primary purpose of Hadrian's tours was to inspect the frontiers and to maintain the armies in a constant state of readiness, he was often simply a royal 'tourist'. According to the *Augustan Histories*: 'he was so fond of travel that he wished to inform himself in person about all that he had read concerning all parts of the world'.

Like any other tourist, he visited famous sites, learning of the civilizations that had gone before. At such sites, he was shown around by local guides and encouraged to buy souvenirs.

In Egypt, in 130–131, Hadrian, publicly inspecting the 3rd Legion, privately held debates with the most renowned Greek intellectuals, even attending meetings at the most famous seat of Classical learning, at the Temple of the Muses or the *Mouseion* (which in its Latinized form gives 'Museum') at Alexandria. He also visited and restored the tomb of Pompey which he found derelict.

He visited the Pyramids and then decided to take an extended cruise up the Nile. For this he was joined by Sabina . His relationship with his wife is vague, but, as emperor and empress, seems to have been professional. *The Augustan Histories* tell us, however, that, '…he was wont to say himself, that he would have sent away his wife on the grounds of ill-temper and irritability had he been merely a private citizen…'

Hadrian was also accompanied on the Nile by his lover, Antinous. On the cruise Antinous drowned under mysterious circumstances. Some said that he was put to death by Hadrian so that the youth would never grow old and ugly, or perhaps Sabina had taken a hand? The likelihood is that he simply slipped and fell in. In commemoration, Hadrian had an Egyptian city built and named after him – Antinoöpolis. He also had him proclaimed a god, and statues of the boy were set up all over the Empire.

Hadrian and Sabina nevertheless continued their tour. At Thebes they heard the 'singing Memnon', a massive statue that whistled every morning.

The Royal court at Alexandria. Hadrian tried to travel with the minimum of fuss, but visiting Egypt with Sabina would have doubled the size of the entourage.

This wondrous event, the cause of which was unknown to the Romans, resulted from air trapped inside the statue expanding with the morning heat and escaping through a crack. Hadrian, Sabina and the imperial party were greatly impressed and carved some graffiti into the statue. The inscriptions are still there. A woman called Julia Balbilla, probably one of Sabina's ladies-in-waiting, wrote, 'Memnon...beheld Hadrian, the all-powerful monarch, before the rays of the sun... Memnon released his piercing voice... the lord Hadrian himself suitably greeted Memnon, and left behind for posterity on a tablet words signifying what he had seen and what he had heard. The gods reveal themselves to the children they love'.

We also read that, 'Sabina Augusta, wife of Imperator Caesar Hadrian, within the first hour heard Memnon twice'.

After Egypt, Hadrian headed north towards Syria.

Not every province, tribe or religious group welcomed the Roman army and administration. When Hadrian had passed through Judaea in 130, on his way to Egypt, he found Jerusalem still in ruins from the Roman siege and ransack of sixty years earlier. He decided to rebuild the city in his own name. On the site of the Jewish Temple he began building a new temple to 'Jupiter and the Emperor'. The Jews could not tolerate such an affront to their ancient traditions and religion. In 132, they rose in revolt and Hadrian was faced with the only major war of his imperial career.

From mountainous strongholds they conducted effective guerrilla operations against Roman troops. It took the Roman legions, which Hadrian had kept fighting fit, three years to stamp out this bitter and bloody rebellion. Eusebius, a bishop and historian who lived in the late third and

early fourth century AD, described how, 'The war reached its zenith in the eighteenth year of his rule… the whole nation was prevented by order of law and by imperial command from entering the land around Jerusalem, Hadrian ordering that not even from afar should it look upon its ancestral foundation… The city changed its name and was called Aelia to honour the ruler Aelius Hadrianus'.

The Romans were brutal: tens of thousands of Jews were allegedly killed. Many others were sold into slavery and the province of Judaea was abolished, and renamed Syria Palaestina.

While Hadrian saw to it that the new 'Jew-less' Jerusalem was completed, hatred between Jew and non-Jew remained intense. The chief beneficiaries of this rebellion were the Christians. Although still perceived as an offshoot Jewish sect, they did not join the Jews in revolt. They were thus not excluded from Jerusalem, which increasingly became a Christian city. Indirectly Hadrian had furthered their cause – a cause that would be taken up by the Emperor Constantine 200 years later.

❖

The Theatre at Dougga. Hadrian loved architecture, and admired theatres, temples and other buildings wherever he went.

Hadrian had returned to Rome in late 133 or early 134. Aged fifty-eight, he had travelled many thousands of miles. The time had come to ease back. He thus settled in to his specially built villa at Tivoli, 24 kilometres (15 miles) east of Rome. Aurelius Victor tells us that: 'Hadrian, as is the custom among the fortunate rich, erected palatial mansions, turned his attention to banquets, statues and paintings. Finally, he looked forward most carefully to everything connected with luxurious living and self-indulgence...'

Tivoli was indeed the height of Roman luxury and magnificence, a paradise laid out over more than 2.5 square kilometres (1 square mile). Its many buildings varied considerably in architectural character. Started by Hadrian on his previous stay in Rome eight years before, the complex was a reflection of his personal tastes. It included an imperial palace; large-scale accommodation for guards, servants and guests; bath-houses; two libraries (one Greek, one Latin, with an additional private study); a sports stadium, a swimming pool, a theatre, an art gallery; numerous temples, shrines and altars; and a miniature villa-retreat on an island in a small lake, connected to the shore by a removable bridge.

It seems likely that parts of the estate were named after sections of the eastern empire he had visited. These names included the Academy (Plato's school), the Lyceum (Aristotle's school), the Prytaneum (a government building in Athens), the Vale of Tempe (a beautiful valley in northern Greece), Canopus (a town in Egypt). A large pond symbolized the Mediterranean. At one point on the lake, Asia was represented by copies of famous statues from the Temple of Artemis at Ephesus, one of the Seven Wonders of the World, and a city on which Hadrian had lavished much attention.

Tivoli was not so much the 'Empire in miniature' (there were no western provinces represented, nor Italy) but more the 'edited highlights', the emperor's personal favourites, that he could wander among, reflecting on the years gone by and the many thousands of miles travelled.

In 135, Sabina died. Though their relationship had not been close, her death served to remind Hadrian of his own mortality. These concerns were reflected in some of the poems he wrote, one of which reads:

Dear fleeting, sweeting, little soul
My body's comrade and its guest
What region now must be thy goal
Poor little wan, numb, naked soul,
Unable, as of old, to jest? [6]

Nevertheless, though Hadrian's travelling may have ended, his rule continued. One of the many orders he sent to the provincial governor of Egypt in AD136 read: 'Imperator Caesar Hadrianus…father of the country, declares… Whereas I have learned that at the present time the Nile has risen quite inadequately – as also last year… I thought it necessary to make some beneficent concession to the farmers… know that the tax for this year will be deferred…'

Hadrian was in great pain, possibly from tuberculosis. He apparently considered suicide but was preoccupied with anxieties about the succession – Rome's (perhaps any monarchy's) enduring weakness. Without children or any close male relatives, he feared plots and intrigues. He alleged that his brother-in-law, Servianus, a rival ever since he had broken Hadrian's chariot wheels as he tried to reach Trajan to be first to congratulate him on his accession, was attempting to secure the succession for his grandson, Fuscus. Hadrian still had his ruthless side: he ordered both to commit suicide, even though they were ninety and eighteen years old respectively. Servianus had been a distinguished senator and thrice consul, and his death, together with the arrest of other senators, earned Hadrian the renewed hatred of the Senate. He, however, was probably too ill to care. According to Cassius Dio: 'He now began to be sick; for he had been subject even before this to a flow of blood from the nostrils, and at this time it became distinctly more copious'.

In summer 136, Hadrian adopted Lucius Commodus as his successor. He was Hadrian's favourite and a companion on his travels. Cassius Dio again:

The substantial remains of Hadrian's Villa at Tivoli. In Hadrian's day it was the height of Roman luxury and magnificence, and a reflection of his personal architectural tastes.

HADRIAN

The Emperor convened at his house the most prominent and most respected of the senators; and lying there upon his couch, he spoke to them as follows: 'I, my friends, have not been permitted by nature to have a son, but you have made it possible by legal enactment. Now there is this difference between the two methods – that a begotten son turns out to be whatever sort of person Heaven pleases, whereas one that is adopted a man takes to himself as the result of a deliberate selection. Thus by the process of nature a maimed and witless child is often given to a parent, but by process of selection one of sound body and sound mind is certain to be chosen'... [7]

The Senate, however, bitterly resented the fact that excellent candidates had been passed over in favour of a man who, they claimed, merely shared Hadrian's literary tastes and, according to some, his bed. The months passed, and Hadrian did not die but Commodus did. Hadrian was stunned – and angered at the huge amount of money he had wasted bribing the army and populace at large to support Commodus. 'I have leaned against a tottering wall,' the emperor complained.

Hadrian then turned to Antoninus, a fifty-one-year-old senator. This choice was much more popular with the Senate. In return, Hadrian demanded that Antoninus adopt his own sixteen-year-old nephew, Annius Verus, later Marcus Aurelius.

Hadrian ailed. He travelled to the Bay of Naples, probably to partake of the hot, sulphurous springs there, but they seemed to have little effect. Nor did he have much confidence in physicians. Cassius Dio quotes him as saying: 'Many physicians have slain an emperor'.

On 10 July 138, while still at the Bay of Naples, the sixty-two-year-old Hadrian died.

Herodian, describing a later emperor's funeral, gives us an idea of the splendour of Hadrian's last journey:

...noble ladies intone hymns to a sad solemn tune... then the [remains are put] in a wooden structure...like a pyramid...spices, incense, perfumed fruits, and herbs being heaped around it... After ceremonies, a torch is thrown...flames soon begin to devour the whole building... At this juncture an eagle rises into the air from the highest storey...and

carries the soul of the dead Emperor to heaven from that moment he partakes of the honours of the gods. [8]

Hadrian's ashes were eventually deposited back in Rome in the massive new mausoleum he had constructed on the other side of the Tiber.

The Senate showed its latent distaste for Hadrian by refusing him the usual divine honours. It seems it only did so when Antoninus released those senators awaiting execution and refused to take up government unless the Senate honour his adoptive father.

Hadrian had called a halt to further imperial expansion and had 'fixed' the Empire's frontiers. However, this only changed the nature of the pressures facing Rome. How was the army to be dealt with? Could it be kept on a permanent war footing for the purposes of defence but without the possibility of further, potentially lucrative, conquest to motivate it? This policy was not only extremely expensive, it also required a man of Hadrian's drive and energy to maintain the necessary loyalty and battle readiness. Hadrian's immediate successors (the new dynasty of the Antonines) were able to manage this, until the Emperor Commodus (180–192) failed, and his assassination sparked off a series of damaging civil wars and an upsurge in military autocracy.

Rome's problems were not going unnoticed. Enemies beyond its frontiers saw their time was coming. At Hadrian's death, all was quiet but there were dark clouds on the horizon. Within two generations, this storm would break.

Hadrian's feet keeping a barbarian firmly in place.

171

CHAPTER V

CONSTANTINE

Bearing the Cross

O<small>N</small> a cold October morning in the year 312, two Roman armies marched towards one another. Only a few miles north of Rome itself, these armies were preparing to fight for the future of the Empire, which was racked by internal division and external invasion. It was in need of a remarkable man who could divert it from what looked like an inevitable path of decline and set it on a course of renewed strength and vitality.

❖

Constantine was born, probably in February 272, in the provincial town of Naissus, about 130 kilometres (80 miles) south of the River Danube. His father, Flavius Constantius, was an army officer. His mother, Helena, was probably a barmaid.

While Constantine grew up in this provincial Roman town, his father travelled, working his way up through the army officer ranks. Just as Constantine entered his teenage years, his father, hundreds of miles away, decided to back Diocletian, the commander in the Imperial Bodyguard, in a coup attempt to become the next emperor.

Diocletian was successful. Once again, Rome had been swayed by the power of the sword. Only 150 years before, the Emperor Hadrian had created a stability that had brought Rome to its zenith, but the Empire was now being assailed by such coups and palace assassinations. Rome's great weakness had always been its lack of an effective system of succession, and

Constantine (c. AD 272–337), the first Christian emperor, believed that the Empire could only gain from using – rather than persecuting – the Christian Church's power. His reign was beset by division and discord, which his public support of Christianity helped him overcome.

it had begun to seem that no one man was capable of establishing long-lasting legitimate rule over such a vast and troubled expanse of land. In the absence of any effective central authority, the legions had become accustomed to acclaiming their own generals as emperors. Legions along the Danube, the Rhine and elsewhere each tried to impose the rule of their commanding officers on the other provinces.

In the fifty years following the murder in 235 of the Emperor Alexander Severus (and thus the end of the Severan Dynasty that followed the Antonine Dynasty), there were at least nineteen 'legitimate' emperors and as many usurpers. The year 238 alone saw six emperors, five in the first two months. Very few of these had empire-wide authority; some were 'emperor' of little more than a single province. Few lasted long – on average two and a half years. Only two died at the hands of Rome's enemies; one died of disease; and the others were all assassinated or killed while fighting fellow Romans.

In this chaos lay great opportunity for Rome's enemies. The armies stationed on the

Diocletian, a military commander, proclaimed emperor by his troops, decided that the pressures of the Empire should be shared by a co-emperor.

frontiers were frequently withdrawn to the interior to fight increasingly complex and bitter civil wars, thus leaving the Empire's borders weakly defended at a crucial moment in history.

In the East, Rome's old enemies, the Parthians – once powerful but now fragmented by Roman assaults over the decades – were overthrown by the Sassanians, a new and vigorous line of warlords determined to restore the ancient glories of their nation. Rome's eastern provinces soon began to suffer from Sassanian attacks, and Roman failure to defend its provinces against this new threat created a power vacuum which was filled by the dominating city-state of Palmyra, the major camel-train centre in Syria. From its desert oasis, Palmyra, by 270, came to rule much of the East, from Egypt to Asia Minor.

In Europe, movements of Franks, Alemanni and other Germanic peoples southward and westward began to put pressure on Rome's northern frontiers. New and larger confederations of barbarians, principally Goths, breached the depleted frontier defences and began causing widespread destruction. Cities were destroyed, agriculture disrupted, and, in a striking reversal of fortune, provincial Romans were now carried off into slavery. The repeated passage of these armies – the barbarian invaders and the Roman defenders – caused immense destruction and depopulation. To accentuate the despair, a long and vile plague ensued.

Funding the defence of the Empire had always been a problem for emperors. But the third-century fight against barbarians, and the desire of emperors of dubious legitimacy to buy the loyalty of the legions, caused increased financial problems. In order to augment the money raised by taxation, emperors repeatedly minted more coins from the same quantity of precious metal. The effects of such actions were not properly understood; and the coins simply lost their value as prices rose. A vicious circle of debasement and inflation ensued (to differing degrees throughout the Empire) – until coins that were once 90 per cent silver carried barely a trace – and inflation in some areas reached 1000 per cent.

Many government employees, especially soldiers, preferred to be paid in food or clothing, rather than in increasingly worthless coinage. Rome's government was forced to make frequent unpaid levies of produce and materials from the provinces. This, in turn, only served to worsen the state of the economy.

The situation seemed impossible to remedy. Central government's failure to provide defence prompted more areas of the Empire to break away from central authority, in the belief that they stood a better chance by fending for themselves. In 260 the provinces west of the Rhine severed their links with Rome, and began their own line of emperors, who minted their own coins and defended their own borders.

Rome was rescued from the brink of total collapse by a line of vigorous 'soldier emperors', men of humble origins, who rose to prominence through distinguished military service during this third-century crisis. Their ability to fight off the barbarians and bring rebel provinces back under imperial control was valued more highly than their family backgrounds.

The Tetrarchy: the 'rule of four'.

Thus the nature of the emperor had changed once again. Once he had been an aristocrat or noble Roman, then a bourgeois Italian, then a senator of provincial origin, and now, like Diocletian, a military commander irrespective of class, descent or background.

Having been proclaimed emperor by his troops in 284, Diocletian began a series of reforms, the most important of which concerned the very nature of imperial rule. In 286, he decided that the pressures the Empire faced could only be managed by sharing responsibility between two men. These co-emperors were both to be entitled *augustus*. Diocletian chose Maximian as colleague: Diocletian was to be the senior *augustus* in the East, and Maximian the junior *augustus* in the West.

Growing up in this world of major political change, the young Constantine could not remain unaffected by his father's ambition for long. In 289, the seventeen-year-old's mother was cast aside so that Flavius Constantius, who had been made governor of Dalmatia by Diocletian, could marry into a politically more acceptable and useful family.

Constantine's father married Theodora, the stepdaughter of Maximian, the *augustus* of the West. Four years later, Flavius Constantius's astute marriage proved beneficial. Diocletian had decided that even two rulers could not manage the administration and defence of the Empire. Each *augustus* was now to receive a deputy, entitled *caesar*. The system as a whole was called the Tetrarchy (meaning 'rule of the four'). Maximian chose his new son-in-law Flavius Constantius to be his *caesar*, while Diocletian chose Galerius.

Flavius Constantius, thinking of the future, decided that his son should marry Fausta, another daughter of Maximian. But Constantine refused; he was already betrothed.

The next request Flavius Constantius made of his son could not be refused. He was ordered to travel to the court of Diocletian, officially as a 'guest', but in reality as a hostage to ensure his father's continued loyalty to his imperial colleagues. This time Constantine had no choice; he dutifully headed east. There he would remain for twelve years.

❖

Diocletian's court was at his new capital at Nicomedia, on the Sea of Marmara (western Turkey). In the third century, Rome had ceased to be the centre of the Empire that bore its name. It remained the ideological and symbolic capital, but the Empire had become so large that Rome was considered too distant from its threatened frontiers for Diocletian or his co-emperor Maximian to live there.

Diocletian had chosen to have his court at Nicomedia; Maximian spent most of his time at Milan; the *caesar* Galerius watched the eastern frontier from Antioch; while Constantine's father, the other *caesar*, remained at Trier, close to the Rhine. The benefit this system offered in securing the defence of the Empire's borders was clear but the cost and increase in bureaucracy was huge. Each man had his own court, officials and armed forces, and the provinces were expected to pay.

A contemporary author Lactantius was only one of those to complain bitterly. Although he was prone to exaggeration there was probably some truth in his observations:

[Diocletian] appointed three men to share his rule, dividing the world into four parts and multiplying the armies, since each of the four strove to have a far larger number of troops than previous Emperors had had when they were governing the state alone...with farmers' resources exhausted by the enormous size of the requisitions, fields became deserted and cultivated land turned into forest... the activities of all these people were very rarely civil; they engaged only in repeated condemnations and confiscations. [1]

The nature of imperial leadership had also changed. Constantine was dazzled not only by Diocletian's magnificent palace but by his deportment. He was a very different ruler from Augustus or Hadrian. He and other members of the court wore cosmetics, wigs, glittering garments and jewellery. The emperor even demanded that all who approached him prostrate themselves at his feet (and consider themselves privileged to do so). Unlike Julius Caesar, four centuries earlier, Diocletian accepted the name 'king'.

Diocletian had introduced such ceremonial innovations (partly in imitation of Persian monarchs) in the hope that they would restore the remote, almost divine status of emperor – supposedly helping to prevent rebellion.

According to the fourth-century Christian historian, Eutropius: 'Diocletian was the first who introduced into the Roman Empire a ceremony suited rather to royal usages than to Roman liberty, giving orders that he should be adored whereas all emperors before him were only saluted. He put ornaments of precious stones on his dress and shoes, when the imperial distinction had previously been only in the purple robe'.

Initially the Tetrarchy worked; the senior and junior *augustus* and their *caesars* controlled the Empire so firmly that Diocletian felt confident enough to send Galerius on the offensive.

He struck first against the Sarmatians north of the Danube. With Galerius went Constantine who was proving as fine a soldier as his father. An anonymous author wrote: 'when Constantine, then a young man, was serving in the cavalry against the Sarmatians, he seized by the hair and carried off a fierce savage, and threw him at the feet of the Emperor Galerius. Then, sent by Galerius through a swamp, he entered it on horseback and made a way for his comrades to the Sarmatians, killing many and winning the victory'.

Then, again with Galerius, Constantine successfully campaigned eastward, deep into the Sassanian Empire, helping to capture their magnificent capital at Ctesiphon.

These were notable victories and Constantine must have felt part of a renewed and vibrant Empire. Back at the palace, he awaited news of the next foe. To his surprise, perhaps, the next enemy was an internal one – a religious group called the Christians.

The Roman Empire had united Europe, North Africa and the Near East to an extent not seen before – or since. An excellent road network connected all parts of the Empire. It was a single political and cultural entity, with Latin and Greek as its common languages. Within the Empire there was considerable movement: army units switched from province to province; trade criss-crossed seas, mountains and rivers; and migrants from all over the Empire travelled to the big cities. With these movements, it was not only goods that were transported; it was also ideas, among them religious beliefs like Christianity.

This new religion was notable for being a 'religion of the word' with written texts. Whereas traditional Roman religion had a few magic texts known only to priests, by the end of the first century, the Gospels had already roughly assumed their present form. Few religious leaders in the ancient world had even one biography but Jesus of Nazareth had four 'official' accounts, and several others. The authors of the Gospels deliberately chose to write in Greek, the language of the entire eastern empire and one widely spoken among the educated classes in the West, even though Greek was neither their own first language nor that of Christ, who spoke Aramaic.

For many, the pagan gods remained as important as they had always been. Others, however, had chosen alternative faiths with perhaps greater personal involvement. In the traditional Graeco-Roman religion, great emphasis was placed on performing the rituals correctly, and worship often amounted to little more than a formulaic sacrifice or attendance at a priest's recitation.

Over the years, there had been a gradual movement towards belief in one god, or the belief that different gods were merely different aspects of a single deity. This 'greater god' took various, often quite traditional forms. Helios, the Sun, was a particular favourite with the military. There also developed other, less traditional, alternatives. The three most popular were the worship of Isis, an Egyptian deity; the worship of Mithras, originally a Persian god; and Christianity.

Christianity's great attraction lay partly in its promise of redemption, resurrection and after-life. This had a special appeal for the lower orders, whom the Roman elite had traditionally ignored, and who relished the idea of some form of compensation for what was often a miserable existence on earth. It is not surprising that Christianity's earliest converts were drawn from those whose lives were troubled – the poor, unemployed and slaves. Women were also particularly attracted to a religion which was unusual in deliberately seeking their involvement.

The Emperor Nero had been the first to persecute Christians, making them the scapegoat for the Fire of Rome in AD 64. But from then on persecution of Christians had been rare and sporadic, for, even at a local level, it caused upheaval and was not conducive to law and order. Indeed, the state tolerated practically all forms of worship. The problem with Christianity was that it was the most exclusive and intolerant of religions, declaring all other gods to be false. It shared this view with Judaism but, whereas the Jews were considered a defined ethnic group, anyone could become a Christian (as perhaps 10 per cent had done) – and that was what made it seem so dangerous. Moreover, because they considered it blasphemous to award divine honours to a mortal, Christians refused to take part in the emperor cult, the worship of the emperor as a god, which was particularly prevalent throughout the East.

From the middle of the third century, the intermittent persecution grew more intense. Diocletian – and his *caesar* Galerius – were convinced pagans

Representation of a pagan ritual: a bull being taken to sacrifice. For many, the pagan gods remained as important as they had always been.

and believed that the Empire's difficulties had been caused by the loss of their gods' favour, because of Christian impieties. They firmly believed that religion was an integral part of national life, with the gods upholding the natural order of things, and they were distinctly troubled by the rise of eastern, Oriental and secretive alternatives. They also saw the Christians as likely informers to the Persians (in whose country Christianity was able to grow in relative safety).

They therefore ordered the Christians to be punished and made an example of.

Diocletian decreed that all churches were to be demolished, all bibles and scriptures burned, all Church property confiscated, and Christians who refused to recant were to be deprived of their status and privileges. Anyone who refused to co-operate was to be imprisoned, tortured and even executed.

In the Empire at large, however, the persecution had little popular support. Many governors, even if they were not Christians themselves, were half-hearted about putting these orders into effect. Constantine's father did little to enforce Diocletian's instructions (though there were few Christians in his western domain anyway). As a consequence, the cohesion of the Tetrarchy was weakened.

At Nicomedia, Constantine would have been unable to ignore the flames of persecution – whether he supported them or not is unknown, but his later ruthlessness indicates that he could quite easily have been as brutal as Diocletian. Certainly, as he watched the full horror of the persecution, amazed by its martyrs who went almost willingly to their brutal deaths, he saw just how powerful the Christian faith could be.

❖

In 303, Diocletian celebrated his twentieth anniversary as emperor. To mark the occasion, he visited Rome for the first time. Constantine, aged thirty-one, accompanied him.

One author, Ammianus, noted Rome's decline:

Rome first began to rise into a position of worldwide splendour, destined to live so long as men shall exist... Then, entering upon adult life, after many toilsome years, they crossed the Alps and the sea. Grown to youth and manhood, from every region which the vast globe includes, they brought back laurels and triumphs. And now, declining into old age, and often owing victory to its name alone, it had come to a quieter period of life. Thus the venerable city, after humbling the proud necks of savage nations, and making laws, the everlasting foundations and moorings of liberty, like a thrifty parent, wise and wealthy, has entrusted the management of her inheritance to the caesars, *as to her children...* [2]

Constantine would nevertheless have been impressed by the ancient capital.

Vast monuments were still being constructed – for example, the Baths of Diocletian, started over a decade before and nearing completion at the time of this visit, were as sumptuous as anything built in the first century.

Constantine would also have seen the Aurelian Wall, built only a generation before. The fact that an emperor of Rome had deemed it necessary to fortify the city so heavily underlined the unpleasant reality that the Romans were becoming increasingly nervous of assaults, especially from the Goths (north of the Danube).

Nevertheless, with its rich aristocracy and enormous appetite for luxury goods from all over the known world, Rome would have been the grandest and most conspicuously wealthy place Constantine had ever seen. He does not, however, seem to have felt remotely at home there. He had little time for the social niceties of Rome's arrogant, landed aristocrats. Ammianus's description of Rome's inhabitants helps to explain Constantine's disdain:

The few houses that were formerly famed for devotion to serious pursuits now teem with the sports of sluggish indolence, re-echoing to the sound of singing and the tinkling of flutes and lyres. In short, in place of the philosopher the singer is called in, and in place of the orator the teacher of stagecraft, and the libraries are shut up forever like tombs...

Of the multitude of lowest condition and greatest poverty some spend the entire night in wineshops, some lurk in the shade of the awnings of the theatres...or they quarrel with one another in their games at dice, making a disgusting sound by drawing back the breath into their resounding nostrils; or, which is the favourite among all amusements, from sunrise until evening, in sunshine and in rain, they stand open-mouthed, examining minutely the good points or the defects of charioteers and their horses... [3]

Together, Constantine and Diocletian left Rome before the celebrations had been completed, and returned to Nicomedia. En route, Diocletian developed a chronic illness and decided it was time to retire. He persuaded his fellow *augustus*, Maximian, also to stand down.

According to the rules of the Tetrarchy, the eastern *caesar* Galerius succeeded Diocletian as *augustus* in the East, and Constantine's father, Flavius Constantius, succeeded Maximian in the West.

But who would now become the two new *caesars*? Lactantius, a Christian, wrote: 'Constantius had a son, Constantine, a young man of the highest integrity, entirely worthy of the rank of *caesar*. His distinguished and becoming presence, his military application, his upright habits, and his extraordinary affability made him the object of the soldiers' affection and of the private citizens' choice…'

But, the writer continued, the young man was in for a shock: 'Diocletian and Galerius held a parade to publish the names of the *caesars*. Everyone looked at Constantine, for no one doubted the choice would fall on him. The soldiers were called to order…and Diocletian [told] them he was going to resign… Suddenly he declared that the *caesars* would be Severus and Maximinus Daia. There was universal amazement'.

Lactantius's account cannot be entirely trusted but Galerius had certainly ensured the choice of a friend and a nephew instead of Constantine. As a result, Galerius dominated the Empire; not only was he *augustus* of the largest quarter, but his dependants were the *caesars* in the other two. Only Flavius Constantius remained independent as *augustus* of the West, but he was known to be ill. Lactantius describes the events that followed:

…seriously ill, Constantius had written to Galerius asking him to send his son Constantine back for him to see, as he had not seen him in a long time. There was nothing Galerius was less keen to do. Although he did not dare take any action against Constantine, in case this stirred up civil war against himself and – what he feared most – made him unpopular with the troops, he had already made several covert attacks on the young man, exposing him under the pretence of exercise and sport to wild beasts… [4]

Constantine decided to escape: 'when Galerius was resting after dinner, he made a hurried departure and sped on his way, getting rid of the horses of the public post at the many staging points he passed…'

Constantine rode to the coast of the English Channel. There he joined his father, who was on his way to Britain to defend the province against attacks from the Picts, a people of northern Britain. Hadrian's Wall, which divided the Roman south from the barbarian north, was never intended to

A portrait of a female, perhaps Constantine's mother Helena, the 'Queen Mother' of the Empire.

protect against such a concerted onslaught. Father and son were forced to campaign to the north of the Wall, which they did with success. On 25 July 306, however, Flavius Constantius succumbed to ill health and died at York.

His troops wasted no time, immediately proclaiming his popular son as the new western *augustus*. Galerius had little choice but to accept; the Empire and its government were so completely militarized that the legions could not be ignored.

Whereas the eastern empire was rich with resources and opportunities, the West seemed, in comparison, to be the reverse, its lands racked by civil war and economic disruption. As ruler of Britain and Gaul (and, within two years, Spain), Constantine's first act was to officially end the persecution of Christians within his domain. He granted complete toleration, and even returned to them all the rights and property that they had lost since 303. This was an important moment. Constantine, already a usurper with no legal authority, was now legislating without consulting the other Tetrarchs.

❖

When Constantine became part of the Tetrarchy, Maximian's son, Maxentius, envious of Constantine's achievement, could not see why he should be left out. He turned to the Praetorian Guard for support. (The Guard had, for decades, had the final say in who controlled Rome. The nadir had been reached in 192–193, when they had murdered the reigning emperor and sold the office to the highest bidder – a businessman.) Maxentius was able to secure their backing and so overthrow the authorities in Rome, and proclaim himself *augustus*. His father, the retired *augustus* Maximian, decided to re-enter public life to assist him.

At first Constantine co-operated with them both, offering assistance or at least neutrality in their struggle with the eastern Emperor Galerius. Constantine cemented the alliance by marriage. His first wife Minervina now dead, Constantine married Maximian's daughter (Maxentius's sister) Fausta. This was the very woman his father had tried to make him marry over a decade earlier.

When not touring his domain, Constantine and his wife lived at Trier. Many of Rome's earliest settlements were legionary forts, usually at important crossing points or frontiers, such settlements benefiting from the many traders who passed through. In what is today Germany, these included Cologne, Bonn, Mainz and Trier.

Trier (*Augusta Trevirorum*) had originally been the base for a unit of Spanish cavalry, stationed on the River Moselle by Augustus. By the second century, Trier had become a key trading centre, and by the late third century an imperial 'capital' due to its proximity to the Rhine frontier. In 260–274 it had even been 'capital' of the breakaway Gallic Empire. Trier was much damaged in an invasion by the Alemanni around 275–276, and then retaken and rebuilt by the Roman Empire.

For Constantine, this city of 70,000 was a convenient base for operations, as it was the Rhine frontier that demanded the most attention. Tribes in Germany were themselves under threat from the east. They were therefore fighting on two fronts – as well as among themselves. Constantine realized he could take advantage of his enemy's weaknesses and reminded them that crossing the Rhine would mean death or slavery. He not only repelled incursions by the Franks but also built a bridge across the Rhine and led ruthless expeditions into their territory. His aim was to create a devastated wilderness on the other side of the river, so that it could not serve as a base for raiding the Empire.

Some of those he captured were brought back to Trier and publicly put to death in the town's arena. Eutropius gives this account of events: 'Constantine, who was ruling in Gaul with great approbation both of the soldiers and the people of the province, overthrew the Franks and Alemanni with great slaughter, and captured their kings, whom, on exhibiting a magnificent show of games, he exposed to wild beasts…'

An anonymous source gives another account: 'Countless were slain, very many captured. All of their herds were seized or slaughtered; all of their villages consumed by fire. The adult males being offered for punishment in a spectacle, by their very multitude exhausted the savage beasts'.

Constantine was clearly ruthless against barbarians; he was soon to prove he could be equally ruthless against his fellow Romans. The harmony between Maxentius and his father Maximian in Rome was short-lived. They could not resolve which of the two had seniority. Eventually Maximian assaulted his son, tearing his purple cloak from him during a parade, and then fled to join his son-in-law, Constantine.

Any friendship between Constantine and Maximian was short-lived too: after attempting to overthrow his host, Maximian was found hanging in his apartments.

Within a year, Constantine received the gratifying news that the senior *augustus*, Galerius, had died of a long and agonizing illness. Constantine now had everything to play for. Galerius's successor in the East was Licinius, and

NIMEIV
TELEGENI
PROLEOPARDO
MERITVMHA
BEANTVESTRI
FAVORISDONA
TEEISDENARIOS
QVINGENTOS

DERETVAMV
NVSEDES
STADIES
MAGERIVSDO
NATHOCISTHABE
REHOCESTPOSSE
HOCESTIA · NOXEST
IAMVNERETVO
SACCISMISSOS

MAGERI

VICTOR

BVLLARIVS

CRISPINVS

HILARINV

Unlike gladiators who fought wild beasts with a chance of surviving, Constantine threw captured prisoners to their deaths, unarmed, to be mercilessly savaged by these animals.

Constantine duly courted the new *augustus*, betrothing his stepsister Constantia to him. Notwithstanding their new 'brotherly' relationship, both Constantine and Licinius began to look covetously upon the weak regime of Maxentius in Italy and North Africa. Constantine knew he had to destroy Maxentius and conquer his domain before Licinius did.

In early 312, Constantine marched over the Alps into Italy with 40,000 men. He defeated Maxentius's forces twice in hard-fought battles in northern Italy, and then marched on Rome, forbidding his soldiers to sack any cities en route. Maxentius had no wish to face Constantine again in the field and, after demolishing all the bridges over the Tiber, settled down for a siege. But the Roman populace rioted at the idea of the imperial city being besieged, especially by Romans. Maxentius was forced to risk all in pitched battle.

The night before battle Constantine alleged he had a vision. Lactantius described how: 'Constantine was directed in a dream to cause the heavenly sign to be marked on the shields of his soldiers, and so proceed to battle. He did as he had been commanded, and marked on their shields the letter

X with a perpendicular line through it, turned over at the top, this being the monogram of Christ...'

There are many versions of the story. What is certain is that, unwisely crossing the Tiber on a bridge of boats beside the demolished Milvian Bridge, Maxentius engaged Constantine. The battle was brief and a complete victory for Constantine. As Maxentius's forces fled back to Rome in total disorder the bridge of boats broke and many drowned, among them Maxentius. Constantine was to claim the victory as irrefutable evidence of divine support. He entered Rome in triumph. The whole of the western Empire was his.

❖

The Roman world was now divided in two: Constantine in the West; Licinius in the East. Few thought it possible that either of them would be able reunite the Empire alone – Constantine was to prove them wrong.

His first concern, however, was to inaugurate several extravagant building projects in Rome: erecting a huge bathing complex; completing a vast basilica; restoring the Circus Maximus. At the same time, as punishment for supporting his rival, Constantine abolished the Praetorian Guard.

The disorder of the previous decades had brought to political dominance a class of military men who completely overshadowed the earlier civilian elite. Senators were now barred from military command and provincial governorships: thus had Rome's ruling elite finally lost its power. Nevertheless Rome's Senate continued to cling to a sense of importance. About half the Senate was, in fact, non-Italian, from North Africa, Gaul, Germany. The prestige of senatorial life meant more to them than to those born in Rome itself. To appease Constantine and, ostensibly, to thank him for liberating them, they built him a massive arch. Many of its reliefs were stripped from earlier emperors' triumphal monuments and physically amended to suit Constantine. It was to be the last, and the largest, triumphal arch erected in Rome, and the inscription read: 'To the Emperor Caesar Flavius Constantine who, being imbued with divinity and by the greatness of his spirit, with his forces avenged the commonwealth in a just war on both the tyrant and all his party...'

Constantine, the soldier from the Balkans, continued to have little time for Rome or Romans. But it was this rough soldier who now had the task of managing an enormous Empire. One of his first actions involved the Christians. As Eusebius tells us: 'Those who in the time of trial had distinguished themselves by the fortitude of their souls in the cause of God, and had therefore been condemned to the labour of the mines, or consigned to the solitude of islands, or compelled to toil in public works, all received an immediate release from these burdens…'

Property was returned, and gifts offered. He gave the Bishop of Rome the Lateran palace which became home to the Popes for 1000 years.

Despite all this activity, Constantine stayed in Rome less than three months. He knew he still had the eastern Emperor Licinius to defeat if he was now to achieve his goal of becoming emperor of the whole Roman Empire.

Constantine had to move carefully. In early 313 they met in Milan and agreed a universal toleration of Christians. Licinius also now married Constantine's sister Constantia. However, the peace between the two men remained precarious and it was not long before Constantine claimed to have discovered a plot to assassinate him by some of his courtiers, including his brother-in-law, Bassianus. He alleged that Licinius was behind the plot and soon the two men were preparing their armies to face one another. In 316, Constantine launched his assault. Though he was the weaker (20,000 against 35,000), his superior military knowledge enabled him to defeat Licinius in a very bloody night-time battle at Cibalae in the Sava Valley. Licinius withdrew to Mardia.

After a second, indecisive, battle, Licinius fled and sued for peace. He had no choice but to recognize Constantine as the senior emperor, *augustus maximus*, and to cede a very large section of his domain to him: most of his Balkan provinces, which were major military recruiting grounds. The frontier between the two emperors had thus moved dramatically eastward.

Peace temporarily prevailed, the most visible sign of which was that the two emperors and their sons shared the consulship each year. Constantine's coins bore the legend 'Blessed Tranquillity'. But Constantine was preparing for the final assault. He moved his capital to Serdica (modern Sofia), declaring, 'Serdica is my Rome'. It was clear that the frontier with his 'colleague' was the one requiring his greatest attention. The Rhine he entrusted to Crispus, the son of his first wife.

The years slipped by until, around 324, Constantine felt able to declare war once again. The forces involved were much larger this time, perhaps double or triple the previous encounter. The clash came at Adrianople and was among the largest battles of the entire fourth century.

The fifty-two-year-old Constantine was active throughout the battle and, despite being wounded with a spear through the thigh, led his men to victory. Licinius, reported to have lost over 30,000 men, withdrew to the city of Byzantium, at the point where Europe meets Asia. Here Constantine besieged him. Licinius's position became untenable when Crispus, with fewer than 200 warships, drove back Licinius's 350 warships in one of the biggest naval battles in antiquity. Licinius regrouped but was totally defeated, losing another 30,000 men.

Licinius's wife (and Constantine's stepsister) Constantia persuaded him to surrender. She then pleaded with Constantine to spare her husband's life. Constantine, having won his complete victory, was prepared to be merciful, but only temporarily. The stay of execution lasted a mere few weeks until, claiming that Licinius had begun plotting with the Goths, Constantine successfully incited the soldiers to 'demand' Licinius' execution.

It had taken eighteen years of struggle since the death of his father but, by 324, the Roman Empire was entirely in Constantine's hands. Eusebius expressed the general belief that a new era was beginning:

Thus the Emperor VICTOR, *for he had himself adopted this name as fitting appellation to express the victory over all who hated or opposed him, assumed the dominion of the East, and thus singly governed the Roman Empire, reunited, as in former times, under one head... The sun once more shone brightly after the gloomy cloud of tyrannical power...the whole body of the Roman Empire was graced...with a single supreme power...* [5]

Constantine decided to mark his triumph by building a new city. It was to be built on top of the ancient Greek colony of Byzantium where he had defeated Licinius. The new city was to be called Constantinople ('Constantine's city'). Constantinople was to be an extra capital, added to Trier, Serdica, Antioch and Milan. But Constantine wanted 'his' capital to be grander than the others.

Constantine's head, part of a colossal statue.

He wrote to provincial governors and ordered them to send their best artisans. Then he set up schools of science, architecture and building to ensure a steady flow of skilled workers. Simultaneously, he looted art treasures from all over the Empire. The famous bronze horses that now sit in the Loggia of St Mark's, Venice, were looted from Chios in Greece to sit in Constantinople's Hippodrome.

He sought to attract new citizens to build their homes in the city. He even appealed to the old Roman senatorial families, with whom he had so little in common, to come and form a new urban aristocracy. He offered them grants of land in the neighbouring provinces of Asia Minor (Bithynia and Pontus), food rations for life, exemption from all taxation, and even promised to build new palaces for senatorial families by the southern waterfront – replicas of their palaces in Rome. The policy, however, seems to have been fairly unsuccessful. The Romans did not want to move east.

Constantine also encouraged ordinary settlers – they, too, were exempted from taxation and conscription, and given free food rations. Eunapius, an author hostile to Constantine, recalled:

He collected at Byzantium a population from the cities subject to him, so a great corps of drunkards could applaud him in the theatre one minute and throw up their wine the next. He was quite satisfied with the applause of those who had lost control of their faculties, and was happy to hear his name shouted, even though only by men who knew it merely because it was impressed on them every day... [6]

The cost of building the city and encouraging settlers was huge. Throughout the Empire, Constantine's officials strove to make sure that all the taxes were collected, thus encouraging people to move to Constantinople in order to enjoy the tax exemptions there. Nevertheless, the population only slowly edged towards 50,000, while Rome's remained at around a million. But the move was vital – it further highlighted the demise of Rome as the Empire's centre. The Roman Empire was being re-orientated towards the East. Latin-speaking, pagan, western Rome was gradually being superseded by Greek-speaking, eastward-looking, increasingly Christian, Constantinople.

Constantine, the gruff, Balkan soldier, decided it was appropriate to imitate Diocletian and take on eastern customs: wearing elaborate costumes, heavy jewellery, wigs and perfumes, a pearl crown. His nephew Julian later claimed that these ornaments looked utterly ridiculous and became a source of great amusement. Around Constantine hovered courtiers and, in particular, eunuchs, whose role in palace affairs was growing all the time. Having been castrated, they could not hope to establish a dynasty – and therefore posed much less of a threat to the emperor. It would not be long before they were essentially running Constantine's imperial household.

At the same time, as Eusebius tells us, the influence of Christianity was reflected in Constantine's home: 'in the imperial palace itself, on a vast tablet displayed in the centre of its gold-covered panelled ceiling, he had fixed the symbol of Our Saviour...composed of a variety of precious stones richly set in gold. The symbol he seemed to have intended to be, as it were, the safeguard of the Empire itself'.

At his palace, surrounded by his gold and his eunuchs, Constantine took stock of the situation. He knew his position was vulnerable, as shaky as many of the buildings that were being hurriedly constructed in his new city. He recognized that the problems of the Empire did indeed seem too great for one man but, unlike Diocletian, he was unwilling to share the imperial crown – certainly not with the nobility who he considered effete and ineffectual.

Constantine's view was echoed by Ammianus:

Others, resplendent in silken garments, as though they were to be led to death…are followed by a throng of slaves, amid noise and confusion. When such men, each attended by 50 servants, have entered the vaulted rooms of a bath, they shout in threatening tones: 'Where on earth are our attendants?' If they learn that an unknown prostitute has suddenly appeared…they all strive to be the first to reach her, and caressing the newcomer, extol her with such disgraceful flattery as the Egyptians their Cleopatras…

Their houses are frequented by idle chatterboxes, who with various pretences of approval applaud every word of the man of loftier fortune… They, admiring the rows of columns hanging in the air with lofty facade, and the walls gleaming with the remarkable colours of precious stones, raise these noble men to the gods. Sometimes at their banquets the scales are even called for, in order to weigh the fish, birds and dormice that are served, whose great size they commend again and again, often repeating it to the weariness of all present… [7]

Constantine preferred to look to his family for assistance. He had several sons whom he hoped he could trust. By his first wife he had Crispus, still only in his early twenties, the hero of the sea battle against Licinius, and the stalwart defender of the Rhine border. By Fausta he had five children: Constantine, Constantius, Constans, Constantia and Helena. The sons were now to share some of the burdens of government.

Constantine, however, continued to fear plots. Under him, the Empire increasingly came to resemble a police state, with the Imperial Bodyguard and Imperial Secret Police always on the lookout for conspiracies. In this suspicious and nervous atmosphere, Crispus, in 326, was suddenly sentenced to death for, as one source wrote, 'an undisclosed reason'.

What actually happened is impossible to say. Palace scandals are rarely known in full to the outside world. All we can be sure of is that, in 326, Crispus was taken off to Pola (at the top of the Adriatic), tried and executed.

We know that Constantine's wife Fausta was also involved. By far the most likely explanation is that Fausta, wishing to supplant Crispus with her own children, had poisoned Constantine against him. Crispus, though still young, had, for some time, played a big part in his father's successes. Along with his stepbrother, Constantine junior, he was made a *caesar* in 317, when he was probably only about twelve years old, and from Trier was given a thorough military training on the Rhine frontier. Later, as victor at Byzantium, he contributed substantially to his father's defeat of Licinius. His achievements were widely celebrated in speeches, and his victorious image was common on coins. His fall was thus very sudden. It is possible that Fausta feared for her own children's inheritance, or at least that they would not get as big a share as Crispus. Fausta was an old hand at political intrigue, and it may not have taken much for her to convince Constantine of possible disloyalty from Crispus.

Constantine's mother, Helena, allegedly once a prostitute, became a Christian convert and was vital in establishing pilgrimage to holy sites.

Whatever Constantine's reason for executing Crispus, we can be sure that he almost immediately regretted it. Although several court figures seem to have been disgusted by the murder, it is Constantine's mother, Helena, who is mentioned in connection with this change of heart. Probably it was she, aggrieved by the death of her eldest grandson, who persuaded Constantine of Fausta's false motives. Whatever changed Constantine's mind, Fausta herself soon met a nasty end – either immersed in a scalding bath or suffocated in a deliberately overheated steamroom in the baths at Trier. Both Crispus and Fausta suffered the final indignity of having their names chipped out of inscriptions everywhere.

This only helps to prove – if further proof were needed – how ruthless Constantine was. He had killed his father-in-law Maximian in 310; his

St Catherine's Monastery on Mount Sinai. Here the 'burning bush' was enclosed in a chapel by Helena and the walls were added later by Justinian.

brother-in-law Bassianus in 316; his other brother-in-law Licinius in 324–5; his son and wife in 326; as well as numerous friends and courtiers.

As Eutropius saw it: '…the pride of prosperity caused Constantine greatly to depart from his former agreeable mildness of temper'.

The frontiers were holding firm. There were ten years left to run of a forty-year truce signed with the Sassanians in 297. The army was loyal – if expensive. Constantine, however, feared for the unity of the Empire and was prepared to use any method at his disposal to secure its future. He thus increasingly turned to religion.

Since his father's death two decades earlier, Constantine had shown favour to the Christians and granted them religious toleration. He had also continually tried to exploit the extremely strong organization of the Christian Church (which remained the only organized body in the Empire apart from the army). Though still a minority, its structure made the Church a far more vocal and powerful force than its size might otherwise imply. It was this that had enabled the Church to survive the full, albeit uneven, force of nearly a decade of state-backed persecution.

Constantine believed that the Empire could only gain from using this Christian unity and he sought to 'channel' the Christian Church's power by taking it over at the top – by becoming its 'head', just as he was already head of the traditional pagan cults as *pontifex maximus*. Constantine began to project himself as God's 'representative' on earth. Eusebius recorded his words to the leaders of the Church: 'You are bishops whose jurisdiction is within the Church, I am also a bishop, ordained by God to oversee whatever is external to the Church'.

Constantine remained equivocal as to the nature of this ultimate deity. At first, like many military men, he identified it with the god of the sun, *Sol Invictus* – 'the Unconquered Sun'. One theory suggests that the 'vision' he saw at the Battle of the Milvian Bridge was a solar halo, and that Constantine saw this as a sign of his god. A few years after that battle, it is noteworthy that he made Sunday – the day of the Sun – a public holiday: 'All magistrates, city-dwellers and artisans are to rest on the venerable day of the sun'.

One implication for later Christianity was that Christmas (which was never as important as Easter) was celebrated on 25 December, the day of the old pagan festival of *Sol Invictus*.

The ambiguity of Constantine's religious position is further demonstrated by the fact that throughout his entire reign he retained the title *pontifex maximus*. Whatever his declared personal beliefs, he also had to show respect for the traditional gods, as these gods were still revered by most of the army and administration.

Until 330, Constantine restricted his 'anti-pagan' measures. He had passed a law against certain forms of magic, but allowed others to continue. Some things he banned, not because they were pagan but because they were secret. Some temples were closed and there were substantial confiscations of temple property. Some cults were banned, but these were largely Syrian cults and so less likely to offend Roman traditionalists.

Simultaneously, there was considerable pro-Christian legislation, much of it of a seemingly 'modern' humane character. Convicts could no longer be branded on the face, 'which,' Constantine wrote, ' is formed in the image of heavenly beauty', and there was another law prohibiting brutality to prisoners. Masters lost the ancient right to kill their slaves. Crucifixion was abolished. Gladiatorial combats, once so exploited by emperors, were prohibited.

❖

Constantine had churches built – at vast expense – throughout the Empire, particularly in Rome. These churches were filled with hugely expensive gold and silver artefacts, mosaics and marbles. Constantine also constructed a number of churches on the burial sites of Christian martyrs, including that of St Peter, and put them under the guidance of the thirty-third Pope, Silvester I.

Constantine's mother, Helena, allegedly once a prostitute but now the effective 'Queen Mother' of the Roman Empire, was also a convert. In 326 she had been on a pilgrimage to the Biblical sites and founded some important and expensive churches in the region, most notably the Church of the Holy Sepulchre, Jerusalem.

Constantine wrote to Bishop Macarius of Jerusalem, urging him to ensure that it was built to the highest standards:

It will be well...that the decorations of the building may be of such a kind that the fairest structures in any city of the Empire may be excelled by them... As to the columns and marbles, whatever you shall judge...to be especially precious and serviceable, diligently send details to us in writing, in order that whatever quantity or type of materials we shall judge from your letter to be needed, may be procured from every quarter, as required, for it is fitting that the most marvellous place in the world should be worthily decorated. [3]

Helena and Constantine also saw to the construction of the Church of the Nativity, Bethlehem, and the small chapel of the Burning Bush in the Sinai Desert in Egypt. Helena's pilgrimage was so successful – she even claimed to have found pieces of Jesus's cross – that she caused a flood of pilgrims to follow in her footsteps.

There were some Christians who criticized all this opulence, among them St Jerome, the great theologian and scholar, who commented later that the Church had become, 'richer in possessions and power but poorer by far in virtue'.

Constantine's backing, however, certainly led to an enormous increase in

Christian converts. Many who were indifferent chose to follow the emperor's lead. Christianity appeared a safer bet on the path to wealth and social advancement; the ambitious did not require much persuasion to give up their pagan religions and become Christians. As Vettius Praetextatus, a militant pagan Roman of the fourth century, put it: 'Make me bishop of Rome, and I'll become a Christian tomorrow'.

Constantine made a career in the Church even more attractive by relieving clergymen of the onerous duties of military service, the financial obligations of local government and the payment of taxes. He also revoked Augustus's ancient law penalizing celibacy and childlessness, so that clergymen would not suffer. However, such exemptions were to cost the Empire dear, for tax income was affected and many talented men, who would otherwise have automatically joined the army or government, became priests instead.

The unity Constantine sought through Christianity did not come easily. If Constantine thought being head of the Church would be straightforward, he had not counted on the intolerance of this faith. Unlike all previous emperors of the religiously heterogeneous pagan world, Constantine found himself championing an exclusive and intolerant religion: all other gods were false; there was only one way to worship, one creed to believe.

Nor was Christianity a united religion – it was riven by dispute and rivalry. Most notably, there was Arianism, a heresy which questioned whether Christ was not at one with God but inferior to God the Father; after all, Christ was His creation and instrument. Bitter arguments and power struggles followed these claims. As head of the Church, Constantine had to summon Church councils to seek concord. He now found himself embroiled in extremely detailed and frustrating debates as to the nature of Christianity.

One of his letters to the cause of the problem, Arius, and Bishop Alexander of Alexandria, reveals this frustration, when he begs them to: '...Restore my quiet days and untroubled nights to me, so that joy of undimmed light, delight in tranquil life, may once again be mine...'

In another letter to the same bishop he says: '...Let me hear what I desire and yearn to hear, that there is peace and concord among you all...'

In 325, Constantine had called the Council of Nicaea, the first Ecumenical Council of the Church, in an attempt to define certain doctrinal points. Eusebius gives us this description of his dramatic entrance:

When the whole assembly was seated with fitting dignity, a general silence prevailed in expectation of the Emperor's arrival... at last he himself proceeded through the midst of the assembly, like some heavenly Angel of God, clothed in a garment which glittered as though radiant with light, reflecting the glow of a purple robe, and adorned with the brilliant splendour of gold and precious stones... [9]

The common language of the Council was Greek but Constantine was a poor Greek-speaker, so he wrote his speech in Latin and then handed it to it his team of translators. According to Eusebius, he began by saying: 'My friends: it

Constantine became embroiled in extremely detailed and frustrating debates as to the nature of Christianity. As a result, he presided over the assembled bishops at Nicaea, the first Ecumenical Council of the Church.

has long been my supreme desire to see you come together, and now it is fulfilled. I publicly give thanks to the King of the Universe who, capping all his other blessings, has granted me this supreme blessing of seeing you all gathered together in a single spirit of concord…'

In the end Constantine forced the participants to condemn Arianism. The orthodox beliefs of the Church were formulated in the Nicene Creed which decreed that Christ and God were one (the formula still accepted by most Christian denominations today). Once a solution had been arrived at, Constantine swept out of the Assembly Hall again, a gruff, bad-tempered soldier wrapped in his bejewelled, embroidered, powdered, perfumed, purple cloak.

❖

In 330, the city of Constantinople was officially dedicated. At the same time, the fifty-eight-year-old Constantine had to turn his attention to the Empire's frontiers.

The weaker Rome appeared, the stronger the external threat became. Constantine was determined to prevent further incursions by large bodies of ever more mobile 'barbarian' forces. He therefore chose to reorganize Rome's once near-invincible army.

Constantine was, in effect, only accelerating a process that had begun in the previous century. He divided the army into two groups. The first group were frontier soldiers – generally infantry units, positioned along the frontiers, in a similar manner to the legions of the Empire in its first two centuries. The second group were field armies, smaller army units, often cavalry, positioned in cities behind the frontiers. These changes were not without their critics. Zosimus, a later historian who, believing the decline of Rome was due to the abandoning of the traditional gods, wrote:

Constantine abolished security by removing the greater part of the soldiery from the frontiers to cities that needed no auxiliary forces. He thus deprived of help the people who were harassed by the barbarians and burdened tranquil cities with the pest of the military, so that several straightaway were deserted. Moreover, he softened the soldiers, who treated themselves to shows and luxuries... Indeed, he personally planted the seeds of our present devastated state of affairs... [10]

However, Constantine's reasoning was partly strategic, and a direct reaction to the events of the third century. In the first and second centuries the legions had been strung out along the borders, offering a 'perimeter defence' against raids by relatively small neighbouring peoples. The purpose of Constantine's frontier soldiers was to provide general security for the frontiers but, if these were breached, then the field armies, based at some distance from the frontier, would move to intercept and defeat the invading force.

Constantine was determined not to suffer the fate of so many of the previous generation of emperors. He therefore continued the policy of his predecessor Diocletian, of increasing the number of provinces by dividing existing provinces into two or sometimes three. Governors thus had a much smaller power base and armed force under their control, preventing attempts to usurp the emperor. Constantine also made sure that his field armies, which were as much for internal security as external defence, were commanded by himself, members of his family or trusted friends.

Constantine left the Rhine frontier to his eldest son, and took responsibility himself for the Danube line, the most threatened sector, partly due to the presence of the Goths.

The Goths, who had invaded the Empire in the third century, had at that time been politically fragmented. But the different, disorganized groups had become settled, and were now more politically and culturally advanced. Some were even literate and it would not be long before a Gothic alphabet was devised (the first work to be produced in it being the Gospels, leading to the rapid Christianizing of the Goths).

The Goths had taken advantage of the civil wars in Constantine's early life to carry out raids deep into the Empire. Constantine was now able to retaliate, taking violent military action against them. He constructed a mile-long bridge (the world's longest at that time) over the central Danube and its surrounding marshes and then, using a road built two centuries earlier by the Emperor Trajan, he pursued them deep into their own lands. Ultimately his armies were strong enough to enforce a humiliating peace upon the Goths, forcing them to recognize Constantine as their ruler.

Constantine could now claim that he had 'reconquered' the 'whole of Dacia'. The term 'Victoria Gothica' began to appear on coins. However, despite building great new fortifications along the Danube, these victories were not, in the long term, to prove decisive. The Goths and others had become too large and powerful to be more than temporarily pacified.

Constantine thought he could help solve the Empire's problems by assimilating some of the barbarians. It had been done before and it would reduce their military threat, provide a good source of recruits to an army that was increasingly unattractive to Roman citizens, and encourage the

A mosaic from Santa Sophia, Istanbul (Constantinople) showing Constantine on the right holding a model of the city he rebuilt. This also shows Justinian with a model of Sancta Sophia which later, during his reign, he had rebuilt.

agricultural exploitation of unused land. In 334, only a year after famine and plague had vividly demonstrated that the eastern provinces could barely support the existing population, Constantine offered farming lands to an estimated 300,000 Sarmatians. Eusebius, for one, admired this bold move: 'Do I need to describe, however briefly, the way in which he subjected barbarian peoples to the authority of Rome? He was the first to subdue the Scythian and Sarmatian tribes which never before had known servitude... He enrolled the men of military age in his army, and to the others gave land to provide for their needs...'

Constantine also decided to pay some tribes to remain loyal or peaceful. An increasingly long queue formed at his palace doors, and one source recorded: 'We ourselves, sometimes happening to be at the gates of the palace, have seen lines of barbarians of remarkable aspect standing there, with distinctive types of appearance, hair and beards, grim faces, terrifying glance, and surpassing bodily size; some with red complexions, some pale as snow, some blacker than ebony...'

In the short term, this strategy may have turned enemies into allies but in the long term it weakened the unity of the Empire. These subsidies only added to the massive increase in imperial expenditure, which Constantine, like others before him, had done nothing to reduce. There were no effective controls on state spending and these accumulating costs were now placing an intolerable burden on the Empire.

The number of taxes and their enforcement increased but that only encouraged tax avoidance and left fewer people to pay. Zosimus described the effects: '[Constantine] imposed a tribute of gold and silver on all who engaged in commerce, even on the pettiest tradesmen in the towns... the scourge and rack were used against those whose extreme poverty could not support this unjust tax. Mothers sold their children, and fathers prostituted their daughters...'

Despite all these economic pressures, the Empire remained powerful enough to allow Constantine to consider reopening the conflict with Persia

Religious syncretism: here Christ has many of the attributes of the sun god, Helios.

in the East. Their forty-year peace treaty was about to expire and the Persian king, Sapor II, seemed keen to re-engage in hostilities. Perhaps Constantine saw a solution to his difficulties in Sapor's treasury. The emperor began to concoct slanders and offences in order to provoke renewed war. But before the armies were fully prepared, fate took a hand.

Soon after spring 337, Constantine, now in his mid-sixties, complained of feeling unwell. He travelled to a number of hot springs but did not improve. Temporarily at Nicomedia, he decided his hour had come. After much confession and prayer, he requested the long-delayed baptism from his accompanying bishops. Eusebius reported his words:

The moment I have been waiting for so long, earnestly desiring and praying that in it I might receive the salvation of God, has come at last. Now I may receive the seal of salvation. I wanted to receive it in the waters of the River Jordan, where our Saviour is said to have been baptized as an example to us. But it pleases God – who knows what is best for us – that I should receive it here. So be it then. Let there be no further delay... [11]

He took off his purple robe, was baptized naked, and donned the white robes of the newly baptized. According to Eusebius:

...at the end of the ceremonies, he clothed himself in radiant imperial robes as shining as light, and reclining on a couch of the purest white, refused ever to clothe himself in purple again. He assured his soldiers that he was happy to die, then went on to put the final touches to the necessary disposition of his affairs...and sharing out inheritance of the Empire among his own children, just like any patrimonial estate, and, in short, arranging everything just as it pleased him... [12]

The baptism had been so long delayed because Constantine wanted to die in a state of purity; baptism on the point of death left limited time or opportunity to sin again.

On 22 May 337, near Nicomedia, Constantine died.

The body was taken to the palace in Constantinople to lie in state. There, great lines of dignitaries filed past, each performing obeisance to the dead emperor.

Constantine had left instructions for his burial in the Church of the Holy Apostles, Constantinople. The funeral was conducted with great pomp. Soldiers, ministers, bishops, ambassadors and, of course, his sons all attended. In either transept lay six sarcophagi, representing the twelve Apostles of the Lord. Constantine had sent agents all over the Holy Land to collect suitable relics of the Apostles to fill these. His own sarcophagus lay in the centre, beneath the central drum. The symbolism was blatant. Constantine had called himself 'Equal of the Apostles' for some time. In the positioning of his tomb he could now even be perceived as a 'substitute' for Jesus Christ himself.

Nothing remains of the church now. Like many of the original buildings of Constantinople, it was hastily constructed. Within a few decades, it began to collapse, and Constantine's body was moved elsewhere.

Like his city, Constantine's Empire was unstable. Rome's neighbours were becoming ever more numerous and Rome's own provinces were showing signs of exhaustion under the weight of imperial taxation and mismanagement. Constantine had sanctioned Christianity in an effort to unite his people but although it was to prove to be one of the Roman Empire's greatest legacies, it did not prove the immediate success Constantine had hoped for. He named his three sons and his two nephews as his successors but they were by no means his equals in energy or intellect, and his bequest to them was double-edged. Constantine must have known they would never rule together – perhaps he was simply leaving it to fate to sort out who would prove strongest.

Constantine's struggle to become emperor had been matched only by his struggle to rule once power was his. The Empire was subject to huge internal and external pressures, and Constantine had done his best to shore up its walls. For some, this was a vital and productive period of Roman history; for others it was an era of division and discord. Constantine had reunited the Empire under his sole leadership but, ultimately, while helping to establish a strengthened eastern Empire, he had done little to prevent the imminent collapse of the western Empire.

CHAPTER VI

JUSTINIAN

The Last of the Romans

THE Emperor Justinian looked down from his imperial box with a mixture of pride and jealousy. The procession passing before him was marking a great victory in North Africa. It was a Triumph the like of which Constantinople had never seen. Slaves, looted treasure, proud soldiers, all paraded along the race track. Although Justinian envied his general, Belisarius, who was leading the Triumph, he also felt grateful to be emperor at such a time, a time of greatness and rejuvenation. But it was an illusion. The Empire was not the Empire of Augustus, or even Constantine – and it would never be so again.

❖

Though few empires have definitive conclusions, Justinian's reign, in many ways, represents an appropriate point at which to take leave of Rome's long story. Other emperors were to follow him but Justinian can be considered the last truly Roman emperor – the last emperor to speak Latin rather than Greek, the emperor who ended the Roman consulship after a thousand years, the emperor who failed in his hopes of reuniting the Roman Empire.

What caused the decline and fall, or perhaps, more correctly, the decline and transition, of an Empire which had lasted over a thousand years is one of the most hotly debated of historical questions. Historians have put forward many explanations to account for it, from 'barbarian invasion to moral degeneration, from the impact of Christianity to that of inflation, from

Justinian (c. AD 480–565) had a wide-ranging mind and showed a keen interest in all aspects of his Empire. But, despite his successes in almost every field, he failed to recreate the lost grandeur of the Roman Empire.

soil erosion to lead poisoning. Some have claimed the Empire was dead even before Justinian was born; others point out that it was constantly changing and adapting, to the extent that there was no end – it simply became something else.

❖

The Emperor Constantine probably felt he had done more than enough to safeguard the future of the Roman world. However, in bequeathing the Empire to his three sons and two nephews, he re-opened a schism that could not be healed. Though the reasoning behind such power-sharing is understandable, it rarely results in leadership as strong as that of a single ruler. Despite this, it became standard practice and, after the death of Constantine in 337, Rome's vast expanses were rarely ruled by one emperor alone. The norm became at least two co-emperors, one in the West at Milan or, later, at Ravenna; the other in the East, at Constantinople. The Emperor Theodosius the Great (379–395) briefly united the Empire under his sole rule, but then he too divided it between his sons. The Roman Empire was never to be united under one ruler again.

Less than a century later, in AD 476, the line of Roman emperors that had persisted in Western Europe since the time of Augustus, 500 years earlier, came to an end. The last incumbent, Romulus, a powerless teenager, ironically named after the legendary founder of Rome, was pushed aside by one of his own barbarian generals and forced to 'retire' to the country. The event was significant because no new emperor was proclaimed in his place. However, at the time, few saw this situation as permanent. It was only later, with the benefit of hindsight, that people claimed this was the moment at which the Western Roman Empire truly fell.

The western kingdom subsequently ruled by the Goth Theodoric the Great (493–526) was far from barbaric and he attempted to fuse the two peoples of his realm. The talents of both peoples were maximized: the army was the exclusive preserve of Ostrogoths, while only Romans could enter the civil service. Although much of the best land was distributed to the Ostrogothic nobles, the Italian aristocracy retained their great estates. While the

Ostrogoths were subject to their own laws and customs, Theodoric's Roman subjects were judged according to Roman law, and life generally proceeded unaltered. Theodoric lived in splendour at the former imperial Roman 'capital' at Ravenna, his court staffed by educated senators, patricians and scholars. To the vast majority it did not matter whether they paid their taxes to the emperor or to the King of the Ostrogoths.

The Roman Empire of the East was more stable. At its political heart lay Constantinople, an immense and wealthy city whose population had, in 150 years, grown from 50,000 to 500,000. This was a 'New Rome', rivalling the 'Old' in its grandeur. The eastern territories were wealthy and productive, and though their frontiers required constant vigilance, the area was at relative peace. It was into this strong and prosperous eastern Empire, in around AD 480, that Petrus Sabbatius, later to become the Emperor Justinian, was born.

Petrus Sabbatius's birthplace was a farm near the small town of Bederiana in Illyricum, in modern Serbia. Of obscure peasant origin, his first language was not Latin, but a Thracian dialect. The population as a whole was Thracian in origin, though Romanized, and several of Petrus's relations bore Thracian names. Little is known of the boy's youth. We do know however, that he was very fortunate to be able to escape the drudgery of this provincial life thanks to the favour and influence of his uncle.

His uncle Justin, his mother's brother, was a self-made man, an ordinary soldier who had risen through the ranks. He was thus typical of the later Roman Empire.

According to the historian and high-ranking official Procopius:

When Leo occupied the imperial throne (457–474), three young farmers of Illyrian origin, Zimarchus, Dityvistus and Justin, who came from Bederiana, had been waging an endless war with poverty at home. So they determined to get away from it all and went to join the army. They covered the whole distance to Constantinople on foot, carrying on their shoulders their cloaks, in which they had nothing on arrival but some dry biscuits put in before they left home. Their names were entered in the army registers, and the Emperor picked them out to serve in the Palace Guard, as they were all men of exceptional physique. [1]

Justin's career was slow and largely uneventful, but by around 490 he commanded a regiment. Although he probably never returned to Bederiana, his strong sense of family loyalty led him to find appointments for many of his younger relatives. One of these was the young Petrus Sabbatius, who was transferred from his obscure home to Constantinople. He was hardly to set foot outside the city walls for the next seventy years.

The boy was probably little more than ten years old and few details are known of his new life in the capital, but the change must have been baffling. In addition, he spoke little Greek, a language which he now had to learn and which, it was later claimed, he always spoke 'barbarously'. Nevertheless, the move to the capital was a great opportunity, and he certainly received the best education money could buy. The peasant boy became immensely cultured, proving how civilizing life in a Roman city could be.

The boy became a teenager. In the words of Procopius: '[He was] of normal height; rather plump, with a round face that was not unattractive…'

After his education he undertook military service – that he should do anything else was probably never considered. But, like Justin's other nephews, he did not begin in the ranks. Instead, he was enlisted in one of the elite regiments of the Palace Guard. By this time, these better-paid, highly privileged soldiers never saw active service and were kept largely for show. One somewhat exaggerated account, by the contemporary historian Agathias, recorded this change: 'Though they are called soldiers and have their names entered on the rolls, most of them are merely civilians in splendid uniforms and perform such purely decorative functions as enhancing the pomp of the royal progress'.

The real task of guarding the emperor (at this time Anastasius) fell to the *excubitores* (literally 'those outside the chamber'), a crack fighting unit. Petrus's uncle had become their commanding officer which helped to make Petrus's life at the palace even more comfortable. Being little interested in military life, he found his ornamental parade duties arduous and frequently skipped them. Despite this, he rose to the rank of officer whose duties included attendance, dressed in white robes, on the emperor himself.

When the Emperor Anastasius died, on 9 July 518, Justin, as commander of the Imperial Guard, was in a very advantageous position. The political manoeuvrings that went on that night cannot now be deciphered, but the next morning Justin emerged into the Hippodrome, the race course adjoining the palace. There the *excubitores* raised him on a shield and the crowd acclaimed him 'the Emperor Caesar Justin, victorious'. It was a carefully stage-managed affair, in which his nephew no doubt played a part.

At some point, the sixty-eight-year-old Justin appears to have adopted his nephew, who thereafter styled himself Flavius Petrus Sabbatius Justinianus (Justinian). After the accession, Justinian was made Count of the Domestics, an important figure in the court and a member of the Emperor's Imperial Council. In 521 Justinian, now in his thirties, became consul, a prestigious though not politically powerful post; his chief function was to organize games in the Hippodrome. Justinian took advantage of his power (as Julius Caesar had in a similar position almost 600 years earlier) and put on extraordinarily lavish games in a bid for social standing and popularity.

Although the *excubitores* had made Justin emperor, this did not necessarily qualify him for the job. He was a rural, military man, who had little in common with the city's aristocracy. The subtleties of diplomacy and ecclesiastical controversy tired him. It is also possible that he became senile shortly after his accession. These circumstances provided the perfect opportunity for his nephew whose upbringing had given him considerable experience of the capital's ruling class. It was later argued that the nine-year reign of Justin was simply the first nine years of Justinian's reign. Though this

The palace guards at Constantinople.

is probably an exaggeration, which disregards other important figures in government, there can be no doubt that during this period Justinian was steadily becoming the chief power behind the throne.

According to Procopius: 'Justin was not capable of doing any harm to his subjects or any good either. He was uncouth in the extreme, utterly inarticulate and incredibly boorish. His nephew Justinian, though still quite young, used to manage all the affairs of state...'

In 525, Justin gave Justinian the title *caesar*, and later *nobilissimus* ('most noble'), indicating that he was to be his successor. Then, on 1 April 527, the mortally ill Justin officially proclaimed his nephew co-emperor. After another few weeks his uncle died and Justinian became sole emperor.

Procopius, from whom we get most of our detailed knowledge of Justinian's life, grew to despise the new emperor. The historian represented upper-class opinion and it was this class which, during Justinian's reign, was to suffer from the emperor's financial demands. As a result, Procopius clearly felt a deep and bitter resentment, if not hatred, of the emperor, claiming that: 'when [Justinian's mother] was about to conceive she was visited by a demon...'

Procopius was equally damning about Justinian's wife, Theodora, whom Justinian had married two years before becoming emperor. Justinian was nearing forty and she was just over twenty. However, it was not the age difference that appalled the aristocracy but the 'fact' that she had been a child prostitute. According to Procopius: 'Theodora [had been] too undeveloped to be capable of sharing a man's bed or having intercourse like a woman; but she acted as a sort of male prostitute to satisfy customers of the lowest type, and slaves at that...'

Her father was the keeper and trainer of the dancing bears in the Hippodrome. He was employed by 'the Greens', one of the four circus factions. These were the supporters of the different chariot-racing teams in the Hippodrome, each distinguished by a team colour. The two most powerful circus factions were the Blues and the Greens, who hated one another and frequently rioted.

These sports hooligans dressed in team colours and had outrageous haircuts (bald at the front, long at the back). The factions were very well organized, with their own hierarchy and recognized slogans and chants. Senators, while publicly decrying them, privately sought to manipulate them. The state too, in times of emergency, would sometimes call upon them to man the walls of the city, which further served to increase their sense of worth and bravado. They were not a phenomenon restricted to the capital – all the large cities of the Empire suffered from their activities. They often caused great damage to property, terrorizing and robbing the citizens of Constantinople. Each faction had its own entertainments, including dancing bears and dancing girls. In his later attacks on Justinian, Procopius branded Theodora one such 'entertainment':

...she would spread herself out and lie face upwards on the floor. Servants would sprinkle barley grains over her private parts, and geese trained for the purpose used to pick them off one by one with their bills and swallow them...

Often she would go to a bring-your-own-food dinner party with ten young men or more, all at the peak of their physical powers, and with fornication as their chief object in life, and would lie with her fellow diners in turn the whole night long [and] reduce them all to a state of exhaustion... [2]

Despite this alleged background in prostitution and erotic dance, by the time Justinian met her she had reputedly retired from the stage. Justinian's work at the Hippodrome had led to him meeting people from all levels of society and, born of a humble background himself he was perhaps more at ease mixing with all classes of men than other emporers such as Augustus had been. His wish to marry Theodora was not based on political advantage but love. Nevertheless, he still had to overcome enormous resistance to the marriage, and indeed had to change the law which prevented someone of the senatorial class marrying an actress or a prostitute. It is a sign of his determination that he persisted and won. These events scandalized the upper classes of Constantinople but this did not stop Justinian being appointed emperor: the choice was unchallenged – he was related to the

The Empress
Theodora and her
magnificent retinue.
No busts or statues
survive of either
Justinian or Theodora.

previous emperor, he was well connected at court, he was on the spot, and he had the Palace Guard on his side.

Justinian was a secretive, unsociable and private man who enjoyed the luxury of his apartments, as described by Procopius: '…the whole interior of the building, as far as the mosaics above, is clothed with handsome marbles, not only the walls, but the whole pavement as well. Some of these marbles are of Spartan stone which rivals the emerald, while some simulate the flame of fire, but most of them are white in colour, yet not plain white, but set off with wavy lines of blue…'

His behaviour was typical of late Roman emperors. The position of emperor had become so unstable and precarious that emperors had deliberately made themselves into remote, semi-divine figures, spending much of their time in the palace.

Synesius, a fourth-century bishop, had recognized the reason: 'You hide in your apartments in case men discover that you are mortal'.

In the maze-like, mosaic-covered palace only the emperor's advisers, foreign ambassadors and palace eunuchs had direct contact with him. Political and military positions had been separated and the legions, which emperors ignored at their peril, were dangerously left to military generals. Justinian never led his armies in person and only once travelled more than a few days' journey from the capital.

His isolation bred paranoia: a fear of usurpers and assassins. Consequently his public life was carefully stage-managed – the people of Constantinople might briefly see him passing from the palace to Sancta Sophia across the Augusteum, the central square of the city. Or he would appear in the imperial box at the Hippodrome, to be ritually saluted by the circus factions. Decked in silks, gold and gems, wearing the imperial diadem, and surrounded by his brightly clothed guardsmen, the white-robed *candidati*, eunuchs or churchmen, he would have looked an impressive, if distant figure. The intimacy (albeit staged) of an emperor like Hadrian had gone.

John Malalas, a Christian chronicler at the time, described him thus: 'In appearance he was short, with a good chest, a good nose, fair-skinned, curly haired, round-faced, handsome, with receding hair, a florid complexion, with his hair and beard greying. He was magnanimous and Christian...'

John Malalas was a supporter of the emperor because he was a devout believer in Christianity. In the 150 years since it had received the immense boost of Constantine's edict of toleration and later his conversion, Christianity had become the state religion and since that time all emperors, except one, had declared themselves followers. But their belief in Christianity had not radically changed the nature of imperial rule. It remained autocratic, without even lip-service being paid to constitutional forms. When Constantine had founded Constantinople he had copied many of the institutions and features of the old Rome, including its Senate. This was originally intended simply as a city council, but his son Constantius II (337–361) raised its status to the eastern equivalent of the Roman Senate. However, emperors had little time for legislative restraints. By Justinian's day, the Senate's powers and duties had been severely limited to all but ceremonial and prestigious duties. It no longer even sat in one of the Senate Houses (Constantinople, for reasons that are unclear, had two Senate Houses), but actually met in the palace, sometimes separately, sometimes simply as an extension of the Imperial Council.

Having senior rank often entailed spending vast amounts on public works and entertainments. Not surprisingly, the vast majority of those with senatorial rank remained on their estates and tried to avoid taking an active, and thus expensive, role in politics. Only the highest rank of senators – 'the Illustrious' – took their seats, and most of them held other posts anyway. In Caesar's day the ambitious politician had devoted most of his time and energy to ascending the strictly regulated ranks of hierarchical power. But, from Constantine onwards, there had been a huge proliferation of ranks, titles and precedence that were of greater importance. The ambitious politician in Justinian's day no longer regarded the old titles with unqualified respect; being a senator or consul was a distinction he picked up along the way, rather than an end in itself.

From the time of Constantine, the relationship between emperor and Senate had been very clear and Justinian's reign was no exception. Procopius tells us: 'when the Senate came into the presence of Justinian and Theodora all of them had to fall on the floor flat on their faces, stretch out their hands and feet as far as they could, touch with their lips one foot of each of Their Majesties, and then stand up again'.

Once a decision had been taken, it was left to the civil service to enact it. It is estimated that the 'civil service', which had rarely stopped growing since Augustus's era, now amounted to about 10,000 men, placing a considerable strain on the state budget. Like the whole of late Roman society, the civil service was extremely conscious of rank. All important officers belonged to a particular order which carried with it certain honours and privileges.

In addition, there was a large number of 'domestics' who had duties associated with the imperial person. Many of these were eunuchs, who had acquired considerable influence simply from their proximity to the emperor. Since castration was illegal within the Empire, the vast majority were foreigners and often despised by the public. This worked to the emperor's advantage as the eunuchs therefore became totally reliant on the palace for their positions. The domestic staff, however, soon realized that their power was greatest as intermediaries between Justinian, Theodora and their courtiers and councils. They did their best to keep such people apart, in different wings of the palace, while they scuttled between them with messages and notices.

Of all the personages to whom the staff delivered their messages, it was Theodora who inspired the greatest fear. It became well known that she had a network of spies answering only to her and it was certainly suspected that she had a pool of supporters ready and willing to act on her behalf. Theodora was clearly more than the emperor's wife; she was, in her opinion at least, co-ruler. This was another source of annoyance to Procopius: 'To her bodily needs she devoted quite unnecessary attention. though never enough to satisfy herself. She was in great hurry to get into her bath, and very unwilling to get out again… At lunch and supper she indulged her taste for every kind of food and drink…though she strayed thus into every path of self-indulgence for so great a part of the day, she thought fit to run the whole of the Roman Empire!'

While his wife concentrated on building her position of power, Justinian made genuine efforts to improve the domestic state of affairs. His first – and ultimately his greatest – actions concerned revising and updating the Empire's laws. He established a law commission which, in a very short space of time, codified 1000 years of Roman legal statute and precedence. *The Digest* (533) and the *Codex Justinianus* (534) were to become the basis of European law.

Simultaneously, Justinian began to push the Empire towards an intolerant Christian society. His attitudes were a far cry from the tolerance of Augustus's and Hadrian's eras. John Malalas tells us that:

...The Emperor issued a decree and sent it to Athens, ordering that no one should teach philosophy, nor interpret the laws, nor should gaming be permitted in any city, for some gamblers who had been discovered in Constantinople had been indulging themselves in dreadful blasphemies. Their hands were cut off and they were paraded around on camels...

The Emperor immediately ordered that those detected in pederasty should have their genitals amputated. At that time many homosexuals were arrested and died after having their genitals amputated. From then on there was fear amongst those afflicted with homosexual lust... [3]

Justinian also sought to see that his Treasury received its taxes. His chief agent in the collection of monies due was the hated John of Cappadocia. Not only did he ensure that offences were punished, he also presided over the wholesale trimming of a system that had become swollen with dead men's names still left on the payrolls of provincial governors. John of Cappadocia attacked the privileged position of the rich, exposing corrupt dealings between the provincial aristocracy and the governors' staffs. He even breached this class's long-standing immunity from corporal punishment, and had them flogged for tax-evasion. The rich could no longer bend the system quite so much in their interests, and so they were vociferous in their

complaints that the demands were 'excessive'. John of Cappadocia, together with his assistants Alexander 'the Scissors' and John 'Leaden Jaws', as their names suggest, were universally hated.

Five years after his accession, Justinian's reforms and changes were, in part, responsible for a major uprising. Attempting to curb the violent and uncontrolled activities of the circus factions, he had arrested some leading Greens and Blues. The ensuing disturbance escalated into the worst riot the city had ever seen. For two days, large areas were looted and destroyed by fire.

Procopius gave this account of events as they unfolded:

These mosaics from Ravenna were commissioned by the Gothic kings, prior to Justinian's reconquest.

...at this time the officers of the city administration...were leading away to death some of the rioters. But the members of the two factions, conspiring together and declaring a truce, seized the prisoners and straight away entered the prison and released those who were confined there... And all the attendants in the service of the city government were killed indiscriminately. Meanwhile, all the sane-minded citizens were fleeing to the opposite mainland, and fire was applied to the city as if it had fallen under the hand of an enemy...

...During this time the Emperor and his consort, with a few members of the Senate, shut themselves up in the palace and remained quietly there ...

Forgetting their rivalries, the Blues and Greens united against the authorities, occupied the Hippodrome and attempted to raise an alternative emperor. Theodora made her views clear, in a speech recorded by Procopius:

May I never be separated from the purple, and may I not live to see the day when those who meet me shall not address me as 'mistress'. If, now, it is your wish to save yourself, O Emperor, there is no problem. For we have much money, and there is the sea, here the boats. However, having saved yourself, consider whether the day will not come when you would gladly exchange that security for death...As for myself, I approve a certain ancient saying that royalty is a good burial-shroud. [5]

Justinian acceded to his wife's demands and delivered a personal plea for a return to order – but it failed. According to the *Chronicon Paschale*, a chronicle written at Constantinople during the reign of Justinian:

...many people remained mobbing outside the palace. And when this became known, the patrician Belisarius, the Master of Soldiers, came out with a multitude of soldiers and cut down many until evening. And thereafter they set fire to the bronze-roofed entrance to the palace, and it was burnt...and similarly the Senate House, by the Augusteum, was burnt, and the whole of the Great Church, together with its awesome and marvellous columns was completely demolished on all four sides... [6]

Justinian felt he had no choice but to order his general, Belisarius, to put an end to the uprising using whatever force was required. As many as 30,000 protestors are said to have been slaughtered.

Such brutality coloured people's perception of Justinian. He, however, saw force as the only way of keeping a lid on the boiling atmosphere of resentment and unrest. The military controlled the streets; Justinian controlled the military. But a diversion would help; a foreign campaign would divert attention from domestic difficulties, and Justinian had such a campaign in mind.

❖

The Empire that Constantine had bequeathed to his successors covered an enormous area, from the Atlantic to the Euphrates, the Danube to the Nile. Such an expanse, stretching over 6400 kilometres (4000 miles) from west to east, almost 3200 kilometres (2000 miles) north to south, had eventually resulted in the Empire being divided between East and West. This was, however, purely for the purposes of administration and defence. There was still only one Empire, for which laws were passed jointly, and, despite the huge distance between them, there was frequent co-operation between the two imperial courts at Constantinople and at Milan or Ravenna. Nevertheless, court intrigues, divergent political and strategic interests, and differing attitudes towards dealing with barbarians led the East and West to become highly suspicious of one another, and, from the fourth century, even hostile. Although they faced similar problems, they adopted different, and often independent, approaches to them. The two halves of the Empire began to diverge – and their fates were ultimately different.

The Empire had long faced barbarian peoples on its European frontiers, who periodically attempted to carry out raids across Rome's borders. There was never a period in which these peoples could be ignored, but, by means of regular defensive campaigns, they were kept at bay. Diocletian and Constantine had both reorganized the armed forces to deal with this threat. They had raised the number of men under arms to perhaps double that of earlier centuries. It was the cost of this expansion – both in money and manpower – that was to plague the Empire for generations to come.

The apparently successful defence system of the early Empire had only worked because there was never a time when all the frontiers were under attack. Legions could therefore be transferred as required. The borders were often so quiet that men could indulge in years of civil war, using the armies for their own gain, rather than for national defence. But in the fourth and fifth centuries, those periods of peace were long gone.

What was the alternative to long drawn-out, expensive, potentially devastating military campaigns? Constantine and others had believed the only real alternative was to let some of the 'barbarians' in, thus lessening the pressure on the frontiers and simultaneously solving the Empire's manpower problems. Consequently, throughout the fourth century, Germanic tribes provided some of Rome's best soldiery. Many Germans saw the Roman Empire not so much as an enemy, but as a career.

The Roman Empire had always welcomed new groups from beyond its borders as long as they were not so large as to pose a threat and could be successfully Romanized. Barbarians and their families were settled in communities within the Empire, often on the borders, and they promised to defend the frontier in return for land. In the West, particularly, the Roman army came increasingly to rely on *federates* as a source of manpower. These *federates* ('those under treaty') were German war bands employed by the Roman government. Crucially, Rome made the apparent mistake of not absorbing them throughout the army or administration but allowing them to stay together, thus keeping their separate identity.

Military service was no longer as attractive an option for many Roman citizens as it had been in the earlier days of the Empire. Service no longer involved wars of conquest with ample opportunities for self-enrichment; a newly appointed soldier was now more likely to find himself doing inglorious garrison duty on remote frontiers.

Furthermore, military pay was lower than it had been. By the fifth century, increasingly fragmented communications, combined with corruption, meant that some soldiers were not paid at all. Earlier in Roman history, one of the main incentives for non-citizens to join the army was the eventual reward of citizenship. However, since an act passed in 212, every free man in the Empire was a citizen anyway. This gave Romans another reason to avoid the army, opting instead to buy their way out of recruitment; giving money so that the state could hire a mercenary, usually a German, as a replacement.

Many, seeking the security and social status once offered by the army, now saw those opportunities in the Church. While recruitment was easier in the East, as there was a greater population and many wished to escape the mountains through military careers (Justinian's uncle Justin for example), in the West it had far less appeal. Those who could not afford to buy their way out of being conscripted went to great lengths to avoid military service, even cutting off their thumbs to make themselves ineligible. The state passed laws to combat these 'draft-dodgers'; there were severe penalties for deliberate self-mutilation or assisting others to avoid conscription. A law was passed making it compulsory to accept recruits even with no thumbs. Some provincial administrations took increasingly severe measures to ensure a supply of recruits – press-gangs, branding new recruits like slaves, even transporting them to their posts in cages.

Although local landowners were required by law to provide army recruits in proportion to the size of their estates, they were often reluctant to co-operate with provincial administrations. For centuries, mass agricultural slavery had been giving way to free tenancy on a 'share-cropping' basis. This was simply a matter of economics: it was now cheaper to employ free men as low-wage labour than to buy and maintain slaves. Army recruitment reduced local manpower – and the landowners wanted to keep as much labour working their lands as possible. If they did produce recruits for the authorities they tended to offer the weakest and most unfit, whom they wished to dispose of anyway. Therefore the so-called barbarians, who wanted to be part of the Roman military, and who retained their ferocity, became preferred as soldiers to the 'soft' or 'civilized' Roman citizens. As St Jerome put it: '[Rome had] purchased her life from the barbarians with gold and precious things'.

In frontier and key cities throughout the Empire, Roman soldiers of Germanic origin passed through the streets, racially distinct from the locals and perceived as being lazy, drunken, violent and undisciplined Roman civilians had always viewed the arrival of soldiers in their neighbourhood, even 'friendly' Roman troops, as a misfortune. The arrival of German troops was considered a punishment.

Matters became worse when a formerly unknown people of Asiatic origin burst in from Central Asia. These were the Huns, and the reasons for their movement into Europe are not properly documented or understood. The Huns were a nomadic Mongolic people, who may be related to (or the same as) the Hsiung-nu, who plagued the northern border of the Han Empire in China until the first century AD. It is thought that difficult conditions on the Steppes of Asia – over-population, lack of grazing land, inter-tribal warfare – may have driven many tribal groups to seek a better existence westwards. The Huns were one of these groups. They entered southern

Russia around the year 370, rapidly overthrowing the Gothic kingdoms there, and provoking a refugee crisis.

The eastern Empire then faced its first large-scale migration with the appearance of the Goths on the Danube in 376. Driven from their homelands north of the Black Sea by the Huns, they appealed to the eastern emperor, Valens, to be allowed to settle south of the Danube within the Empire as *federates*. However there were simply too many of them to be properly controlled and fed. The situation was made worse by the appalling behaviour of the Roman authorities – robbing and extorting money and slaves from the disarmed immigrants. As a result, the Goths revolted. Two years later, there followed the Battle of Adrianople, which was to prove a catastrophic defeat for the east Roman army (the Empire's best troops).

Such a defeat – with the associated loss of manpower and armaments – meant that things would never be quite the same again. Although relations with the Goths were eventually restored and, in theory, they remained *federates*, thereafter there were often large Germanic forces roaming within the Empire. The eastern Empire had the social, economic and military strength to recover from the shock. The western Empire, however, did not have the same resilience, and could do nothing to prevent the endless tide of barbarian movements.

The situation became steadily worse. Whole Germanic peoples gradually, but relentlessly, moved westwards. On the last day of 406, the Rhine froze over and tens of thousands of Vandals, Alans and Suebi took a once-in-a-lifetime opportunity to pack up their possessions and cross over into Gaul. Shortly thereafter, a Gothic king, Alaric, who had been displaced by the East, sacked Rome.

St Jerome lamented the consequences: '...Terrifying news comes to us from the West. Rome has been taken by assault. Men are ransoming their lives with gold. Though despoiled, they are still hounded, so that after their goods they may pay with their very lives... My voice is still, and sobs disturb my every utterance. The city which had once conquered an entire world has been conquered'.

Rome itself was of little strategic importance but its sacking had enormous symbolic impact. The western emperor in Ravenna could do nothing and was fortunate that Alaric died almost immediately, easing the pressure. However, the floodgates had been opened and the sack of Rome gave those beyond the Empire's borders further evidence that Rome's once firm hold on its dominions had significantly weakened.

The rebuilding of cities sacked by barbarians, the subsidies paid to tribes to stay away and keep the peace, and in particular the cost of maintaining the army and bureaucracy, all put severe strain on the reserves of the Roman governments in both capitals. Attempts to cover this ever-rising expenditure by means of increased taxation placed an enormous burden on taxpayers, many of whom could not or would not pay. Emperors passed ever harsher laws against tax evasion, and tax collectors were increasingly brutal in their methods of exaction. Taxpayers, rich and poor, no doubt felt increasingly alienated from central government.

The manpower and finance problems of the western emperors meant that they could not defend themselves against invaders. Local defence forces were increasingly drafted into the field armies to swell their shrinking ranks. This meant that certain regions, even whole provinces, had to fend for themselves, without the assistance of central government. In 410, for example, the Emperor Honorius is thought to have written to the cities of Britain, which had been stripped of their garrisons for service on the Continent, telling them that their defence was now their own responsibility.

Since the army was also an internal police force, its removal from a region also added to the breakdown of provincial administration and law and order. Large areas of the western Empire, especially western Gaul, effectively fell under the control of bandits – ex-slaves, tax-burdened peasants, runaway soldiers. Local forces tended to elevate one of their own officers to the rank of emperor, abandoning the emperor in Italy who had effectively abandoned them. These usurpers sometimes took whole provinces out of the emperor's control, depriving him of their manpower and revenues, and thus depleting his resources yet further, in a vicious circle.

The colonnaded street from Palmyra, Syria. The eastern Roman Empire continued to flourish even after the western Empire had fragmented.

Such dissension caused whole villages and towns to look to powerful local landowners for immediate and effective protection, rather than to what now seemed the ineffective administration of the distant emperor. The rural poor could find greater security by abandoning the land and moving into the confines of a great landowner's estates, which were often heavily defended. In return, the poor became completely reliant on the landowner for protection.

Meanwhile, skilled and talented Germans rose ever higher through the army, becoming officers and generals. Some achieved the highest positions in the army and state, a situation that some 'true' Romans found abhorrent.

Synesius of Cyrene, a fourth-century bishop, wrote:

...the title of senator which, in ancient times, seemed to Romans the climax of all honours, because of the barbarians has become something abject...the same blond barbarians, who in private life fulfil the role of domestic servants, in public life give us orders...They interpreted it as weakness on our part, and that inspired in them an insolent arrogance and unheard-of boastfulness. [7]

Emperors themselves gradually became the puppets of their German generals, who increasingly acted as 'kingmakers'. So large were the numbers that now came in that there soon emerged separate states within the western Empire, owing only nominal allegiance to the emperor. Much of the western Roman Empire was occupied by Germanic, barbarian kingdoms. There was the Kingdom of the Visigoths in Spain and southern Gaul, the Kingdom of the Vandals in North Africa, the growing Kingdom of the Franks in northern Gaul, and several smaller Anglo-Saxon kingdoms were beginning to appear in Britain.

Theoretically, most of these separate kingdoms were still part of the Empire and subject to the Roman emperor. But in reality they were governed by their own rulers, under their own legal codes, and paid no taxes to the emperor. The emperor had no control over them, unless he could impose his will upon their rulers by military force, which few, if any, of the later western emperors could do. Occasionally they could persuade certain barbarian rulers to join them in the field, but this would be due to mutual interest rather than loyalty.

The difficulty for the Empire was how to control all these tribal rulers. One example was Odoacer, a Roman general of German descent. His forces were based around the western capital, Ravenna. In 476, when the child Emperor Romulus Augustulus refused his troops' demands for a third of Italy for them to settle, he deposed the boy. Crucially, he did not appoint a new emperor as his puppet. Instead, he sent the imperial regalia to the eastern emperor, Zeno, saying that an emperor no longer ruled in the West. He himself took the title King of Italy. In Constantinople, the Emperor Zeno could do nothing to respond militarily and instead agreed that Odoacer was to be considered a representative of the Roman state.

Despite the fact that these events had occurred before he was even born, Justinian, like many Romans, regarded the Goths and others as temporary usurpers. He was now determined to reconquer the West, and reunite the Empire.

Before Justinian could look to the West, however, he had to secure his eastern frontiers. That meant dealing with the Empire's formidable eastern neighbours, the Sassanian Persians. The Sassanians had been the eastern Roman Empire's greatest enemy since the third century, and even when they were not actually fighting there was a 'cold war' between these two superpowers. An on-going campaign against them had stalled and the emperor now decided to 'buy' a peace. It was hugely expensive but, by 533, such an agreement was in place and Justinian felt ready to launch his western campaign.

Justinian despatched his trusted general, Belisarius, to North Africa with a modest force of 5000 cavalry and 10,000 infantry. His orders were to reconquer the whole province. North Africa had been the centre of the Kingdom of the Vandals for over a century, but within less than two years Belisarius had completely overthrown Vandal rule, to the extent that they shortly disappeared altogether from historical record. The Vandal king, and the vast accumulated treasures of his piratical kingdom, were sent to Constantinople and carried through the Hippodrome in the most magnificent Triumph to be held for decades. North Africa was once again a Roman province.

Procopius described the celebrations:

Belisarius, upon reaching Constantinople…was counted worthy to receive such honours as in former times were assigned to those generals of the Romans who had won the greatest and most noteworthy victories… For he displayed the spoils and the slaves of war in the midst of the city and led a procession…to the Hippodrome and then from the barriers until he reached the imperial box. And there was booty…thrones of gold and carriages…and much jewellery made of precious stones, and golden drinking cups, and other things used at the royal table. And there was also silver weighing many thousands of talents and all the royal treasure amounting to an exceedingly great sum… [8]

Belisarius's success probably took Justinian by surprise but he did not hesitate to then order him to destroy the Kingdom of the Goths in Italy. Crossing to Sicily in 535, Belisarius took advantage of divisions among his enemies and made rapid gains. By the end of 536 he had captured Rome itself. The once-great capital of the Empire was in a poor state. The city had by now been sacked twice, in 410 by Alaric and the Visigoths and, more systematically, by the Vandals in 455. Few new buildings had been constructed, and some of the pagan temples had been converted into churches. A more serious danger in the long term was that there was little money available to repair existing buildings. This decay became more pronounced in later centuries, when many great buildings became quarries for stone or were stripped of their riches by successive popes. Belisarius returned the keys of the city to Justinian, the first time a Roman emperor had possessed them in over sixty years.

Despite Procopius's dislike of Justinian, he had to acknowledge this achievement: 'In our own age there has been born the Emperor Justinian, who, taking over the state when it was harassed by disorder, has not only made it greater in extent, but also much more illustrious, by expelling from it those barbarians who had from of old pressed hard upon it…'

Justinian, in a state of excitement and flushed with success, initiated a building spree, including, says Procopius, a complete renovation of his own palace:

…practically the whole palace is new…it is impossible to describe it in words…set with tiny cubes of stone beautifully coloured in all hues, which represent human figures and all kinds

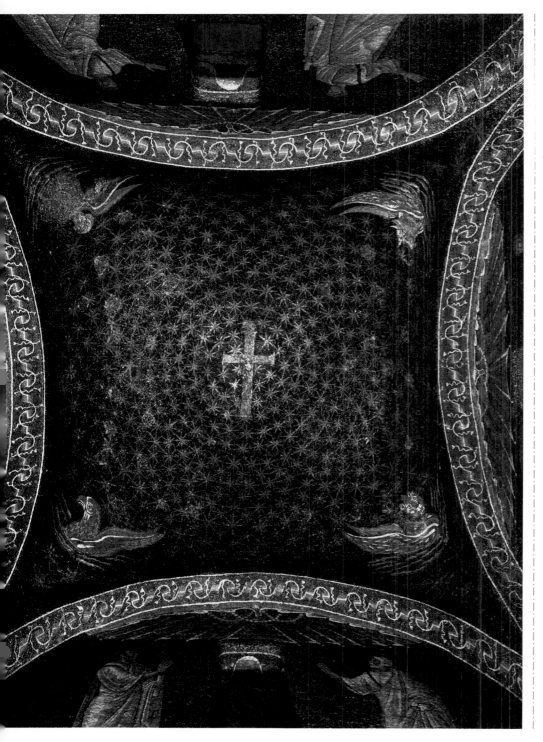

By Justinian's era,
the Empire had
become almost
entirely Christian.

of subjects…war and battle, and many cities being captured, …and the general Belisarius returning to the Emperor with his whole army intact, and giving him spoils, both kings and kingdoms and all things that are prized among men. In the centre stands the Emperor and the Empress Theodora… [9]

Justinian also decided to mark the victory by dedicating a great church he had been rebuilding. Many of Constantinople's most important buildings had been destroyed as a consequence of the earlier riots, one casualty being the old church of Sancta Sophia ('Holy Wisdom'). Justinian had hired the greatest architects of the day to build a new church of unsurpassed grandeur, surmounted by an immense domed structure.

Procopius tells us that money was no object: 'The emperor, disregarding all questions of expense, eagerly pressed on to begin the work of construction, and began to gather all the artisans from the whole world'. According to Agathias:

He was particularly concerned about the Great Church. Previously burnt by the populace, he had built it up anew, right from its foundations, creating a church of amazing beauty, which was further enhanced by its vastly increased dimensions, its majestic proportions and by a lavish profusion of ornamental marble. It was built of baked brick and lime on a structure of iron girders, the use of wood being avoided in order to prevent it from being easily set on fire again… [10]

When the new church was finally finished it was regarded as the most breathtaking building in the world. It had incredible dimensions, arches, domes, windows, mosaics, icons, sacred vessels and relics. Procopius described its glories: 'So the church has become a spectacle of marvellous beauty, overwhelming those who see it, but to those who know it by hearsay altogether incredible. For it soars to a height to match the sky, and as if surging up from amongst the other buildings, it stands on high and looks down upon the rest of the city…'

The enthusiasm surrounding its construction marked the high point of Justinian's reign. The middle-aged emperor thought his new church symbolized a revitalized, reunited, reglorified Empire. But he was mistaken.

Ironically enough, as if to mark his error, there was a severe earthquake soon afterwards, as a result of which the dome of his new church collapsed and had to be rebuilt.

Agathias was one of those who foresaw that Justinian's reign would now be marked by endless war: 'Everyone supposed that the fighting in Italy had been brought to a successful conclusion: in reality it had scarcely begun. I am convinced, for my part, that our generation shall see no end to such ills…human nature being what it is'.

Belisarius had left Rome and moved north to capture Ravenna, the Gothic capital. He deposed their king and seemed on the point of complete victory when he suddenly received orders from Justinian to rush east, to face the Sassanians, who had broken the peace.

Justinian's reign had now started to go badly wrong. He found himself having to fight wars on two fronts: in the East against the Sassanians; and in the West against the Goths. To make matters worse, Justinian was becoming envious and fearful of his own general's success. Consequently, whereas, after the conquest of North Africa in 534, Justinian had staged the most magnificent Triumph seen in generations, with all the booty and captives on display, when Belisarius returned from Italy with similar spoils in 540 Justinian held no Triumph, but merely displayed the captured treasures privately to a select audience. Procopius tells us that:

He merely set it forth for the members of the Senate to view privately in the palace, being envious of the magnitude and splendour of the achievement. And neither did he bring it out before the people, nor did he accord Belisarius the customary Triumph, as he had done when he returned from his victory over the Vandals. But the name of Belisarius was on everyone's lips, and to him were ascribed the two victories, such as had never before fallen to the lot of any one man to achieve. [11]

Justinian was in a strange position, in that these military achievements were claimed as his, even though, like most late Roman emperors, he had taken no personal part in the fighting. His fears about Belisarius were confirmed for him by rumours from Ravenna that his general had agreed to become

'Emperor of the West'. It seems probable, however, that Belisarius was just trying to fool the Goths into surrendering Ravenna by accepting their offer of the western throne in return for his abandoning Justinian.

Belisarius managed to persuade Justinian of his loyalty, but thereafter he was never entrusted with large armies again. In short, Justinian realized that he needed Belisarius's military expertise, but he did not trust him enough to provide him with sufficient manpower to bring the fighting to a conclusion. Justinian had become envious of Belisarius's military talents and feared, unjustly, that he might usurp his power. He was thus shunted from one front to another, trying to continue fighting, despite dwindling resources, unpaid troops and desertions.

At one point, according to Procopius, the long-suffering general wrote to Justinian: 'We have arrived in Italy, Most Mighty Emperor, without men, horses, arms or money, and no man, I think, without a plentiful supply of these things, would ever be able to carry on the war'.

Belisarius never had enough men and materials to end either the war in Italy or the East decisively. Even so, at no point did Justinian contemplate withdrawal from the West. Military operations were even extended to other regions, such as southern Spain, where a new province was carved out of what had become a Gothic kingdom.

Procopius summarized the situation with his usual incisiveness:

Now as long as Belisarius was in command of the Roman army both in Africa and in Italy, he was continually victorious...but the other commanders, being unlike him...had already begun to plunder the Romans and to put the civil population at the mercy of the soldiers, and neither were they themselves any longer giving heed to the requirements of the situation, nor could they secure obedience to their commands on the part of the soldiers. And many blunders were committed by them, and the entire fabric of Roman power was utterly destroyed in a short space of time...

Not only did the Italians become disaffected from the Emperor Justinian, but not one of the soldiers was willing any longer to undergo the dangers of war, and by wilfully refusing to fight they caused the strength of the enemy to grow continually greater... [12]

Just as damaging – perhaps even more so – was the arrival of a horrific plague. Procopius wrote that 'the plague fell upon the whole world' and that is how it must have felt. A natural event can destroy a city, crush a nation, fatally weaken an empire. This plague – probably a form of bubonic plague – was certainly one of the worst in history and should not be underestimated as a factor contributing to the Empire's decline.

Procopius described the huge toll it took:

Pestilence swept through the Roman Empire, wiping out most of the farming community and leaving a trail of desolation...the disease in Constantinople ran a course of four months...the toll of dead reached five thousand each day, and again it even came to ten thousand and more...

...it fell to the lot of the Emperor, as was natural, to make provision for this trouble... And when it came about that all the existing tombs were filled with the dead, then they dug up all the places around the city, one after another, laid the dead there...and departed. But later on, those who were making these pits, no longer able to keep up with the numbers of dead, mounted the towers of the fortifications...and, tearing off the roofs, threw the bodies in there in complete disorder, and they piled up as each one happened to fall, and filled practically all the towers with corpses. They then covered them again with their roofs. As a result of this an evil stench pervaded the city and distressed the inhabitants still more, and especially whenever the wind blew fresh from that quarter... [13]

The actual casualties are impossible to estimate but are likely to have been in the hundreds of thousands. Justinian should have felt very lucky to survive (he actually caught the plague but recovered). Instead he bemoaned the loss of tax-paying subjects. The plague also decimated the ranks of the army and the potential reserves of men who could replace them.

War and plague made Justinian, in his late fifties, a desperate man, constantly in search of funds. Many of the old public offices – *tribune*, *aedile*, *quaestor* – had long been abolished. In 542, Justinian went one step further and, after a thousand years of continual service, the consulate was abolished. There were still people prepared to take on the immense financial burdens of the office but Justinian was jealous of the popularity they might gain through their munificence.

Lesser positions, such as governorships, naturally continued but Justinian sought to exploit these posts by accepting bribes for them. Not only did this undermine good government but it led to those very officials extorting their provincial populations in order to make good the funds they had delivered to Justinian. Corruption – though by no means new to the Empire – helped weaken it further.

At the same time, Justinian tried to combat tax evasion by the richer sections of the community. Their resentment is obvious in the words of men like Procopius:

He was constantly on the lookout, immediately squandering on one foreign tribe or another, or on crazy building schemes, all that he had amassed by his earlier looting...the government was indistinguishable from a tyranny; not, however, a stable tyranny, but one that changed every day and was forever starting afresh. The decisions of the magistrates suggested the paralysis of fear; their minds were dominated by dread of a single man... [14]

Many also feared Theodora. She had decided that John of Cappadocia had become too intimate with Justinian. She and her best friend Antonia, Belisarius's wife, concocted a complex plot which ensured that John was disgraced, stripped of rank and possessions and forced to become a priest, eventually being exiled to Antinoöpolis in Egypt.

Justinian's concentration was elsewhere: the renewed war with the Sassanians was not going well. Preoccupied in the West, there were few Roman forces available. Many of the great Roman cities of the East, notably Antioch, were captured and their magnificent buildings systematically looted, the wealth carried off to adorn Sassanian cities.

Procopius lamented the destruction: 'I shudder when I describe so great a disaster, and pass it on to be remembered by future generations, and I do not know what God's will could be in raising up the affairs of a man or a place, and then casting them down and wiping them out for no apparent reason...'

After a brief truce in 545 the war dragged on. Justinian dispatched ever greater forces to the East, but it was a constant drain on his manpower and resources, lasting nearly until the end of his reign. The war was now concentrated in Lazica (the coast of the modern republic of Georgia). These two great superpowers had a truce along their whole frontier except here. The Romans and Sassanians poured massive forces into the area. At stake was the very security of the Empire – if the Sassanians gained access to the Black Sea they could build a fleet and attack Constantinople.

According to Agathias:

Justinian grasped clearly the alarming implications of a Persian victory resulting in the annexation of the whole area. Should such a thing happen there would be nothing to prevent the Persians from sailing up the Black Sea with impunity and probing deep into the heart of the Roman Empire. Accordingly he stationed a large and powerful army there under the command of his best generals... [15]

This diversion east meant that the western campaigns now suffered from lack of manpower and supplies. It was not long before Justinian decided he did not want to fight the war in the East and he returned to paying vast sums of money to the Persians to persuade them to keep the peace. This was, in effect, tribute.

Procopius claimed that: 'On all his country's potential enemies [he] lost no opportunity of lavishing vast sums of money – on those to east, west, north and south, as far as the inhabitants of Britain and the nations in every part of the known world'.

So strong were the Persians becoming that within a generation they were able briefly to conquer right up to the Bosphorus, Syria, Palestine and Egypt.

Justinian was plagued by these troublesome relations with Persia but a third front required his immediate attention. The Danube provinces had long been under pressure; immense armies of Slavs and Bulgars poured through the imperial defences. This was the first time the Slavs began to make their presence felt and hereafter they remained one of the most important ethnic groups in European history. A generation after Justinian they swamped the Balkans and have been there ever since – another part of the Empire had been lost.

Justinian was fighting wars on three fronts. Small wonder that the aging emperor felt besieged:

Busied as we are with the cares of the Empire, our mind intent on such weighty matters as ensuring that the Persians cause no trouble, that the Vandals and the Moors maintain their allegiance, that the people of Africa continue in possession of their ancient freedom to which they have been restored...we are in addition beset by the multitude of individual problems continually submitted to us by our subjects and for which, in each and every case, we give the appropriate ruling... [16]

A Sassanian king fighting lions, the symbol of the Persian god of evil.

The campaign for Italy continued, as opposing armies rolled backwards and forwards with ever-changing fortunes – Rome itself changed hands five times and suffered irrevocable damage. Eventually, Justinian sent Narses, an Armenian eunuch from his court (and, as a eunuch, unable to usurp imperial power), to Italy with all the resources he required. Narses imposed a crushing defeat on the Goths at Taginae in 552 and, though there were some local sieges during the following decade, this battle spelt the end for the Goths, who – like the Vandals – simply disappeared from history. Italy once again became a Roman province.

The 'Reconquest' was accompanied by an extensive building programme throughout the Empire. The Syrian advocate and historian Evagrius tells us that: 'Justinian is said to have restored 150 cities in Africa, some of which had been altogether, and others extensively ruined; and this he did with surpassing magnificence, in private and public works and embellishments, in fortifications, and other vast structures by which cities are adorned and the Deity propitiated...'

Justinian also hoped to preserve city life and the

loyalty of his citizens by building new facilities – walls, cisterns and aqueducts. Procopius was, for once, pleased by these developments: 'There can be no dispute, but it is abundantly clear to all mankind that the Emperor Justinian has strengthened the state, not with fortresses alone, but also by means of garrisons, from the bounds of the East to the very setting of the sun, these being the limits of the Roman Empire'.

Justinian was both knowledgeable and intelligent, and showed a keen interest in all aspects of his Empire. He achieved something in almost every field – legal reform, building, warfare and defence, provincial administration and his particular intellectual interest of ecclesiastical affairs. Few emperors had such wide-ranging minds. It is true that in each case the actual achievements, strictly speaking, belong to another – the reconquests were achieved by Belisarius and Narses; legal reform by Tribonian; the building projects by Anthemius of Tralles. But Justinian had an undeniable talent as an overall co-ordinator of the Empire's affairs, ruling from the political and administrative centre.

Certain sections of society, notably the aristocracy, nevertheless loathed Justinian. To them he was an upstart, who had made a whore his empress, and whose relentless financial exactions impoverished rich and poor alike. Procopius bemoaned the injustice – as he saw it – of the endless taxes: 'the scales of justice wandered at random all over the place, whichever way the greater mass of gold weighing them down succeeded in pulling them'.

Justinian knew that many hated him and this only served to deepen his sense of isolation. As a result, his suspicions of his closest supporters impaired the effectiveness of his policies.

War, taxation, rioting and a multicultural mix, all added ever-increasing stresses and strains to this tense imperial court. Procopius tells us that Justinian and Theodora now began to take a distinctly puritanical approach to the customary hedonism of their society:

Theodora made it her business also to devise punishments for the sins of the flesh. Prostitutes – more than 500 in all – were rounded up; women who in the middle of the Forum sold their services cheaply, just enough to keep body and soul together…were…confined in the Convent known as Repentance in an attempt to force them into a better way of life…

[Justinian] gave orders that all places of entertainment should be closed down… Both in private and in public there was grief and dejection…all laughter had gone out of life. [17]

These actions were, however, mere sideshows. Justinian's central concern was that his Empire was becoming financially exhausted. He tried to make amends – though it was he who was spending lavishly on building and fighting – but in the process acquired a reputation for greed and parsimony. The charge has tended to stick, but is to some extent unfair. Taxation systems are always easy to criticize and the system Justinian employed was one that he had inherited. Indeed, he only appears to have levied one new tax in his entire reign, a tax on high-rise buildings called the 'air-tax'.

The difference was that he was determined to have the taxes collected. Justinian was far stricter in his enforcement of the system. He always demanded what was due, rarely cancelling bad debts or remitting taxation to those provinces devastated by invasion or plague.

The real key to efficiency was the elimination of waste and corruption. Corruption was now clearly operating at all levels and a network of bribes and illicit payments meant that the imperial treasury received only a fraction of what was collected in the provinces. Furthermore, the main tax burden fell upon those least able to pay – the rural peasants – while the urban population, especially the rich, was still tending to escape the worst of the exactions.

Justinian tried to ensure that money collected and set aside for the towns was actually spent on public works and did not just 'disappear'. Local bishops, who were considered more trustworthy, were put in charge of funds, and special accountants were appointed to supervise expenditure. The latter exercised their authority under the emperor's personal mandate, and local authorities were ordered to recognize no other authority (an indication of the existing levels of corruption and extortion). But these measures still failed to stop the decay of town life and the Great Plague of 542 had so reduced the numbers of taxpayers that some towns were unable to provide the most basic amenities for their inhabitants.

In 548, Theodora had died. During their marriage she had given birth only once but their daughter had died as a baby. Justinian was thus without issue but it was matters of religion rather than succession that concerned him. Procopius, amongst others, noted his preoccupation with theological questions: 'Now, although the emperor did promise to concern himself personally with Italy, yet he was devoting his time for the most part to the doctrines of the Christians, seeking eagerly and with great determination to make a satisfactory settlement of the questions disputed among them...'

Like Constantine, Justinian was a manipulator of religious sentiment. The intention of his religious policy was to achieve some kind of compromise between all sides and establish a united Church, of which he was the head. Unlike Constantine, however, he was fascinated by the minutiae of theological debate. Differing beliefs as to the nature of Christianity also severely divided the western and eastern provinces. He sought a formula that would unite both sides, as well as maintaining his supreme role in the order of things.

His most cynical attempt to work out a formula came at the Council of Constantinople in 553. Having finally defeated the Goths, Justinian used his domination of Italy to 'kidnap' the Pope, bring him to Constantinople, and force him to sign the Acts of the Council. These Acts, however, failed. Christianity, which both Constantine and Justinian had hoped would unite the Empire had, in fact, only deepened the division between East and West.

Justinian had spent vast amounts of time and money on the reconquest of the West. His attempts to restore the Empire's former grandeur, at a time when it was under such financial strain, drained the treasury and left it fatally weakened. Even while claiming to restore the glory of ancient Rome, he had all but bankrupted the state, as well as ending the consulate, closing pagan academies, and raising barbarians to positions of power. The aging emperor must have known he had failed. Even though the long wars in the West had just drawn to a close with the fall of Verona, the last Gothic stronghold, the reconquest had been at the cost of Italy's virtual destruction.

*An imagined view
of the successful siege
of Constantinople by
the Ottoman Turks
in 1453. It can be
argued that this
fall marked the end
of the rule of the
last emperor of
the Romans.*

Justinian was now rarely seen, except for a few prolonged and very rare absences from the capital to inspect frontier walls in Thrace or to go on pilgrimage in Anatolia. In 559, a Hun invasion had brought enemy troops to the walls of Constantinople itself. Barricaded inside his palace, Justinian surely saw the futility of having expended so much time and finance on foreign campaigns when the heart of the Empire remained so fragile.

Justinian struggled on, however. He called Belisarius out of retirement to repel the Huns. Then, in 561, there was peace again with Persia, thanks to a huge gold payment. The borders were agreed and customs posts established at certain cities. The Persian king wrote to Justinian addressing him as 'Caesar, brother'.

It had been many years since the Hippodrome had witnessed the magnificent Triumphs of earlier campaigns. Indeed, the Hippodrome itself lay silent while traditional games remained prohibited. A shadow fell over the city as everyone waited for Justinian to die.

Finally, in 565, Justinian died, aged eighty-three.

❖

Despite his apparent successes, Justinian's wars had failed to recreate the lost grandeur of the Roman Empire. In the West, his victory was transitory: North Africa remained a Roman province until the Arab conquests of 640–680 (the subsequent loss of Egypt and the grain supply was a major blow); the Spanish province held out against the Visigoths for less than a century. Even in the short term, these extremely costly wars were perhaps pointless.

In 568, just three years after Justinian's death, the Lombards, another Germanic people, poured into the exhausted Italian peninsula and took much of it from Roman control for ever. Never again would eastern and western Europe be reunited. Justinian's failure marked the end of Rome as a pan-European reality. The Sassanians remained a menace on the eastern frontier, soon to be replaced by the Arabs, and ultimately by the Turks. The Muslim Arab invasion of the eastern provinces of the Roman Empire around 630 effectively marked the end of a united eastern Empire too.

Nevertheless, while the Empire as a whole, and the West in particular, had fallen, the diminished eastern Empire was to survive for many centuries. Indeed it can be argued that it was the Fall of Constantinople to the Ottoman Turks in 1453, a full 800 years later, that marked the end of the rule of the last Emperor of the Romans. Modern scholars have named this period the Byzantine Empire but, right up to this date, the inhabitants of Constantinople called themselves 'Romans' and their ruler 'the Emperor of the Romans'.

In some ways, perhaps, even that late date does not mark the end of Rome. The Empire's legacy was – and is – enormous. In the West, Latin evolved into the amended forms of Italian, French, Spanish, Catalan and Romanian, while Roman law and Latin literature became features of successor states up to the present. Latin remained the universal language of western scholarship, meeting competition from vernacular languages from the sixteenth century, but surviving as an academic language up to the nineteenth century.

No institution inherited the mantle of Rome more than the Catholic Church. In the absence of an Emperor of the West the Pope soon laid similar claims to universal authority. 'Modern' ecclesiastical vestments derive from Roman aristocratic dress, and the Catholic Church preserved Latin as its official language until 1967. Even the idea of the Roman Empire never died completely, and was revived in 800 by the Frankish king, Charlemagne, as the Holy Roman Empire, an institution which survived until it was dismantled by Napoleon in 1806.

If we take 1453 as marking its downfall, the Roman Empire can be said to have lasted around 2000 years. Without any doubt it was the most influential empire in history and its Caesars among history's most influential men.

Rome's 'decline' alone lasted longer than most empires in their entirety. Yet no empire ever truly ends. Empires adapt, change, and assimilate one another. Rome and the Romans remain with us; their legacy surrounds us. So too does the legacy of individual Caesars. History has subsequently spawned many imitators, who have styled themselves, for good and ill, Czars, Kaisers, emperors. But for sheer boldness, brutality, ruthlessness, brilliance, bravery and imagination, few have matched those called Caesar.

NOTES

CHAPTER I: JULIUS CAESAR

1. Plutarch, *The Fall of the Roman Republic*, trans. Rex Warner, Penguin Classics, 1958.
2. Plutarch, ibid.
3. Caesar, *The Conquest of Gaul*, trans. S.A.Handford, Penguin Classics, 1951.
4. Caesar, ibid.

CHAPTER II: AUGUSTUS

1. Cicero, *Philippics*, trans. Walter C.A.Ker, Loeb Classical Library, Harvard University Press, 1926.
2. Suetonius, *The Twelve Caesars*, trans. Robert Graves, Penguin Classics, 1957.
3. Suetonius, ibid.
4. Suetonius, ibid.
5. Cassius Dio, *The Roman History*, trans. Ian Scott-Kilvert, Penguin Classics, 1987.
6. Virgil, adapted by the author from H.R.Fairclough, Loeb Classical Library, Harvard University Press, 1934.
7. Macrobius, *Saturnalia*, in R.K.Sherk, *The Roman Empire: Augustus to Hadrian, Translated Documents of Greece and Rome*, Cambridge University Press, 1988.
8. Suetonius, *The Twelve Caesars*, trans. Robert Graves, Penguin Classics, 1957.
9. Suetonius, ibid.
10. Seneca, *Moral Essays*, vol.III, trans. John W.Basore, Loeb Classical Library, Harvard University Press, 1935.

CHAPTER III: NERO

1. Tacitus, *The Annals of Imperial Rome*, trans. Michael Grant, Penguin Classics, 1956.
2. Calpurnius Siculus, in *Minor Latin Poets*, vol.I, trans. J.W. and A.M.Duff, Loeb Classical Library, Harvard University Press, 1934.
3. Tacitus, *The Annals of Imperial Rome*, trans. Michael Grant, Penguin Classics, 1956.
4. Suetonius, *The Twelve Caesars*, trans. Robert Graves, Penguin Classics, 1957.
5. Suetonius, ibid.
6. Tacitus, *The Annals of Imperial Rome*, trans. Michael Grant, Penguin Classics, 1956.
7. Cassius Dio, *Roman History*, trans. E.Cary, Loeb Classical Library, Harvard University Press, 1914–27.
8. Tacitus, *The Annals of Imperial Rome*, trans. Michael Grant, Penguin Classics, 1956.
9. Suetonius, *The Twelve Caesars*, trans. Robert Graves, Penguin Classics, 1957.

10. Tacitus, *The Annals of Imperial Rome*, trans. Michael Grant, Penguin Classics, 1956.
11. Cassius Dio, *Roman History*, trans. E.Cary, Loeb Classical Library, Harvard University Press,1914–27.
12. Nero, in R.K.Sherk, *The Roman Empire: Augustus to Hadrian, Translated Documents of Greece and Rome*, Cambridge University Press, 1988.

CHAPTER IV: HADRIAN

1. Cassius Dio, *Roman History*, trans. E.Cary, Loeb Classical Library, Harvard University Press, 1914–27.
2. *The Augustan Histories*, trans. D.Magie, Loeb Classical Library, Harvard University Press,1921.
3. Hadrian, in *Minor Latin Poets*, vol.II, trans. J.W. and A.M.Duff, Loeb Classical Library, Harvard University Press, 1934.
4. Tacitus, *Agricola*, trans. M.Hutton, rev. R.M.Ogilvie, Loeb Classical Library, Harvard University Press, 1914; rev. ed. 1970.
5. *The Augustan Histories*, trans. D.Magie, Loeb Classical Library, Harvard University Press, 1921.
6. Hadrian, in *Minor Latin Poets*, vol.II, trans. J.W. and A.M.Duff, Loeb Classical Library, Harvard University Press, 1934.
7. Cassius Dio, *Roman History*, trans. E.Cary, Loeb Classical Library, Harvard University Press, 1914-27.
8. Herodian, *History,* trans. C.R.Whittaker, Loeb Classical Library, Harvard University Press, 1969–71.

CHAPTER V: CONSTANTINE

1. Lactantius, *De Mortibus Persecutorum*, trans. J.L.Creed, Oxford University Press, 1984.
2. Ammianus Marcellinus, *History*, vol.III, trans. J.C.Rolfe, Loeb Classical Library, Harvard University Press, 1939.
3. Ammianus Marcellinus, ibid.
4. Lactantius, *De Mortibus Persecutorum*, trans. J.L.Creed, Oxford University Press, 1984.
5. Eusebius, *Vita Constantini*, trans. E.C.Richardson, Oxford University Press, 1890.
6. Eunapius, in John Holland Smith, *Constantine the Great*, New York, Charles Scribner's Sons, 1971.
7. Ammianus Marcellinus, *History,* vol.III, trans. J.C.Rolfe, Loeb Classical Library, Harvard University Press, 1939.
8. Constantine, in Eusebius, *Vita Constantini*, trans. E.C.Richardson, Oxford University Press, 1890.

9. Eusebius, ibid.
10. Zosimus, in Michael Grant, *Emperor Constantine*, Weidenfeld & Nicolson, 1993.
11. Constantine, in Eusebius, *Vita Constantini*, trans. E.C.Richardson, Oxford University Press 1890.
12. Eusebius, ibid.

CHAPTER VI: JUSTINIAN

1. Procopius, *The Secret History*, trans. G.A.Williamson, Penguin Classics, 1965.
2. Procopius, ibid.
3. John Malalas, *Chronicle of John Malalas*, trans. E. and M.Jeffreys and R.Scott, Melbourne, Australian Association for Byzantine Studies, 1986.
4. Procopius, complete works, 7 vols, trans. H.B.Dewing, Loeb Classical Library, Harvard University Press, 1914–40.
5. Procopius, ibid.
6. *Chronicon Paschale*. trans. M.and M.Whitby, Liverpool University Press, 1989.

7 Synesius of Cyrene, *The Fall of the Roman Empire*, trans. M.Grant, Weidenfeld & Nicolson, 1990.
8 Procopius, complete works, 7 vols, trans. H.B.Dewing, Loeb Classical Library, Harvard University Press, 1914–40.
9 Procopius, ibid.
10. Agathias, *Agathias' Histories* trans. J.D.Frendo, Berlin and New York, Walter de Gruyter, 1975.
11. Procopius, complete works, 7 vols, trans. H.B.Dewing, Loeb Classical Library, Harvard University Press, 1914–40.
12. Procopius, ibid.
13. Procopius, ibid.
14. Procopius, *The Secret History*, trans. G.A.Williamson, Penguin Classics, 1966.
15. Agathias, *Agathias' Histories*, trans. J.D.Frendo, Berlin and New York, Walter de Gruyter, 1975.
16. Justinian, in ibid.
17. Procopius, *The Secret History*, trans. G.A.Williamson, Penguin Classics, 1966.

BIBLIOGRAPHY

Agathias, *The Histories*, trans. J.D. Frendo, Berlin/New York, 1975.
Augustan Histories, trans. A. Birley, Penguin Classics, 1976.
Augustus, *Res Gestae Divi Augusti*, edited and trans. P.A.Brunt and J.M. Moore, Oxford, 1967.
Appian, *Civil War*, trans. J Carter, Penguin Classics, 1996.
Arrian, *The Campaigns of Alexander*, trans. A. de Selincourt, Penguin Classics, 1971.
Caesar, *Conquest of Gaul*, trans. S.A.Handford, Penguin Classics, 1960.
     The Civil War, trans. J.F.Gardner, Penguin Classics, 1967.
Cassius Dio, *Roman History*, trans. I.Scott-Kilvert and J.Carter, Penguin Classics, 1987.
Chronicon Paschale, trans. M. and M.Whitby, Liverpool, 1989.
Eusebius, *The History of the Church*, trans. G.A.Williamson, Penguin Classics, 1989.
Life of Constantine (*Vita Constantini*), trans. E.C. Richardson in *A Select Library of Nicene and Post-Nicene Fathers*, 2nd Ser., vol. 1, Oxford and New York, 1890.
Horace, *Odes and Epodes*, trans. J.Michie, Penguin Classics, 1964.
Josephus, *The Jewish War*. trans. G.A.Williamson, Penguin Classics, 1981.
Juvenal, *The Sixteen Satires*. trans. P.Green, Penguin Classics, 1970.
Lactantius, *On the Deaths of the Persecutors*, trans. J.L.Creed, Oxford, 1984.
Livy, *The Early History of Rome*, trans. Aubrey de Selincourt, Penguin Classics, 1971.
John Malalas, *Chronicle*, trans. E. Jeffreys, M. Jeffreys and R. Scott, Melbourne, 1986.

Plutarch, *Lives in The Fall of the Roman Republic*, trans. R.Warner, Penguin Classics. 1958.
The Makers of Rome, trans. I.Scott-Kilvert, Penguin Classics, 1965.
Procopius, *Wars, Secret History, and Buildings*, trans. H.Dewing and G.Downey. 7 vols., Loeb Classical Library, 1914–40.
Seneca, *The Apocclocyntosis*, Penguin Classics, 1986.
Suetonius, *The Twelve Caesars*, trans. R.Graves, Penguin Classics, 1957.
Tacitus, *The Annals of Imperial Rome*, trans. M.Grant, Penguin Classics, 1956.
Virgil, *Aeneid*, trans.W.F. Jackson Knight, Penguin Classics, 1991.
Zosimus, *New History* trans. R Ridley, Sydney, 1982.

COLLECTIONS OF TEXT SOURCES

Augustus to Nero: A Source Book on Roman History, 31 BC – AD 68, D.C.Braund. London, 1985.
Documents Illustrating the Principates of Gaius, Claudius and Nero, E.Smallwood, Cambridge, 1957.
From Constantine to Julian, S.N.C.Lieu, and D.Montserrat, London, 1996.
The Oxford History of the Roman World, J.Boardman, S.Griffin and O.Murray, Oxford, 1991.
The Roman Empire: Augustus to Hadrian, Translated Documents of Greece and Rome, R.K.Sherk, Cambridge, 1988.

LIST OF SOURCES

AGATHIAS (c. AD 531–c. 580)
From Myrina in Asia Minor, Agathias pursued a legal career before turning to historical writing. His *Histories*, covering the years 553 to 559 in considerable detail, were a self-conscious continuation of Procopius's *Wars*.

ST AMBROSE (c. AD 339–397)
As Bishop of Milan, Ambrose produced many sermons and over ninety epistles, which are an important source for contemporary political events and social developments.

AMMIANUS MARCELLINUS (late fourth/early fifth century AD)
A Greek from Antioch, Ammianus wrote the last great classical history of the Roman Empire in Latin. His detailed and sophisticated *History*, where extant, covers the period from 353 to 378. An experienced soldier, he greatly admired the last pagan emperor, Julian, though his work is not overtly anti-Christian.

APPIAN (later second century AD)
Appian first held office in his native Alexandria but, on receiving Roman citizenship, he moved to Rome, later becoming an imperial procurator. He was a great admirer of Roman imperialism. Writing in Greek, he composed a long history of Rome from its foundation to the beginning of the Augustan Principate, based upon earlier, now lost, sources. Much of his *History* has not survived, but of the extant books those on the civil wars at the end of the Republic are the most useful.

ARRIAN (c. AD 90–175)
Arrian was a Greek, from Bithynia. He had a successful administrative career, rising to consul and provincial governor. He was a respected military commander, a personal friend of Hadrian, and a prolific author.

THE AUGUSTAN HISTORIES (late third/early fourth century AD)
The *Scriptores Historiae Augustae* or *Augustan Histories* is the title given to a series of imperial biographies by six different authors. In its present form the series begins with Hadrian in 117 and ends with Numerian in 284, with a gap for the years 244–257. The authors often used their sources uncritically, repeated dubious information, and accepted without question eulogizing or damning portraits of past emperors. The work is therefore to be used with care.

AURELIUS VICTOR (later fourth century AD)
Originating in North Africa, Sextus Aurelius Victor enjoyed a successful administrative career. His *Book of the Caesars* is a summary of Roman history from Augustus to Constantius II (337–361). It is useful principally for the later Roman period.

CALPURNIUS SICULUS (mid-first century AD)
A pastoral poet whose verse includes descriptions of spectacles at Rome.

CATULLUS (c. 84–c. 54 BC)
Gaius Valerius Catullus was an aristocratic poet from Verona, who moved in fashionable Roman society. Some of his poems obscenely characterized political figures of the late Republic.

THE CHRONICON PASCHALE
A chronicle written at Constantinople during the reign of Justinian (527–565 AD). It includes many historical details, especially concerning the eastern capital.

CICERO (106–143 BC)
Arguably the greatest Roman orator, Cicero came from Arpinum in Latium. Of relatively humble origins, he used his rhetorical skill and success as an advocate to establish a successful political career, becoming consul in 63 BC. Essentially a 'moderate', he attempted to preserve the Republican system of government. His lack of any real power base, however, meant that he was often a pawn of more important political figures, such as Caesar and, later, Octavian. Having made many enemies in his career, he ultimately fell victim to Mark Antony's rage. His speeches and letters are an invaluable source of information on the political and social life of the late Republic.

CASSIUS DIO (c. AD 163–235)
Born in Bithynia in Asia Minor, Lucius Cassius Dio was a senator, like his father, and twice consul (205 and 229). Over many years he composed a vast *Roman History*, from the origins of Rome to his own time, extensively researching the project from earlier authors. Although some books are lost, and others survive only as later abbreviated versions, what remains is often invaluable. Dio naturally upholds the traditions of the Senate throughout, and he is strongly biased against those emperors who infringed senatorial privilege.

EUNAPIUS (c. AD 345–after 414)

From Sardis in Asia Minor, this pagan philosopher and priest wrote a history of the period 270 to 404, which is especially hostile to Christians and Christianity.

EUSEBIUS (c. AD 260–c. 340)

Eusebius, Bishop of Caesarea in Palestine, was one of the principal supporters of Constantine (306–337). His most famous and most influential work was his *Ecclesiastical History*, the first Church history to be written. His *Life of Constantine* is undeniably an uncritical eulogy of the emperor, which aims to demonstrate that he was divinely directed during his lifetime. Although he deals almost exclusively with religious matters, Eusebius frequently quotes Constantine and his laws and letters directly. He claims he had first-hand knowledge of these, though some scholars have doubted this.

EUTROPIUS (later fourth century AD)

A historian closely connected with the court at Constantinople, Eutropius composed the *Ereviarium*, a short but intelligent summary of Roman history from Romulus to Julian (361–363).

EVAGRIUS (c. AD 536–c. 600)

An advocate and official from Epiphaneia in Syria, Evagrius's *Ecclesiastical History* from 431 to 594 includes much secular history.

FRONTO (before AD 100–after 166)

Marcus Cornelius Fronto was a celebrated advocate and orator, and tutor to Marcus Aurelius. He rose to a position of great distinction and was consul in 143. A large corpus of his letters addressed to Marcus Aurelius and others was discovered in the nineteenth century.

HERODIAN (late second/early third century AD)

Probably an Asiatic Greek, Herodian wrote a *History* of the period from the death of Marcus Aurelius in 180 to the accession of Gordian III in 238. The work is more valuable in its later sections, for which Herodian was probably an eyewitness. Although written in a highly rhetorical style, Herodian's *History* serves as a balance to the senatorial bias of Cassius Dio.

HORACE (65–8 BC)

Quintus Horatius Flaccus was one of the greatest Latin poets. From Venusia in southern Italy, Horace compensated for his humble origins with his poetic talent. His genius brought him to the attention of Maecenas, a friend of the Emperor Augustus, through whom he associated with other poets, including Virgil. Although he refused to write an epic on Augustus's life and career, Horace was prepared to use his poetic talents to extol Augustan virtues.

ST JEROME (c. AD 348–420)

St Jerome (or Hieronymus) is one of the principal fathers of the early Church. Born at Stridon in modern Serbia, after a varied career he eventually rose to become a papal secretary. Jerome's writings are very numerous, but his chief claim to fame is his translation of the Bible into Latin, the *Vulgate*, which became the standard version in the West.

JOSEPHUS (AD 37–c. 98)

A highly educated Jewish priest, Josephus originally fought against the Romans in the Jewish revolt but later became pro-Roman.

LACTANTIUS (c. AD 250–c. 320)

Summoned from his native North Africa by Diocletian (284–305), Lactantius went to Nicomedia to teach rhetoric. Becoming a Christian, he fled to the West to avoid persecution, and later became an influential intellectual at the court of Constantine. His *On the Deaths of the Persecutors*, covering the period 303–314, has the express aim of demonstrating that those who persecuted the Church of God met suitably grisly ends. Lactantius's extreme Christian bias means that much of what he writes cannot be taken at face value.

MACROBIUS (c. AD 340)

Probably a pagan, Macrobius's *Saturnalia* is a large collection of miscellaneous information, which includes otherwise unknown historical details.

JOHN MALALAS (c. AD 491–578)

A resident of Antioch during the reign of Justinian, John Malalas composed a *Chronicle* of world history from the Creation to AD 565. Although uncritical and sometimes confused, his work contains much valuable information on the later Roman Empire, and was immensely influential, being used by many subsequent Byzantine historians, and translated into several languages.

PLINY THE ELDER (AD 23–79)

Gaius Plinius Secundus, from Como in North Italy, served for twelve years in the cavalry on the Rhine, and later rose to distinction under the Flavians. Of his several works, only the encyclopedic *Natural History* survives.

PLUTARCH (c. AD 45–c. 120)

A gentleman of Chaeronaea in central Greece, Plutarch was one of the most prolific classical authors. As both a native Greek and a Roman citizen, he attempted to combine the glories of the Greek past with the achievements of the Roman present. His fame rests largely on his *Parallel Lives*, twinned biographies of famous Greeks and Romans, which aimed to demonstrate the essential similarity of the two cultures. These biographies had a moral rather than historical purpose, demonstrating the effect of certain virtues and vices on human lives.

PROCOPIUS (c. AD 500–after 562)

Procopius of Caesarea in Palestine was perhaps the last great historian of antiquity. As secretary to Justinian's famous general, Belisarius, and later Prefect of Constantinople, Procopius was well placed to describe the events of Justinian's reign. His *Wars* provides a continuous military narrative up to 552. His other works are the *Buildings,* a detailed account of the Emperor's extensive building projects, and the *Secret History,* a scurrilous, and in parts obscene, pamphlet, highly critical of Justinian and his wife, Theodora. Procopius's manifest hatred of the Emperor represents the views of the upper classes who felt oppressed by Justinian's taxation policies.

SALVIAN (c. AD 400–c. 480)

Probably born at Trier, Salvian was a priest at Marseilles. His largely religious works include some contemporary social comment.

SENECA (c. 4 BC–AD 65)

Originally from Cordoba in Spain, Lucius Annaeus Seneca played an important administrative role during Nero's early reign. In his treatise *On Clemency* he attempted to steer the emperor towards moderation in government. A scholar of immense abilities, Seneca was the author of numerous philosophical pamphlets, several tragedies, and a scientific compendium entitled *Natural Questions.* He ultimately fell victim to Nero's paranoia, becoming for later generations a philosophical martyr.

SUETONIUS (AD 70–140)

Gaius Suetonius Tranquillus trained as a lawyer and entered the imperial secretariat in the reign of Trajan (97–117). There he enjoyed unrivalled access to the imperial archives, from which he began to compose his *Lives of the Caesars.* Although dismissed by Hadrian (117–138) for rudeness to the Empress, Suetonius completed his series of twelve biographies from Julius Caesar to Domitian. Sometimes dismissed as a gossip-monger, Suetonius remains one of our most important sources for the lifestyle and personalities of the early Principate.

SYNESIUS (c. AD 370–413)

From Cyrene in Libya, Synesius was Bishop of Ptolemais, also in Libya. His works include hymns, sermons and 156 letters.

TACITUS (c. AD 56–c. 115)

Cornelius Tacitus is arguably the most famous Roman historian. His successful senatorial career, culminating in the consulship of AD 97, is reflected in the senatorial bias of his historical works. These are principally represented by the *Annals,* an account of the Julio-Claudian Dynasty, and the *Histories,* a narrative of the Civil War of 68–69 and the beginnings of the Flavian Dynasty. Although large sections of both works have been lost, Tacitus's account of imperial life is detailed and colourful. However, his particular interest in court intrigue and his dislike of the imperial system make his views far from balanced.

VIRGIL (70–19 BC)

Publius Vergilius Maro has long held an unrivalled placed in Latin literature. His family home near Mantua in northern Italy was confiscated by Octavian for his demobilized legions. Like Horace, he later found fame and fortune through his association with Maecenas, who introduced him to Augustus. After lengthy delays, Virgil eventually produced the epic Augustus had so eagerly awaited. This was the *Aeneid,* undoubtedly the most famous Latin poem, a celebration of the Roman imperial achievement and the majesty of the *pax Romana.*

ZOSIMUS (early sixth century AD)

Zosimus was the last of the pagan historians of Rome. A treasury official, his *New History* attempted to explain the decline of Roman power since the third century, and the subsequent Sack of Rome in 410. His principal thesis was that the growth of Christianity caused the traditional gods to abandon Rome. Although clearly biased, his anti-Christian stance offers an alternative historical viewpoint to the prevailing Christian tradition.

INDEX

References to illustrations are in **bold italic**

A

Acte 111
aediles 36, 237
Aelia (Jerusalem) 165
Aeneas 89-90
Africa, North 12, 13, 21, 22, 51, 65,
    67, 96, 111, 122, 143, 162, 188,
    209, 230, 231, 240, 246
Agathias 212, 234, 235, 239, 250
agriculture 111-12, 136, 178, 204, 225
Agrippa 66, 67, 70, **71**, 72, 85, 91
Agrippina 99-107, **100**, **104**,
    112-14 *passim*
Ahenobarbus, Gnaeus Domitius (Nero's
    father) 99, 101
Ahenobarbus, Lucius Domitius *see* Nero
Alaric, king 226, 227, 232
Alexander, Bishop 199
Alexander the Great 35, 128
Alexandria 50, 69, 163; Royal court at **164**
Ammianus 182, 183, 194, 250
Anastasius 212, 213
Anthemius of Tralles 241
Antinoöpolis 163, 238
Antinous 159, **160**, 163
Antioch 14, 143, 177, 192, 238
Antonia (Belisarius's wife) 238
Antonine dynasty 171
Antoninus Pius 13, 170, 171
Antony, Mark 51, 61-70 *passim*, **63**, 87
Apollodorus of Pergamum 50
Appian 67, 250
aqueducts 85, 157, 159, 160, 162
'Arabia' 162; Arabs 246
aristocracy 11-13 *passim*, 22, 26, 27,
    34, 35, 54, 79-81 *passim*, 88, 105,
    154, 183, 192, 241; *Augustiani* 115;
    hunting **137**; toys **23**
Arius/Arianism 199, 201
Armenia 128, 142
army 13, 14, 28-30, 38, 78-9, 108-9,
    118, 127-31, 133, 139, 144-56
    passim, 171, 178, 196, 202-3, 210,
    223-7 *passim*, 230, 236, 237;
    auxiliaries 78, 153-6 *passim*;
    federates 224, 226
Arrian 155, 250
Asia 225; Minor 21, 32-3, 162, 192
Athens 21, 67, 156, 160, 220
Atia (Octavian's mother) 60
Attianus, Acilius 138, 143, 144
Augustan Histories 141-3 *passim*, 145,
    147-8, 150, 158, 160, 162, 163, 250

Augustus (Gaius Julius Caesar
    Octavianus) 6, 7, 52, **58**, 59-97, **77**,
    88, 99, 100, 105, 112, 131, 133, 135,
    145, 146, 219; and Antony 63-70
    passim; appearance 66, birth 59-60;
    and Caesar 12, 60-2; as consul 63, 76,
    79; death 96; education 60-1; funeral
    97; house **73**, lifestyle 72-4; march on
    Rome 63; principale 12-13, 75-97,
    reforms 84-9; *Res Gestae et Impensae*
    96; second Triumvirate 64-5
Aurelia (Caesar's mother) 20
Aurelius, Marcus 13, 170

B

Balbilla, Julia 164
barbarians **28-9**, **171**, 175, 187, 225
Bassianus (Constantine's brother-in-law)
    190, 196
baths 118, 154, 157, 183, 189
battles 63; Actium 70, 72; Adrianople
    (324) 191, (378) 226; Alesia 46;
    Alexandria 50; Byzantium 191, 195;
    Cibalae 190; Milvian Bridge 189,
    197; Munda 52; Pharsalus 49;
    Philippi 65; Taginae 240
Bederiana 211, 212
Belisarius 209, 222, 231-2, 234-6, 241, 246
Bibulus 39
Bosra, Theatre at **124-5**
Boudicca, Queen 118
boxing **132**
bridges 154, 162, 187-9 *passim*, 203
Britain 45-6, 102, 111, 145, 150-3,
    155-6, 184-5, 227, 230, 239, revolt
    118; Hadrian's Wall 150-3, **152**,
    155-6, 184-5
Britannicus 102, 103, 105, 113
Brundisium, Treaty of 66
Bulgars 239
bureaucracy/civil service 14, 112-13,
    157-8, 177, 210, 218, 227
Burrus 103, 105-7, 110-12 *passim*,
    116, 119
Byzantium 191-3 *passim*; empire 16, 247

C

Caesar, Gaius 20-1, 25, 26
Caesar, Gaius Julius 6, 7, 12, **18**, 19-57,
    60-2 *passim*, 64, 86, 96, 99, 131,
    133, 135, 151, 155; appearance/
    character 31-5, 43 assassination 12,
    19-20, 54-6, **56-7** 59, 61, 74, birth

20-1, **20**; childhood 23-5; *Civil Wars*
    48, 52; *Commentaries* 44-6 *passim*;
    education 24-5; in Egypt 50; march
    on Rome 48; political career, as
    aedile 36, consul 38-9, Dictator
    50-4, 59, governor 37-8, *pontifex
    maximus* 36, quaestor 35, first
    Triumvirate 39, 46-7
Caesarion **53**, 70-1
calendar, Julian 51-2
Caligula 88, 100 101, **101**
Carthage 12, 21, 22, 29-30, 51, 90
Cassius of Palma 60
Cassius Dio 104, 114, 120, 151-2, 250;
    on Caesar 35, 46; on Hadrian 147,
    156, 159, 167, 170; on Nero 104,
    108, 113, 116, 118, 119, 123, 128; on
    Octavian/Augustus 75, 76, 78, 88-9
Catholic Church 247
Catullus, Gaius Valerius 41, 250
chariot racing **127**
Charlemagne 247
China 96, 225
Christianity 14-15, 57, 122-3, 165,
    179-82, 185-6, 189, 190, 193,
    196-201, **205**, 206, 207, 209, 217,
    219-20, **233**, 243
Chronicon Paschale 222, 250
church building 198, 234
Cicero 41, 47, **47**, 48, 54, 61-4 *passim*,
    69, 250
Cinna 26-8 *passim*
Circus Maximus **112**, **127**
citizenship, granting of 30, 53, 111,
    156, 158, 224
Claudia (Nero's daughter) 120
Claudia (Octavian's wife) 65
Claudius 88, 101-5, **104**, 112, 113, 151
Cleopatra 50, 53, **53**, 67-70
coins **63**, 100, 113, 156-8 *passim*, 175, 191
'colonies' 51, 86
Commodus 171
Commodus, Lucius 167, 170
Constantia (Constantine's stepsister)
    188, 190, 191
Constantine, Caesar Flavius 6, 7, 14-15,
    165, **172**, 173-207, **192**, 210, 217,
    223, 243; birth 173; and Christianity
    14, 185-6, 188-90, 193, 196-201,
    206, 207, 217; at Council of Nicaea
    200-1; funeral 207; and Licinius
    188-91; march on Rome 188-9; sole
    emperor 191-207

Constantinople 15, 16, 192-3, 202,
206-7, 209-12 *passim*, 217, 221-3,
234-5, 237, 246; Council of 243; fall
of **244-5**, 247; palace guards at **213**;
Sancta Sophia **204**, 234-5
Constantius, Flavius (Constantine's
father) 173, 176-7, 182-5 *passim*
Constantius II 218
Constitutional Settlement (23BC)
79-80
consulate 22, 26, 38-9, 59, 79-80, 109,
237
Corbulo 128-30 *passim*
Corinth 51, 162; canal 130
Cornelia (Caesar's wife) 26, 35
corruption 27, 34, 35, 99, 220, 224,
238, 242
Cossutia 26
Crassus 37, 39, 46, 47, 64, 87
Crispus 191, 194-5
crucifixion, abolition of 198
Ctesiphon 142, 179
culture 13, 21, 56, 137, 140, 159
cults 153, 197; *discipulina* 148;
emperor 87-8, 180

D
Dacia 142, 146, 203
Danube 95, 139, 142, 145, 146, 162,
174, 203, 226, 239
debt 158; cancellation 37, 145, 156,
158, 242
defeated, policy to 22, 30, 48, 53,
203-4, 223-4
Dido 90
Diocletian 14, 173, **174**, 176-8, 180-4
passim, 203, 223; reforms 14, 176
Domitian 138, 139, 144-5
Dougga, Theatre at **165**
Drusilla 100

E
economy 22, 37, 158, 175, 205, 227,
243
Egypt 21, 50, 68-71 *passim*, 88, 143,
163-4, 167, 239, 246
Elbe 95
Ephesus 162; temple 166
Etruscans 11, 22
Eunapius 192-3, 251
eunuchs 219
Euphrates 146, 162
Eusebius 164-5, 190, 191, 193, 197,
200, 204, 206, 251
Eutropius 178, 187, 196, 251
Evagrius 240, 251
expenditure, state 158, 178, 205, 223,
227, 242, 243

F
famine 7, 204; relief 162
Fausta 177, 186, 195
Favorinus 149-50
Flavian dynasty 13, 138
Forum *17*
Franks 230
Fulvia 65, 66
Fuscus 167

G
Gaius (Augustus's grandson) 91, 94
Galba 133, 138
Galerius 177-80, 183-7 *passim*
games 35, 82, 100-2 *passim*, 106-7,
116-18 *passim*, 130, 145, 160, 213;
Neronia 117
Gaul 12, 13, 42, 44-6, 56, 63, 64, 79,
87, 88, 145, 147, 185, 186, 227,
230; rebellion 131, 133
Germanic peoples 15, 83, 95, 140,
145-7 *passim*, 175, 186-7, 223-6,
230, 246
gladiatorial fights 25, 36, **80-1**, 82,
106, *117*, 118, **188**, 198
Goths 14, 175, 183, 191, 203, 210,
223-6, 230-2, 235, 236, 246
Greece/Greeks 11, 12, 21-3 *passim*, 49,
51, 65, 128, 130, 159, 162

H
Hadrian, Publius Aelius 6, 7, 13, **134**,
135-71, **151**, *171*, 173, 219; appear-
ance/character 148-50; birthplace
136-7; and Britain 150-3; career, as
consul 142, governor 142, 143,
judge 139, tribune 139; education
136-7; funeral 170-1; lifestyle 159-
60, 166; and Senate 141-2, 144-5,
167, 170, 171; and Trajan 138-41,
143; Villa at Tivoli **168-9**, Wall **152**
Hadrianopolis 160, 162-3
Hadrianutherae 150, 163
Hannibal 22
Helena 173, 176, **185**, 195, *195*, 198
Hellenism 12, 150, 159-60
Helvetii 42-4 *passim*
Herodian 151, 170-1, 251
Homer 89
homosexuality 159, 220
Honorius 227
Horace 70, 89, 97, 159, 251
Huns 225-6, 246

I
India 52, 96
inflation 175, 209
invasion, barbarian/foreign 14-16 *passim*,

174, 175, 203, 209, 223, 226, 227
Islam 16
Italica 135-8 *passim*, 159
Italy 12, 30, 41, 53, 65, 88, 188, 231,
232, 235, 246; reconquest of 240, 243
Iuvenalia 115

J
Jerome, St 198, 225, 226, 251
Jerusalem 164, 165, 198
Jesus of Nazareth 179
Jews/Judaism 143, 164, 180
John of Cappadocia 220-1, 238
Josephus 148, 251
Judaea 131, 164-5
Julia (Caesar's daughter) 31, 39, 47;
(sister) 60
Julia (Octavian's daughter) 66, 72,
90-1, 94; (granddaughter) 72, 94
Julia Livilla 100
Julian (Constantine's nephew) 193
Julianus, Salvius 157
Julio-Claudian dynasty 13, 96, 127
Justin 211-14 *passim*, 224
Justinian, Flavius Petrus Sabbatius 6, 7,
16, **208**, 209-47; appearance 212,
217; and Belisarius 231-2, 235-6;
birthplace 211; lifestyle
216-17; reforms 219, 221, 241

K
kingdoms, barbarian 230-1
kings 11, 22; client 146

L
labour, forced 154, 190
Lactantius 177-8, 184, 188-9, 251
land 37, 39, 65, 154, 158, 192, 204, 210
Lazica 239
legal system 31-2, 157-8, 160, 211,
219, 241
legions 13, 14, 28-30, 38, 64, 78, 118,
128, 129, 133, 145, 151, 156, 174,
185, 202, 217, 223
Leo 211
Lepida, Domitia 101, 103
Lepidus 64, 65, 67
Licinius 187-91 *passim*, 196
Livia 66, **67**, 72, 90, 91, 94, 96
local government 87, 136-7
Lombards 246
Lucius (Antony's brother) 62, 65, 66
Lucius (Augustus's grandson) 91, 94

M
Macarius, Bishop of Jerusalem 198
Macedonia 23
Macrobius 70, 251

Maecenas 89
Malalas, John 217, 219-20, 251
Marcellus (Octavia's son) 90-1
Marius 27
Matius, Gaius 54
Maxentius 186-9 passim
Maximian 176, 177, 183, 186, 187, 195
Maximinus Daia 184
mercenaries 15. 224, 225
Mesopotamia 142, 143
Messalina 102
migrants 37, 51, 86, 179, 226
Milan 14, 177, 190, 192, 210, 223
Minervina (Constantine's wife) 186
Mithridates of Pontus 32, 50
Moesia, Lower 139
Molo, Apollonius 32

N
Naissus 173
Narses 240, 241
Nero, Claudius Caesar Augustus
    Germanicus 6, 7, **98**, 99-133, **100**,
    138, 146, 180; accession 105-6;
    appearance 115; childhood 102-3;
    and Christians 122-3, 180;
    education 103, 107; lifestyle 108,
    110-11, as performer 114-16, 118,
    123, 126; portrayed as Pharaoh **129**;
    and Senate 105-6
Nerva 139-40, 142
Nicaea, Council of 200-1, **200-1**
Nicomedia 177, 182, 206

O
Octavia (Nero's wife) 103, 119
Octavia (Octavian's sister) 66-8 passim, 71
Octavian (Gaius Julius Caesar
    Octavianus) see Augustus
Octavius, Gaius 60, 96
Odoacer, king 231
Optimates 27, 49
Ostrogoths 210-11

P
Paetus, Thrasea 127
paganism 15, 179-81, 197
Palmyra 175; colonnaded street **228-9**
Pannonia, Lower 139
Pantheon **161**
Parthians 47, 52, 61, 69, 87, 142-3, 174
Paulina (Hadrian's sister) 138
pax Romana 3, 96, 105, 153, 157
Persians 14, 181, 205-6, 231, 239, 246
    see also Sassanians
Petronius 126
physical training **24**
Picts 184-5

Piso, Calpurnius 126
plague 204, 237. 242
Pliny the Elder 32, 251
Plotina (Trajan's wife) 140, 143
Plutarch 31-5 passim, 41, 43, 45, 52, 55, 251
politics 13, 25-7 passim, 31, 34, 39. 75,
    80-2, 105-6, 110, 183, 218
Pompeia (Caesar's wife) 35
Pompeius, Sextus 66-7
Pompey 39, **39**, 42, 46-50 passim, 55,
    64, 67, 133, 153
Pope 190, 243, 247; Silvester I 198
Poppaea 119-20, **119**, 126
Populares 27
Praetextatus, Vettius 199
praetors 26
Praetorian Guard 82, 103, 105, 133,
    156, 186, 189
Procopius 211, 212, 214, 216, 218,
    221, 231-2, 234-43 passim, 252; on
    Justin 214; on Theodora 215, 219
    222, 241-2
provinces 29, 37-8, 41-2. 76, 78,
    86-7, 127, 130-1, 133, 135-7, 140,
    145-7, 150-7 passim, 159-60,
    162-5, 174-6, 203, 207, 227;
    Romanization of 13, 51, 153-5, 159,
    224; secession 175-6, 186;
    settlements 136, 146, 224
Ptolemy XIII 50

Q
quaestors 26, 35, 237

R
racialism 87
Ravenna 210, 211, 223, 227, 231. 235,
    236; mosaics from **220-1**
Regia **33**
religion 7, 14-15, 37. 81, 153-6 passim,
    179-82, 196-201, 217 243
Remus 89
Republic 11-12, 23-57, 59, 75-6
Rhine 47. 133, 140, 174, 177, 186,
    187, 191, 203, 226
riots 221-2, 234
roads 21, 87, 136, 146, 153, 154, 157,
    162, 179, 203
Rome 15, 21, 22, 37, 83-6, 177,
    182-3, 193, 232, 240; Ara Pacis 91,
    92-3; Aurelian Wall 183; Baths of
    Diocletian 183; building, Augustus
    72, 85-6, Constantine 189, 198,
    Hadrian 160, Nero 121-2;
    Constantine Arch 189; fire 85-6.
    120, 180; Forum **17**, 22; foundation
    11, 22, 89-90, 102; Golden House
    121-2; Lateran Palace 190; Pantheon

160, **161**; sack 226-7, 232
Romulus 11, 22, 89
Romulus Augustulus 15, 210, 231

S
Sabina 140, 159, **160**, 163-4, 166-7
St Catherine's Monastery **196**
Sapor II 206
Sarmatians 178-9, 204
Sassanians 14, 174, 179. 196, 231,
    235, 238-9, 246; king **240**
Scipio 136
Scribonia (Octavian's wife) 66, 90
scrinia 113
Senate 11, 13, 22, 26, 27, 34, 35, 49, 63,
    64, 75, 78, 82, 105-6, 108, 139-42,
    145, 189, 217-18; and Caesar 41, 42,
    47-8, 51-5, 74; and Constantine 189;
    and Hadrian 141-2, 144-5, 167, 170,
    171; and Nero 105-6, 133; and
    Octavian 61-3 passim, 75-6, 79; and
    Trajan 140, 145
Senate House **52**, 55, **84**
Seneca 70, 91, 103, 105-7, 110-12
    passim, 115, 116, 119, 126, 131,
    252; *On Clemency* 106
Serdica 191, 192
Servianus (Hadrian's brother-in-law)
    140, 167
Severan dynasty 13, 174
Severus 184
Severus, Alexander 174
Sicily 21, 162, 232
Siculus, Calpurnius 107, 250
slaves 21, 37, 198, 225
Slavs 239
Spain 13, 35, 37-8, 49, 52, 79, 133,
    135-7 passim, 145, 159, 162, 185,
    230, 236, 246; revolt 133, 138
Spanish War 52
Sparta 21, 53, 156
Sporus 128
Strabo 25, 83
succession 6, 13-14, 91, 94, 96, 103-5, 143,
    167, 170, 173-4, 184, 186, 207, 243
Suetonius 252; on Augustus/Octavian
    60, 61, 63, 65, 66, 72-4 passim, 79,
    82, 83, 87, 88, 91, 94, 95; on Caesar
    31, 35, 36, 43, 53; on Nero 110, 111,
    113-17 passim, 121-2, 126, 131, 133
Sulla 27-8, 30, 33
Synesius 217, 230, 252
Syria 13, 21, 138, 155, 162, 164, 175,
    239; Palaestina 165

T
Tacitus 102. 105-8 passim, 111, 114,
    119-21 passim, 126, 133, 138, 150,

155, 252; on Nero 105, 121-3 *passim*; on Octavian 71, 76
taxation 14, 78, 110, 122, 127, 154, 158, 167, 193, 199, 205, 207, 220-1, 227, 238, 241, 242; exemptions 22, 130, 139, 192, 193; 'farming' 158
temples 72, 87, 160, 197
Tetrarchy 14, *176*, 177-8, 182, 183
theatres 55, *124-5*, 159, *165*
Theodora 214, 215, *216*, 218, 219, 222, 238, 241-3 *passim*
Theodora (Maximian's stepdaughter) 177
Theodoric the Great 210-11
Theodosius the Great 210
Thrace 111, 211, 246
Tiber 11, 21, 22, 85, 188-9
Tiberius 66, 91, 94, 96, 100, 101
Tigellinus 119, 127, 133
Tiridates of Armenia 128
Titus 138

Tivoli 166, *168-9*
toga 25-6, 54, 103, 154, 160, 162
trade 11, 12, 21, 22, 57
Trajan, Marcus Ulpius 13, 135, 138-47 *passim*, 158, 162, 203; Column *141*, *149*
tribes 38, 42, 44-6, 95, 118, 152, 154, 187, 204, 227
Tribonian 241
tribune 139, 237
tribute 136, 205
Trier 14, 177, 186-7, 192
Triumphs 25, 38, *40*, 50, 82, 128, 209, 231-2, 235
Triumvirate, first 39, 46-7; second 64-5
Turks 246, 247

U
urbanization 15, 136-7, 153-4, 157

V
Valens 226
Vandals 226, 230-2 *passim*, 240

Varus, Quinctilius 95
Verus, Annius 170
Vespasian *131*, 133, 138
Victor, Aurelius 108, 166, 250
Virgil 70, 89-90, 252
Visigoths 230, 232, 246

W
war 7, 23, 43, 63, 82-3; civil 12-14 *passim*, 27-8, 48-9, 52, 57, 59, 64-5, 133, 138, 171, 173, 174, 187-91, 223; Dacian 142, 146, 203; Gallic 44-6; Judaean 164-5; Justinian's 16, 231, 232, 235-6, 238-9, 246; Parthian 47, 52, 61, 69, 87, 142; Punic 12, 22, 29-30; Sarmatian 178-9; Sassanian 179, 231, 235, 238-9

Z
Zeno 231
Zosimus 202, 205, 252

BBC Books would like to thank the following for providing photographs and for permission to reproduce copyright material. While every effort has been made to trace and acknowledge all copyright holders, we would like to apologize should there be any errors or omissions.

Page 10 Museo Nazionale, Naples/© Phil Grabsky/Seventh Art Productions; 18 Museo e Gallerie Nazionali di Capodimonte, Naples/Bridgeman Art Library; 20 Museo Arcaeologico, Ostia © Phil Grabsky/Seventh Art Prods; 23 Louvre Museum, Paris © Fiona Kingsman/Seventh Art Prods; 24 Museo Arcaeologico, Ostia © Phil Grabsky/Seventh Art Prods; 28-29 Museo delle Terme, Rome/SCALA; 39 Museo Arcaeologico, Venice/ET Archive; 40 The Royal Collections © Her Majesty Queen Elizabeth II; 47 Capitoline Museum, Rome © Peter Nicholson/Seventh Art Prods; 53 Dendara, Egypt © Phil Grabsky/Seventh Art Prods; 56-57 Museo di Capodimonte, Naples/SCALA; 58 Staatliche Glypothek, Munich/ET Archive; 63 Ancient Art & Architecture Collection; 67 Ephesus Museum, Turkey © Phil Grabsky/Seventh Art Prods; 68 Museo Nazionale Terme, Rome/ET Archive; 71 Ancient Art & Architecture Collection; 73 Casa di Augusto (Palatino), Rome/SCALA; 77 The Vatican/SCALA; 80-81 Galleria Borghese, Rome/SCALA; 88, Museo Nazionale, Rome © Peter Nicholson/Seventh Art Prods; 92-93 Ara Pacis Augustae, Rome/SCALA; 98 Capitoline Museum, Rome © Peter Nicholson/Seventh Art Prods; 100 New York University Excavations at Aphrodisias & the Aphrodisias Museum, Turkey © Fiona Kingsman/Seventh Art Prods; 101 Ancient Art & Architecture Collection; 104 New York University Excavations at Aphrodisias & the Aphrodisias Museum, Turkey © Peter Nicholson/Seventh Art Prods; 109 Museo Arcaeologico, Naples © Phil Grabsky/Seventh Art Prods; 116 Prenestino Museum, Rome/ET Archive; 117 Museo Arcaeologico, Merida/ET Archive; 119 Archaeological Museum, Rome © Peter Nicholson/Seventh Art Prods 124-5 © Phil Grabsky/Seventh Art Prods; 127 Museo Gregoriano Profano, Vatican/SCALA; 129 Temple of Matnor, Dendera, Egypt © Phil Grabsky/Seventh Art Prods; 131 Capitoline Museum, Rome/ET Archive; 132 Museo Arcaeologico, Naples/ET Archive 134 Capitoline Museum, Rome/SCALA; 137 Archaeological Museum, Merida/ET Archive; 141 & 149 National Historical Museum, Bucharest/ET Archive; 151 Museo Arcaeologico, Ostia © Phil Grabsky/Seventh Art Prods; 152 Collections © Graeme Peacock; 153 © Phil Grabsky/Seventh Art Prods; 160 (above) Museo Arcaeologico, Ostia © Phil Grabsky/Seventh Art Prods; 160 (below) Museo Arcaeologico Nazionale, Naples © Phil Grabsky/Seventh Art Prods; 161 Werner Forman Archive; 164 Prenestino Museum, Rome/ET Archive; 165 © Peter Nicholson/Seventh Art Prods; 168-9 Colorific! Photo: Jenny Quiggin; 171 Archaeological Museum, Istanbul © Phil Grabsky/Seventh Art Prods; 172 Museo Nazionale, Belgrade/SCALA; 174 Archaeological Museum, Istanbul © Phil Grabsky/Seventh Art Prods; 176 Ancient Art & Architecture Collection; 181 Museo Arcaeologico, Naples/ET Archive; 185 Diözesanmuseum, Trier/ET Archive; 188 Tunisia Ancient Art & Architecture Collection; 192 & 195 Capitoline Museum, Rome © Peter Nicholson/Seventh Art Prods; 196 © Phil Grabsky/Seventh Art Prods; 200-201 Biblioteca Vaticana/SCALA; 204 Werner Forman Archive; 205 Italica, Spain © Phil Grabsky/Seventh Art Prods; 208, 213 & 216 San Vitale, Ravenna/SCALA; 220 & 221 S. Apollinare Nuovo, Ravenna/SCALA; 228-229 © Phil Grabsky/Seventh Art Prods; 233 Mausoleo di Galla Placida, Ravenna/SCALA; 240 Courtesy of the British Museum; 244-5 Moldovita Monastery, Rumania/ET Archive.